CHORLTON-CUM-HARDY
THROUGH TIME

Steven Dickens

AMBERLEY

First published 2018

Amberley Publishing
The Hill, Stroud, Gloucestershire, GL5 4EP
www.amberley-books.com

ISBN 978 1 4456 4768 5 (print)
ISBN 978 1 4456 4769 2 (ebook)

British Library Cataloguing in Publication Data.
A catalogue record for this book is available from the British Library.

Origination by Amberley Publishing.
Printed in Great Britain.

Introduction

In Anglo-Saxon the meaning of Chorlton-cum-Hardy is probably Ceolfrith's farm, or the settlement of Ceolfrith. It is possible that Hardy was derived from the personal name Hearda, or the Anglo-Saxon word for an island, or its alternative meaning of 'dry ground in a well-watered land'. It is also possible that Hardy could be interpreted as meaning 'by the woods', as the ancient forest of Arden Wood grew on either side of the River Mersey at this location. Although there was an Anglo-Saxon settlement here from the ninth century, there is no record of the use of Chorlton-cum-Hardy as a settlement name before approximately 1700. Therefore we can visualise the site of the modern town as an Anglo-Saxon farmstead, sited on a well-drained area of raised ground, close to surrounding marshes, woodland and the River Mersey, fed by a network of localised streams and brooks. Indeed, as with most of the neighbouring urban areas of Manchester, it was the arrival of the railway in 1880 which initiated Chorlton-cum-Hardy's suburban development of the latter part of the nineteenth century. Before that much of the district was utilised as farmland, with many of the farmhouses surviving as private dwellings today. The township of Chorlton consisted of several districts – Martledge, Barlow Moor, Hough End and Hardy – and in the case of the more substantial and influential manor houses of the area, such as Hough End Hall and Barlow Hall, they have now been utilised as public facilities.

The biggest change to take place in Chorlton-cum-Hardy post-urbanisation was the relocation of the centre of the settlement away from Chorlton Green, towards what is now known as 'Chorlton Cross' (a recent designation not appreciated by all residents), where Wilbraham Road and Barlow Moor Road converge at the crossroads. This convergence was more commonly known as 'Bank Corner' on account of a bank being located on each corner of the crossroad's junction; and before that it had the title of Kemp's Corner, named after the pharmacy that was located here for many years. Therefore, for many residents it could be named from a tangible entity that served a genuine purpose in the village. It was also close to the newly established railway station and was at the centre of Chorlton-cum-Hardy's business and retail activities. All of which suited commuters much better, being conveniently located close to the expanding residential developments of the suburb. A division between 'old' Chorlton at Chorlton Green and the 'new' Chorlton of commuter development quickly established itself. Although it is a generalisation, many of the old farming families continued to carry on with their separate way of life, while the commercial 'newcomers' passed them by. This 'push and pull' existence is exemplified by St Clement's Church, which had been sited at Chorlton Green since at least 1512, together with a churchyard and later the lych-gate. The rapidly expanding population of Chorlton-cum-Hardy soon began to outgrow the existing parish church and it was not long before a replacement was proposed, at the corner of Edge Lane and St Clement's Road. Many villagers objected to this, with the new church not consecrated for another thirty years after its construction. The ancient parish church continued in use until 1940 and it was not demolished until 1949, with the 'new' St Clement's then firmly established as the parish church. Of course, with the passage of time these divisions will be consigned to the history books only! History tells us that Chorlton Green, in the centre of the 'old' village, had been a popular location for bear-baiting until the arrival of bull-baiting and the construction of a bullring in the centre of the Green, near where the lamp now stands. A large stone was sunk into the ground, onto which a ring was fixed at the top, with a chain attached to the bull. These were hired by landlords of the Horse & Jockey, who recognised just how lucrative this 'entertainment' could be, until the sport was made illegal in 1835.

In 1904 Chorlton-cum-Hardy was incorporated into the city of Manchester, this move initiating some (but not all) of the road name changes in the area. It also led to the development of the electric tram system throughout the district and, together with the railways, led to Chorlton-cum-Hardy having excellent transport links to the city centre of Manchester and beyond. As a result of these links Chorlton-cum-Hardy became a centre of entertainment in its own right, with several cinemas being established, including the old Pavilion cinema, which became Chorlton Theatre and Winter Gardens, at the corner of Wilbraham Road and Buckingham Road. Included in the book are certain areas which today are on the general periphery of Chorlton-cum-Hardy. These include Brooks Bar, which travellers heading towards Manchester would have encountered when changing trams, for example; St Bede's Catholic college, which receives students from across Manchester and trained for the priesthood, thus having a wide-ranging influence, as well as prominent architecture; Chorlton (Withington) Hospital, which received many generations of Chorlton-cum-Hardy's poor and destitute; and Lloyd Street South, a classic example of early twentieth-century development. Cosgrove Hall Film Studios was based in Albany Road, with the animated children's television series *Chorlton and the Wheelies* (1976–79) named after the suburb. Today Chorlton-cum-Hardy has a reputation for being popular with the young and aspiring professional, as well as providing a home for an eclectic mix of beliefs and cultures, ranging from various Christian beliefs, 'New-Age' philosophies, providing a home for an Islamic high school for girls, and also catering for Buddhist traditions, among others. Hopefully, the postcard selection presented in this volume will appeal to an equally wide-ranging variety of readers.

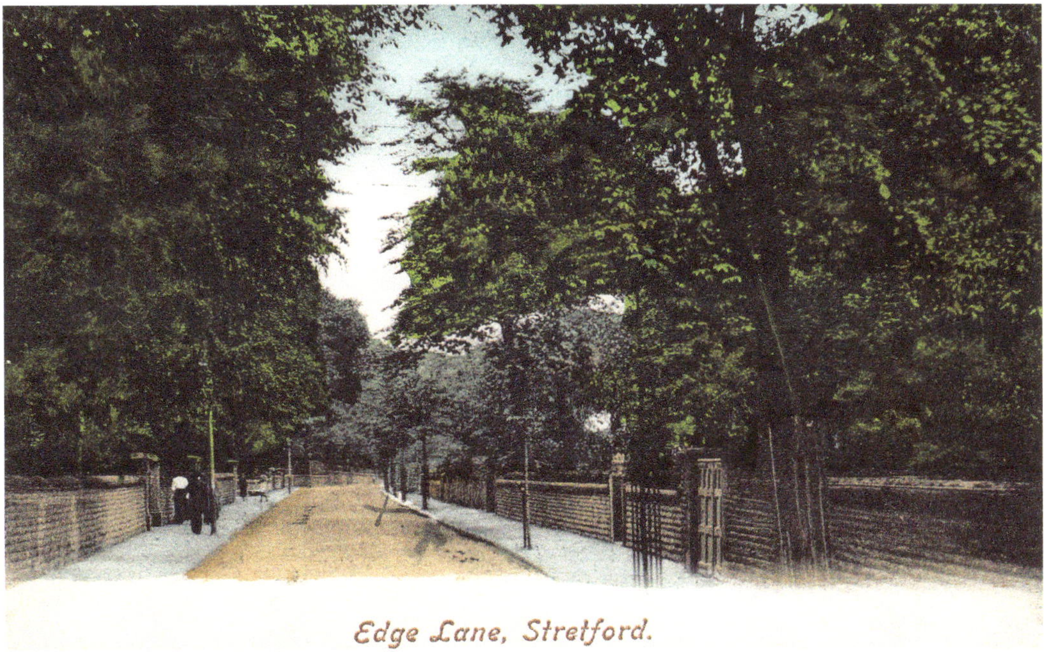

Edge Lane, Looking Towards Chorlton-cum-Hardy from Stretford, *c.* 1905

Edge Lane acted as a general boundary between Longford and Turn Moss, and is a main route into Chorlton-cum-Hardy, via High Lane and Wilbraham Road. Local legend has it that a boggart, representing a wagon with headless team and headless teamster, haunted Edge Lane, to the township boundary posts with High Lane and Wilbraham Road. Edge Lane provides access to Stretford Cemetery, Stretford Metrolink station and the town centre, as well as to Longford Park and the Bridgewater Canal.

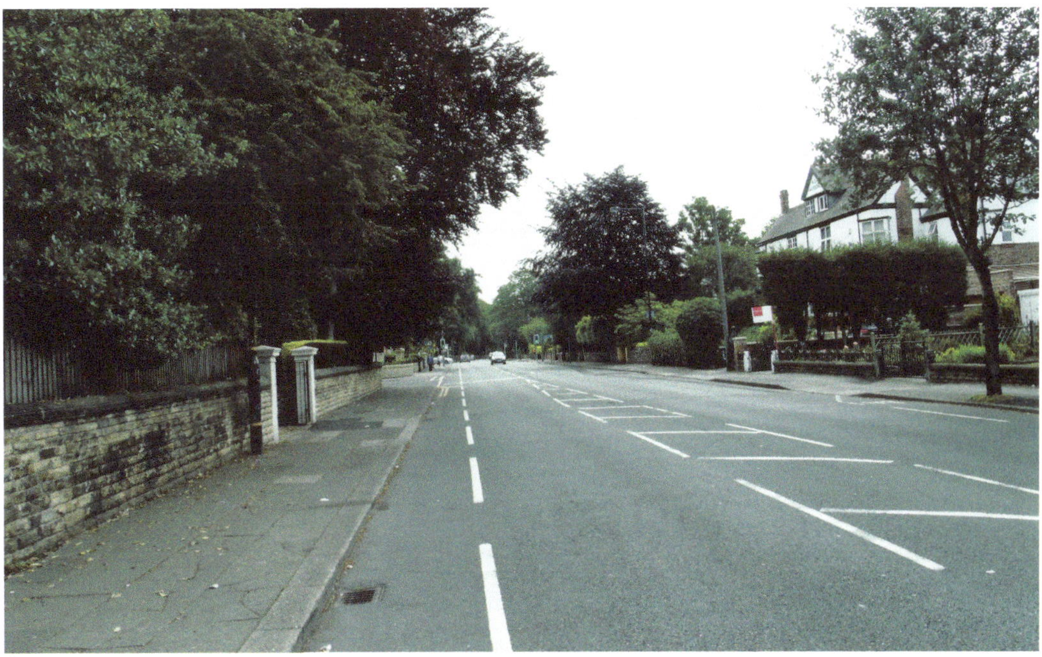

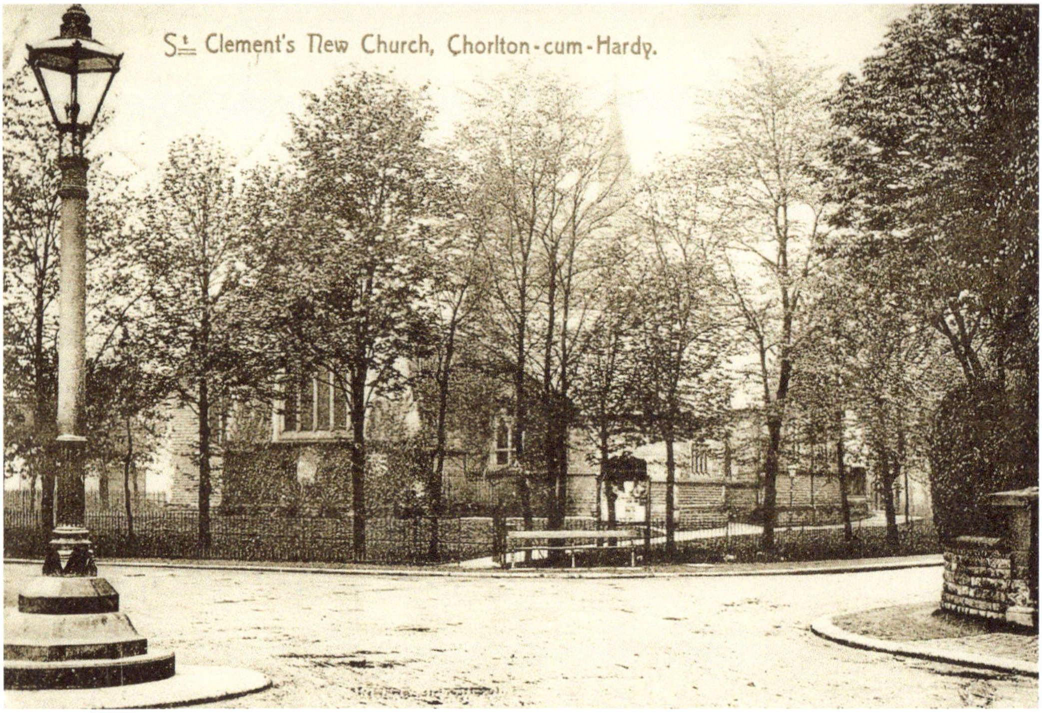

St Clement's 'New' Church, Edge Lane/St Clement's Road, Chorlton-cum-Hardy, 1906
A chapel was founded by the Barlow family around 1512. Chorlton became a parish in 1839 but by 1860 the existing chapel had become inadequate for the needs of a growing population. Lord Egerton gave land in order to build a replacement church, but not all parishioners were in favour of this and the old chapel remained after the new church was completed in 1865–66. It was not until 1949 that the old chapel was demolished and St Clement's became the new parish church.

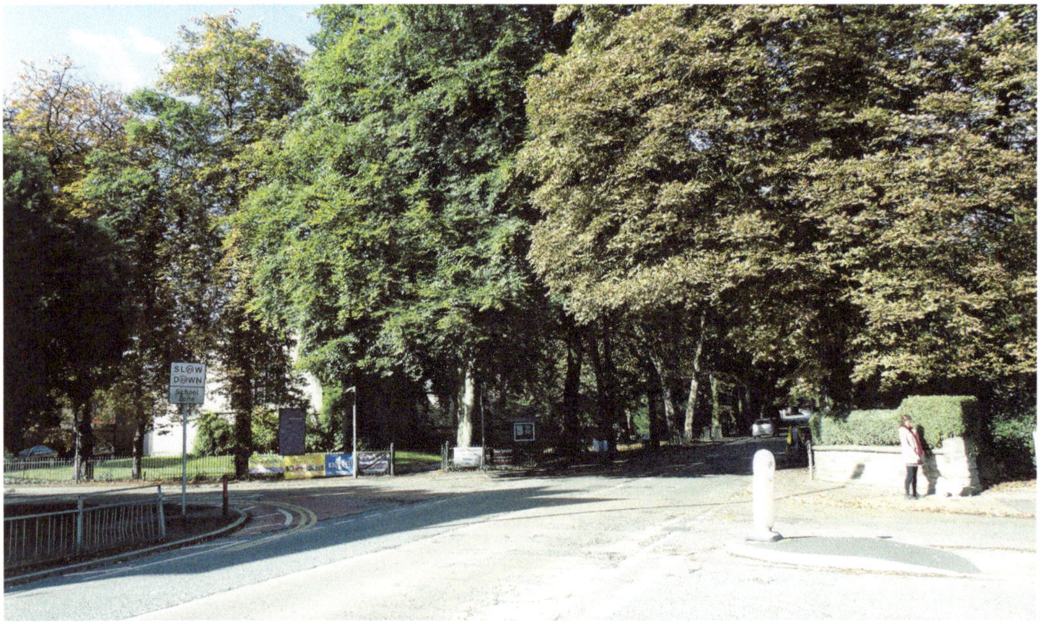

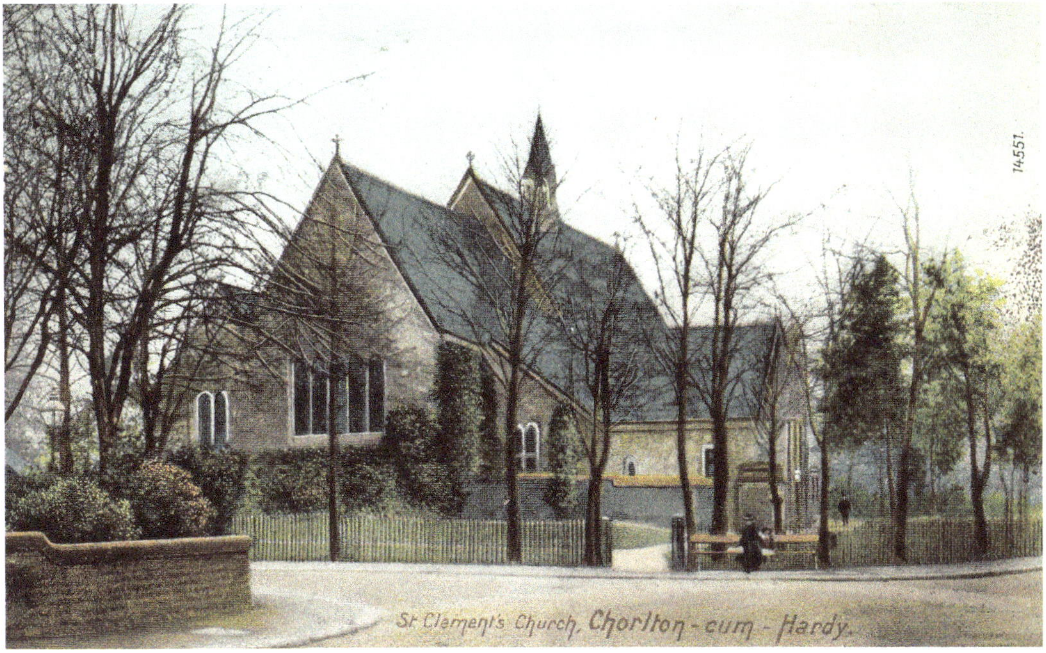

St Clement's Church, Edge Lane/St Clement's Road, Chorlton-cum-Hardy, 1909

In 1860 plans were produced by Pennington & Bridgen, and a site at the corner of Edge Lane was given by Lord Egerton. After delays, the new church was eventually completed in 1865–66, seating 650. It opened on 23 June 1866, although there were many more additions until its eventual consecration by the Bishop of Manchester on 22 April 1896. For example, seating was increased to 900 in the 1890s. However, it was 1940 before the old chapel closed, with the parish transferred in 1949.

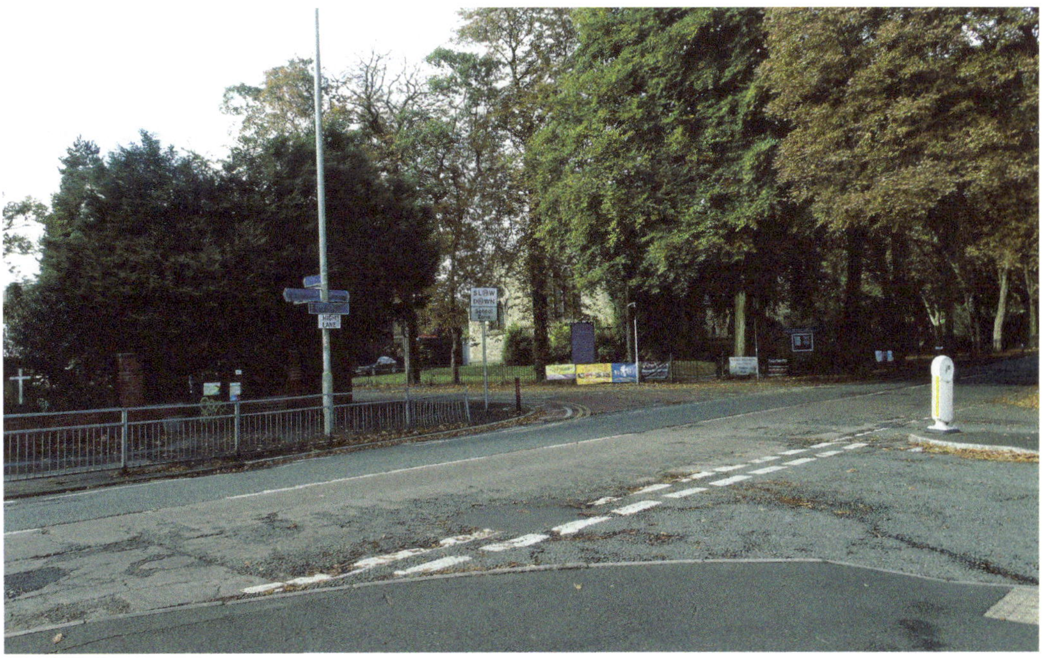

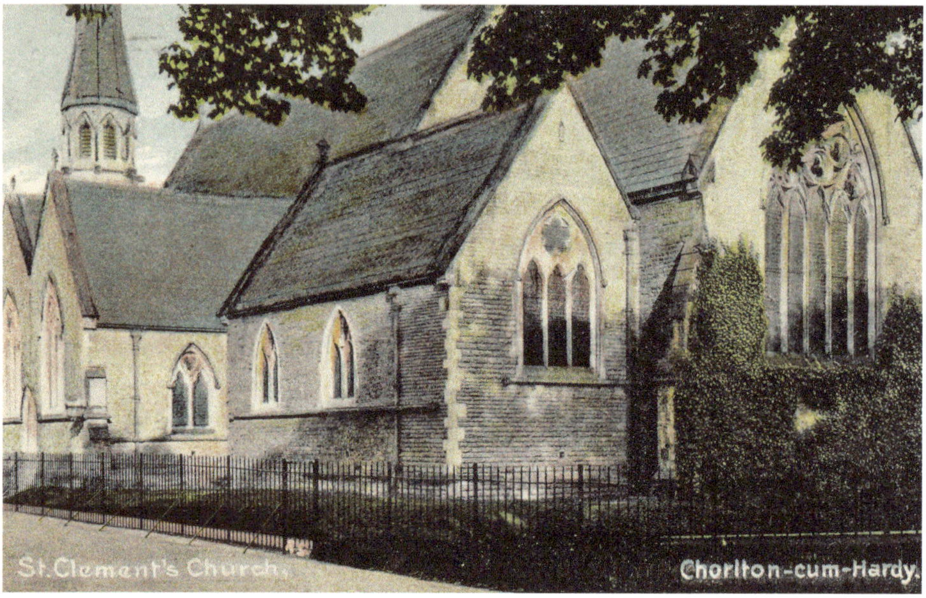

St Clement's Church, Edge Lane/St Clement's Road, Chorlton-cum-Hardy, 1906

The nave and chancel of the recently built St Clement's Church were completed in 1865 and an organ, constructed by Messrs Connacher, was provided for the church at the same time. Further improvements included a north transept and a choir vestry, built in 1883. In 1896 a south transept was added and improvements to the side chapel were made, all of which increased the seating capacity of the church. As the population increased, a new parish was established at St Werburgh's, Wilbraham Road, around 1900 (*inset*).

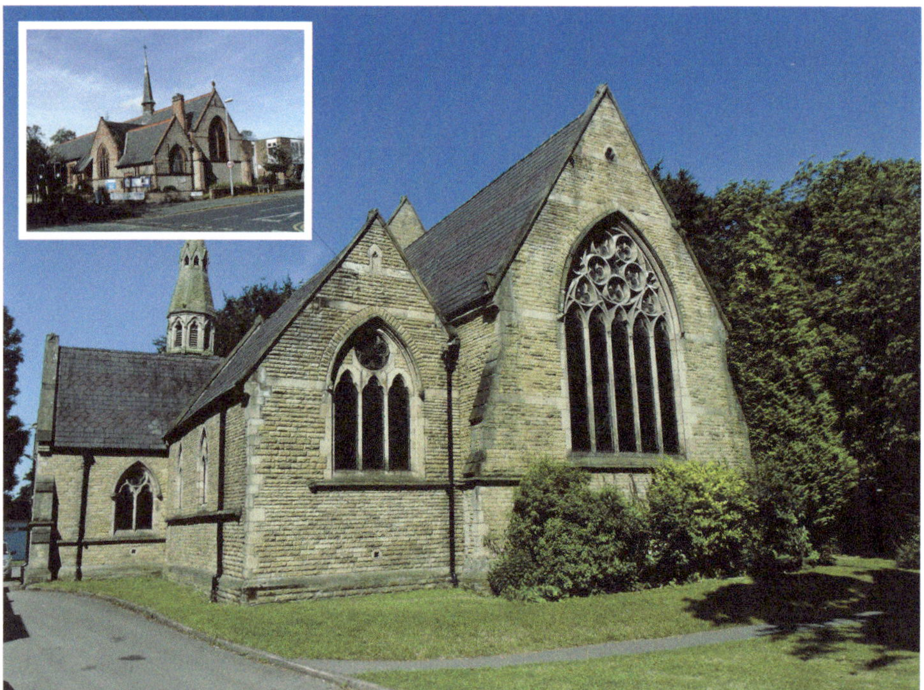

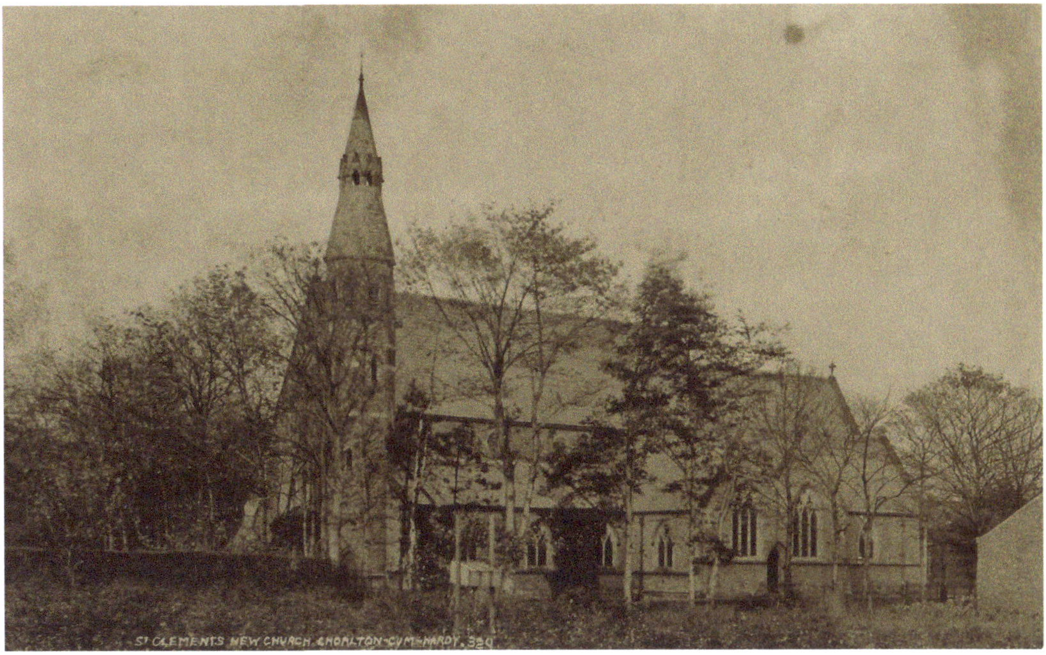

St Clement's Church from Vicars Road, Chorlton-cum-Hardy, *c.* 1900

This photograph shows St Clement's Church from Vicars Road, where Chorlton Church of England Primary School is located today. In 1901 a new church school was built at St Clement's Road, with the old building it replaced at Chorlton Green used for infants and juniors, until it was no longer needed. Now at the junction of St Clement's Road and Vicars Road, the modern image looks across the school playground, towards Edge Lane. Today the view is obscured by school railings.

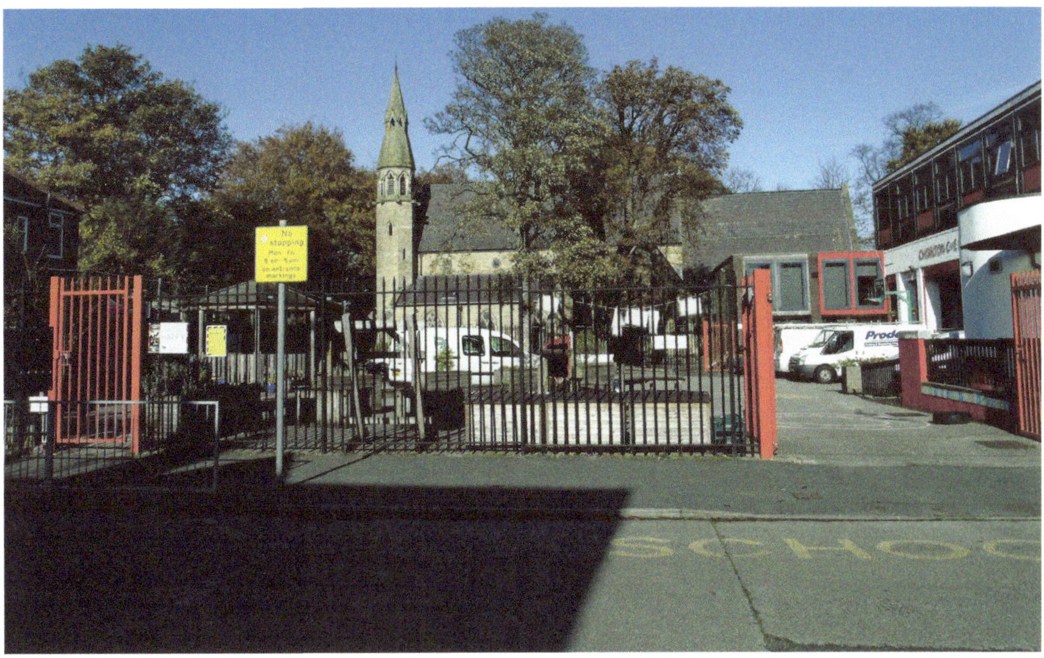

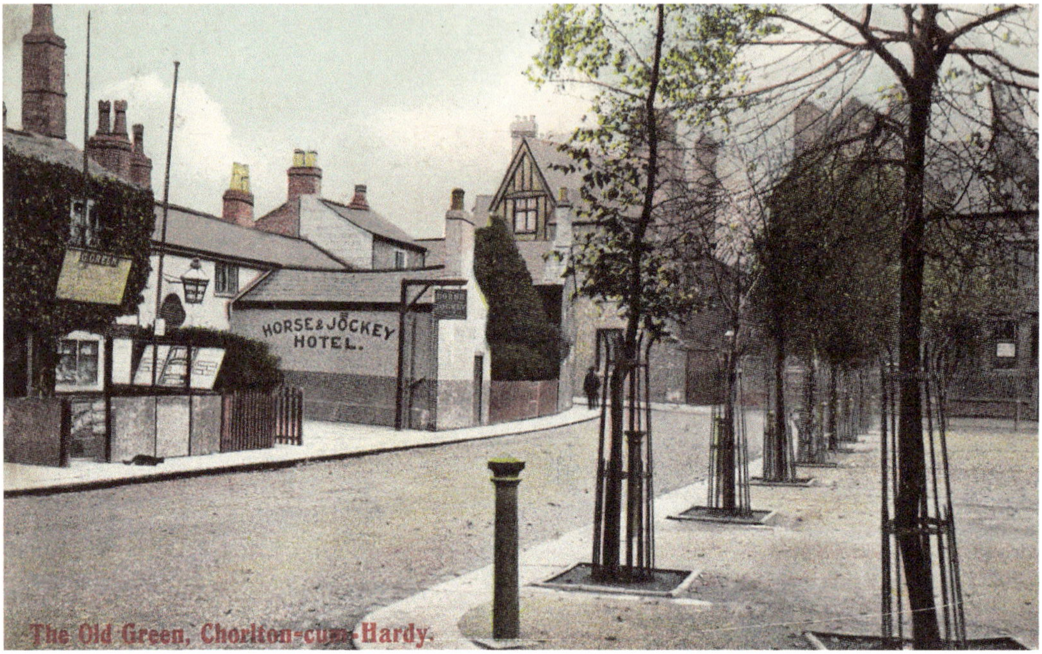

Horse & Jockey, 'The Old Green', Chorlton-cum-Hardy, 1909

The Horse & Jockey was originally a school and first became licensed as an inn and coach house around 1800. The three cottages which form the front part of the building are said to date back to 1512. They were converted into one building for use as a schoolroom. The public house takes its name from the horse racing that used to take place in nearby Chorlton Park. The Green was also popular for the 'sport' of bull-baiting.

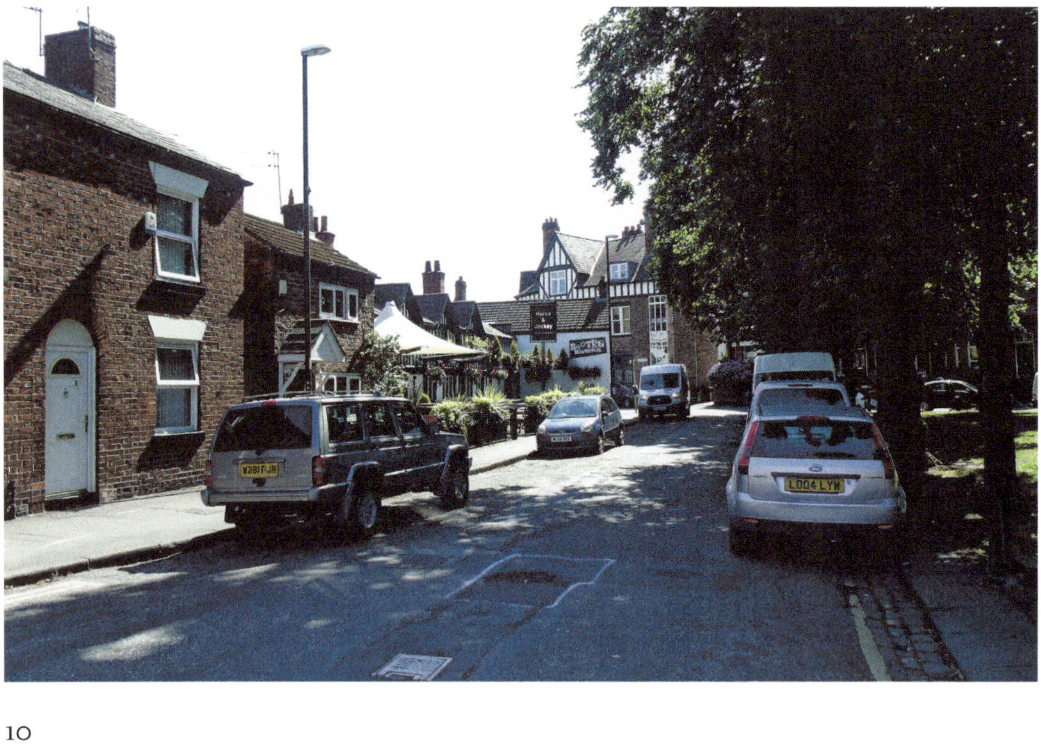

Bootleg Brewery, Chorlton Green, Chorlton-cum-Hardy, 2010

Established as an independent microbrewery in 2010, this is the only brewery in Chorlton at present. It was converted from the shell of the tower shown in the modern photograph below, where the old disused brewery of the Horse & Jockey public house once stood. The brewery has won many awards for its ales, which are popular at the many local beer festivals in the region. The brewery continues to expand and has recently begun to grow its own hops.

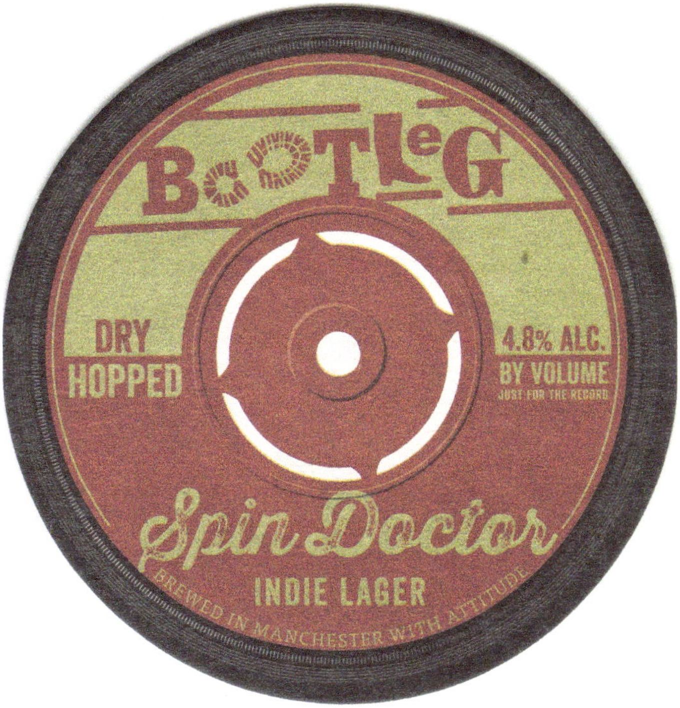

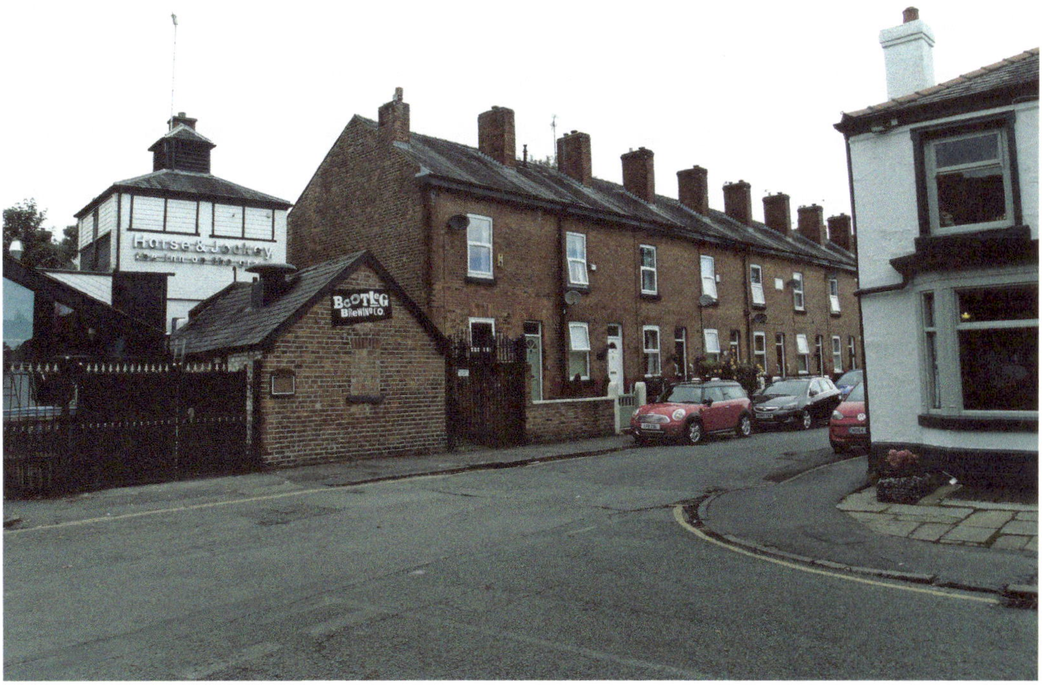

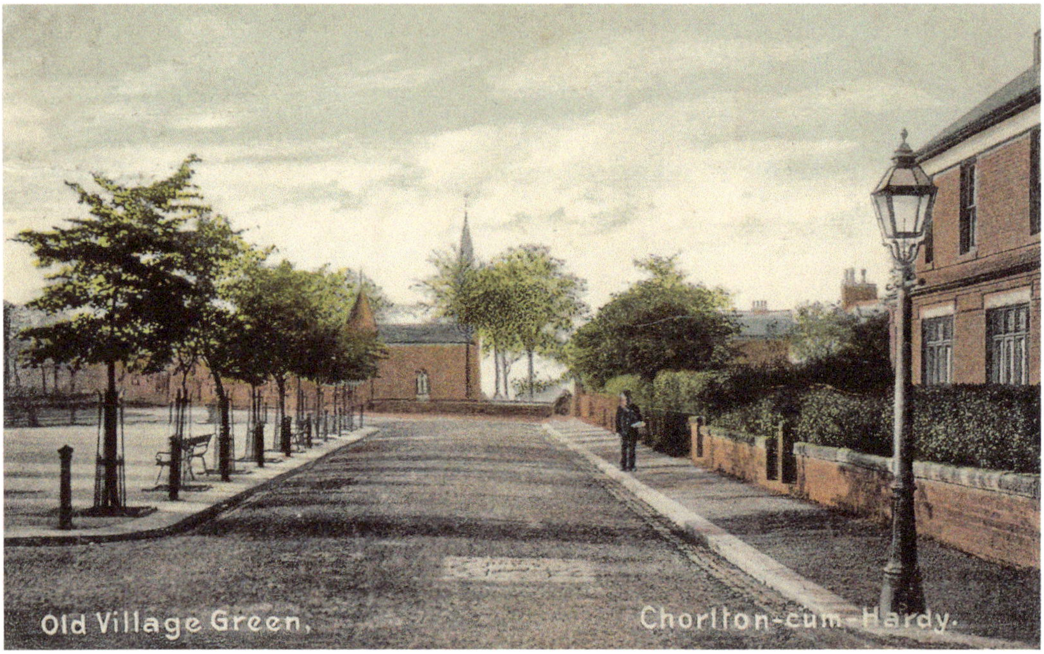

'Old Village Green', Parish Church, Lych-Gate and Old Churchyard (*inset* 2017), Chorlton Green, *c.* 1905

The old churchyard lych-gate is a listed building, noted for its octagonal, half-timbered bell tower. It was built in 1888 as a jubilee gift from influential banker Sir William Cunliffe Brooks, of Barlow Hall, who lead a faction objecting to the resiting of the new church. The old church spire and lych-gate can be seen in the above view. Beyond the lych-gate, the Bowling Green Hotel claims to have been licensed since 1693, though the present building dates from 1908.

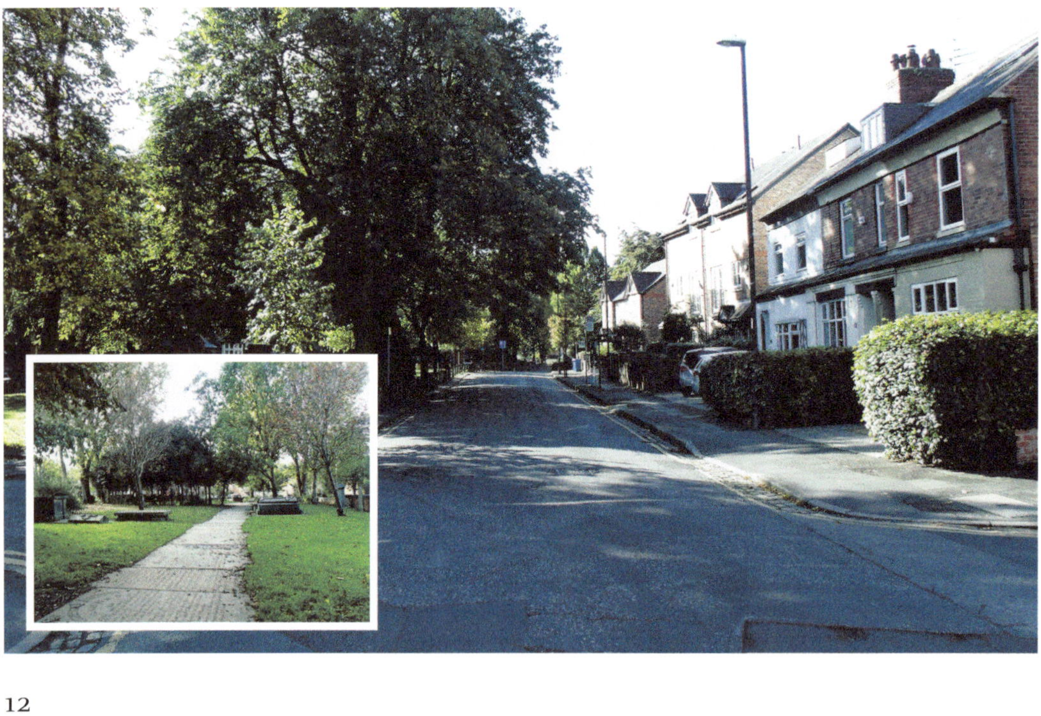

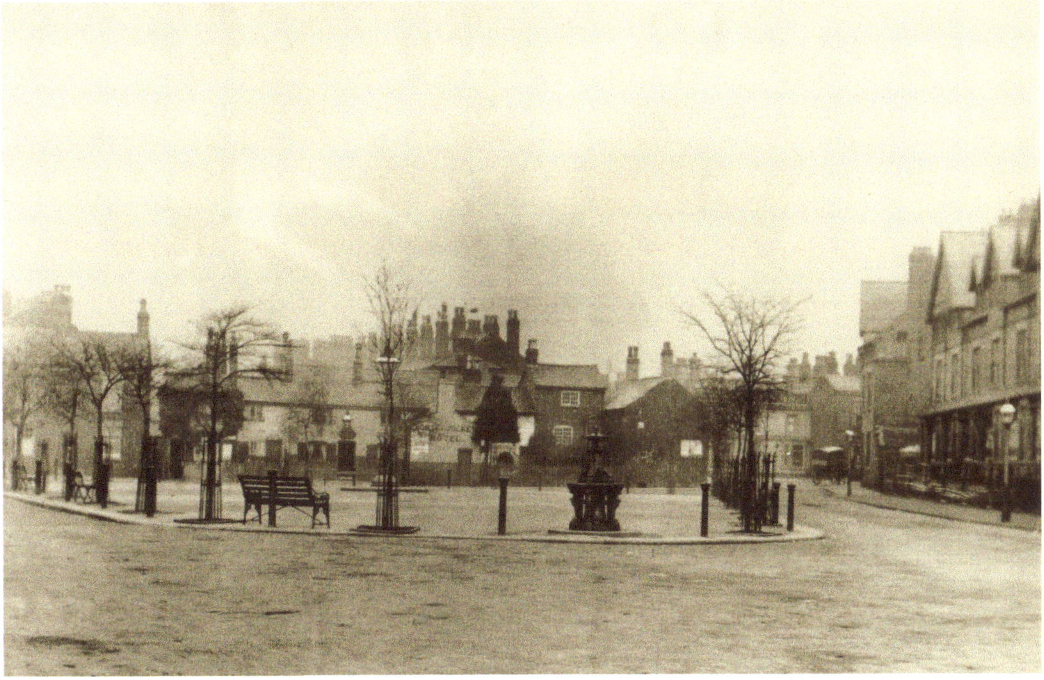

Chorlton Green, *c.* 1900. *Inset*: Central Lampost, 2017

The original features of the Horse & Jockey are now hidden behind a mock-Tudor façade, which was constructed in 1907, together with a redevelopment of the site which led to the institution of a brewery on the premises. The equipment and machinery from this enterprise survives in the outbuildings seen today, and the tradition continues with the establishment of a microbrewery at the Horse & Jockey. However, the past, in the form of a ghost, still prevails into the present.

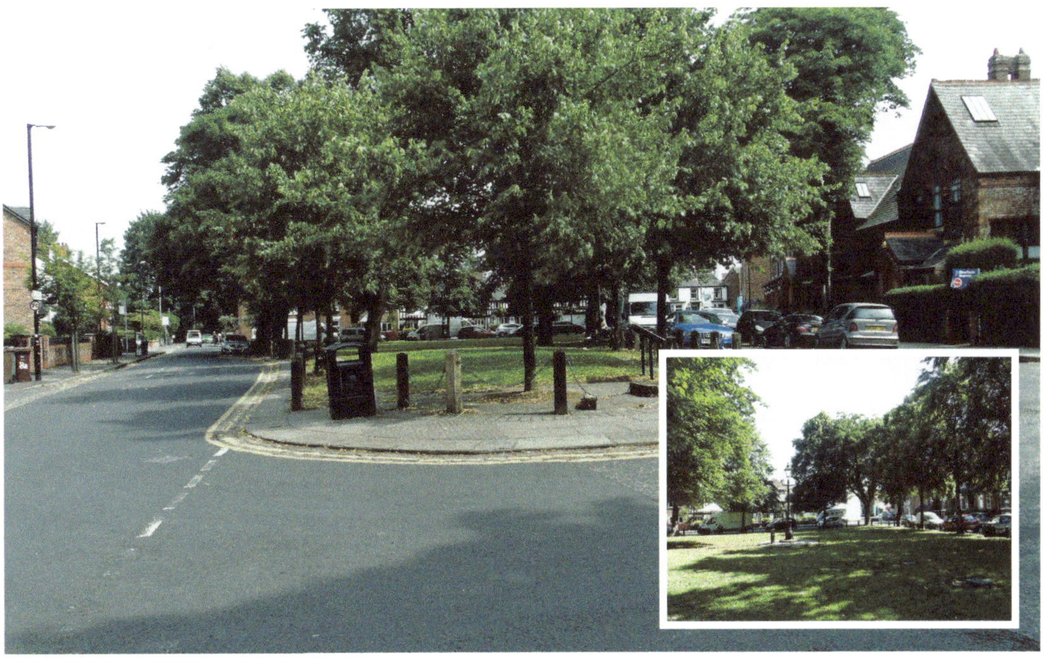

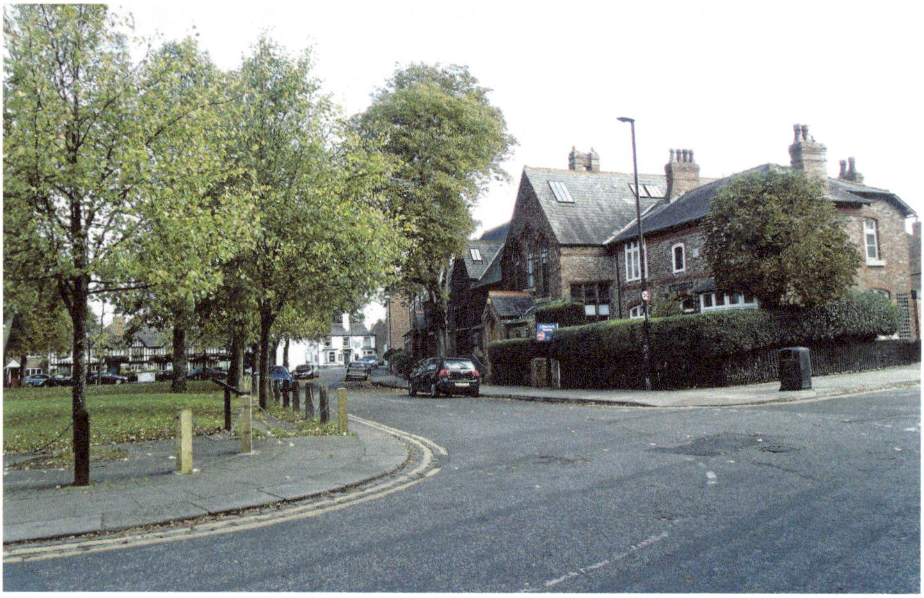

Former Chorlton Green National Board Schools, 2017

On the east side of the Green are late nineteenth-century buildings, one being the former Church of England school opened in 1879. This was later converted into offices, workshops and houses. The commemorative stone on the image below reads 'National Schools erected by subscription A.D. 1878. Revd J.E. Boothe M.A. Rector'. This building replaced a Church of England school built on the Green in 1845 which was condemned because it became too small. Today there is a school on St Clement's Road.

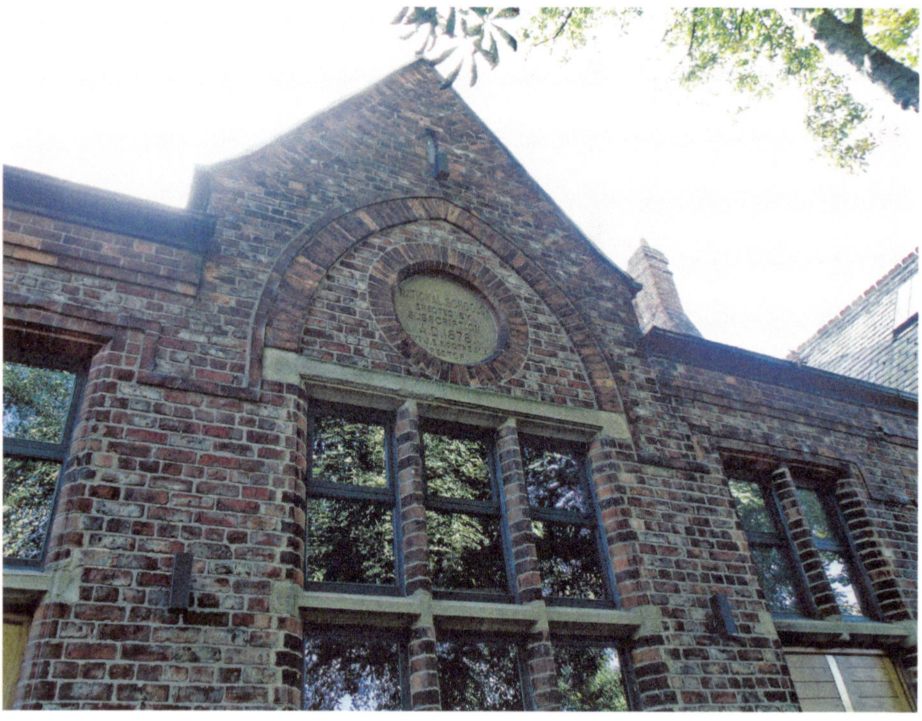

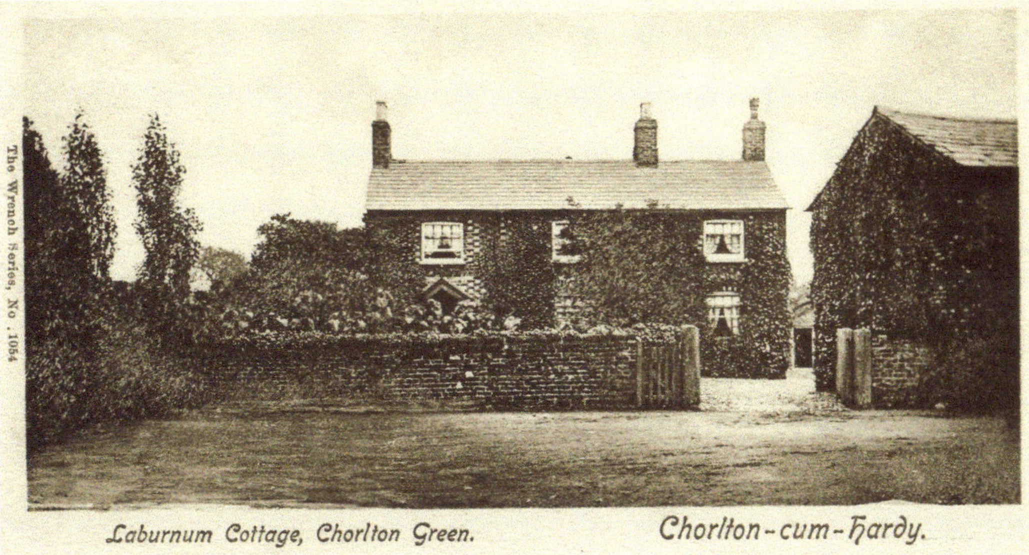

Laburnum Cottage, Chorlton Green, 1904

Laburnum Cottage was also known as Ivy Green Farm and then, later on, as Greenwood's Farm (J. Lloyd). As Chorlton Green began to be 'taken over' by suburban developments, Laburnum Cottage was the only farmhouse around the old village centre to be demolished, with the site now being occupied by a development of town houses. Close to the site is the old church lych-gate and the old churchyard, which are located next to the Bowling Green Hotel. Nothing remains of the original site.

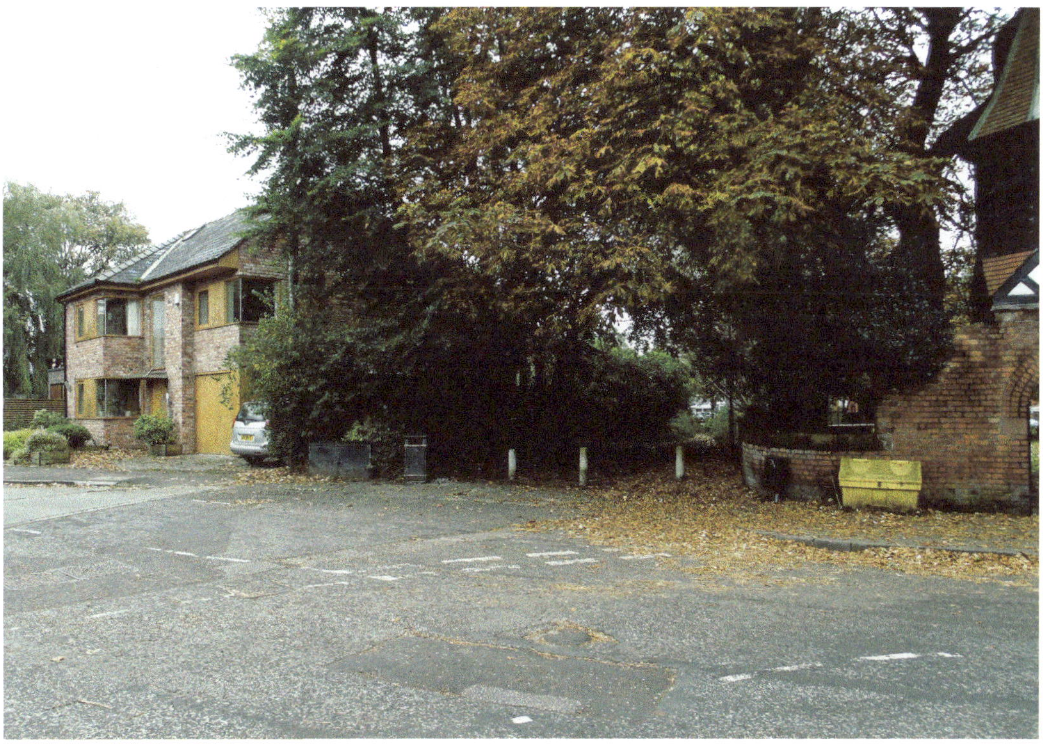

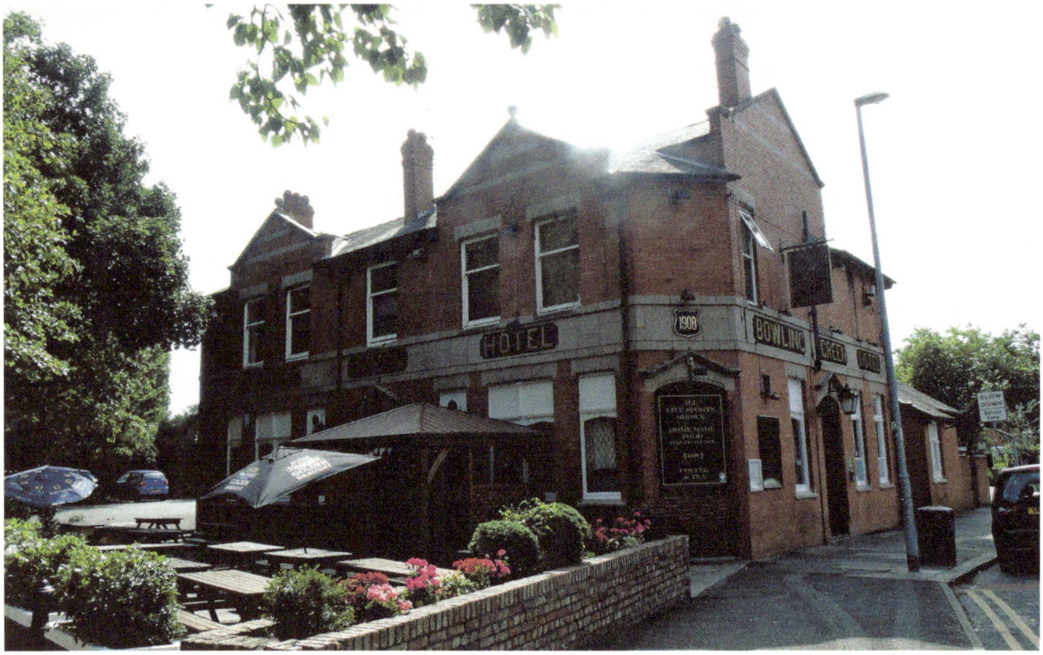

The Bowling Green Hotel (above) and Lych-Gate (below), Chorlton Green, 2017

The first St Clement's was south of Chorlton Green, with the old churchyard next to the Bowling Green Hotel. It was used extensively in the eighteenth and nineteenth centuries, with internments ending in 1882, except for spaces in existing graves. In 1930 bodies remaining in the churchyard were exhumed and reburied in Southern Cemetery. In the 1980s some of the 380 gravestones were used to landscape the churchyard, while others were left in place. The hotel, built in 1908, replaced a building of around 1780.

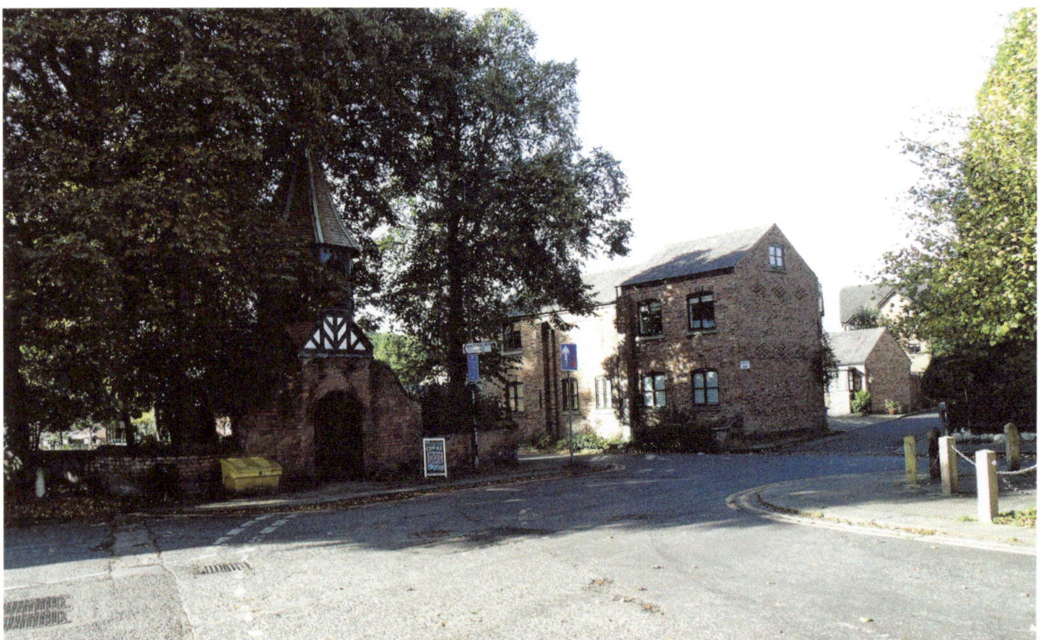

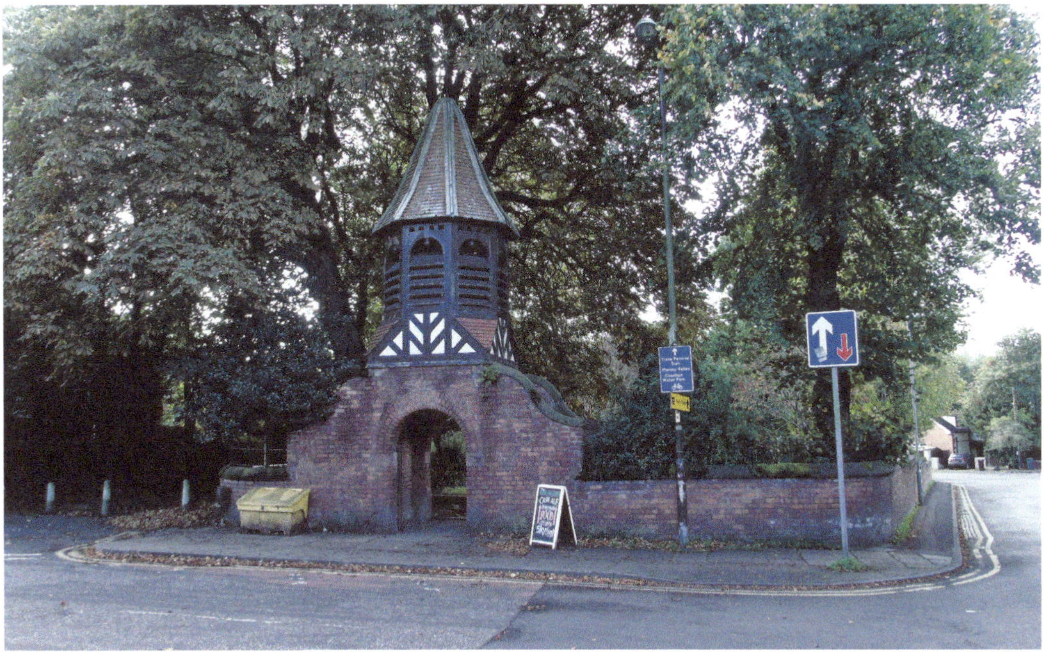

Chorlton Green Lych-Gate (above) and the Bowling Green Hotel from the Old Churchyard (below). ***Inset*:** **Old Churchyard and Lych-Gate, 2017**

The present Bowling Green Hotel dates from 1908 and replaced a building dating from around 1780. The bowling green that gave the hotel its name remains today, behind the hotel. The first Bowling Green public house dated to 1693 and was established to satisfy the recreational needs of villagers. They gathered here to play bowls on an area of land sectioned off by the creation of the old chapel of ease and churchyard (around 1512) directly in front of the inn.

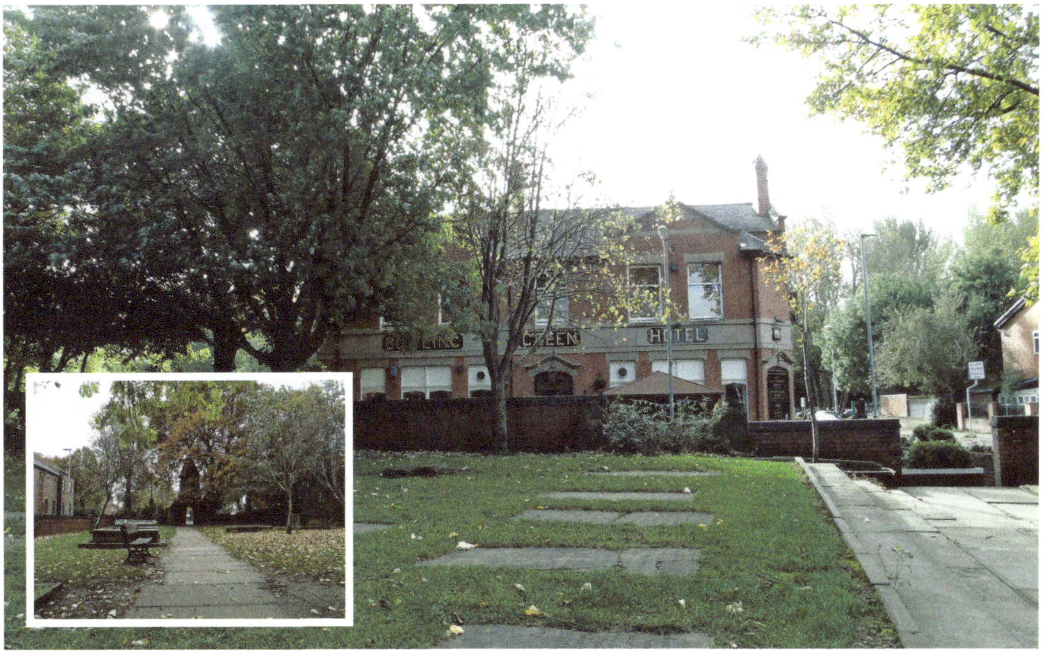

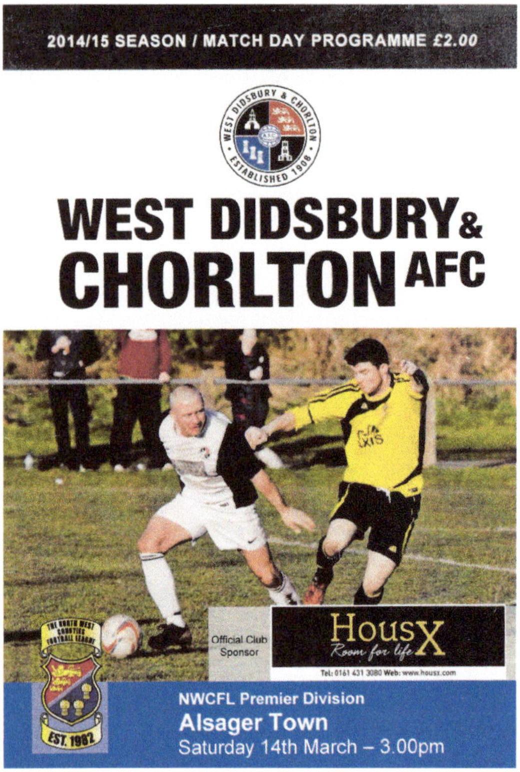

West Didsbury & Chorlton AFC, Recreation Ground, Brookburn Road, Chorltonville, 2015

The club was founded in 1908, as Christ Church AFC. In the 1920/21 season they joined the Lancashire and Cheshire League, as West Didsbury AFC, remaining in the top flight until 1951/52. A semi-professional club, they are currently members of the North-West Counties League, being accepted in 2012/13 and gaining promotion to the Premier Division after just one season. They moved to their current stadium at Brookburn Road, Chorltonville, in 1997, changing their name at the same time.

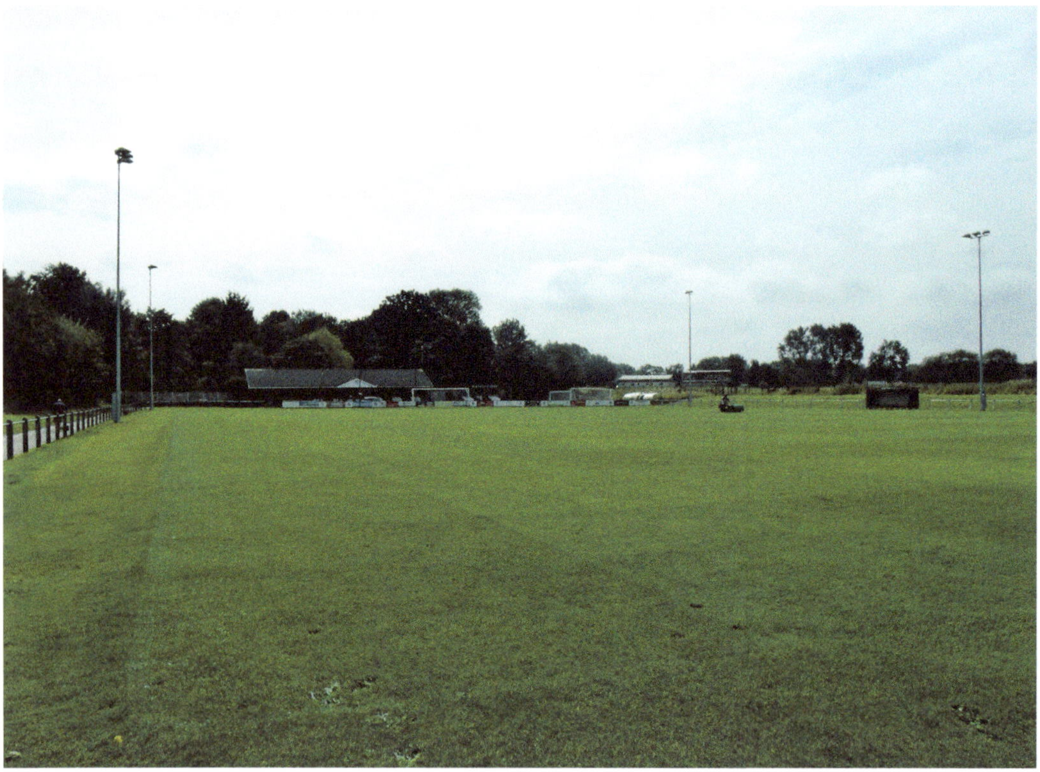

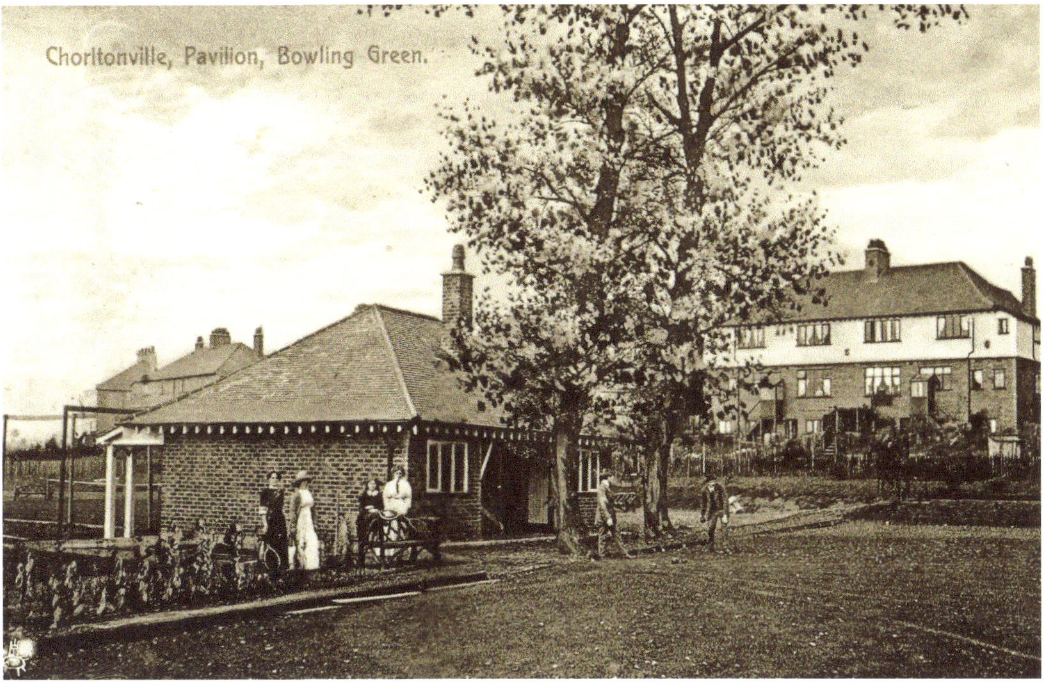

Pavilion and Bowling Green, Chorltonville, 1915

The idea behind the laying-out of tennis courts and a bowling green for Chorltonville, and the construction of a pavilion, was that they would provide for the social well-being of the tenants. After the Second World War the owners' committee sold off the tennis courts and recreation area. The area occupied by the tennis courts was then absorbed by the gardens of adjoining houses, with the recreation area becoming the football ground of West Didsbury & Chorlton AFC.

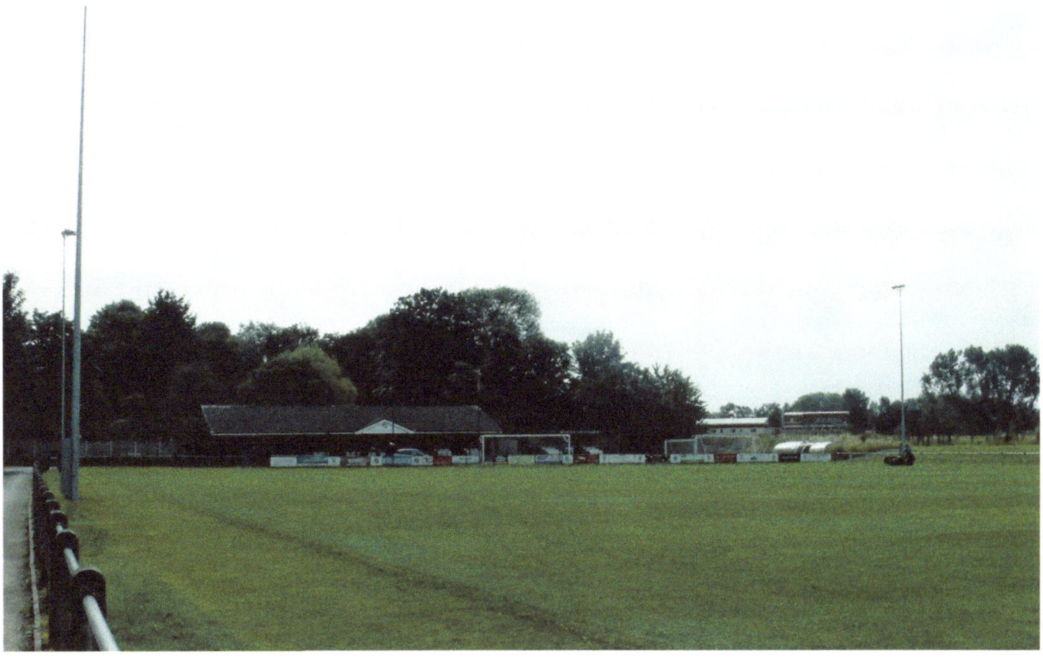

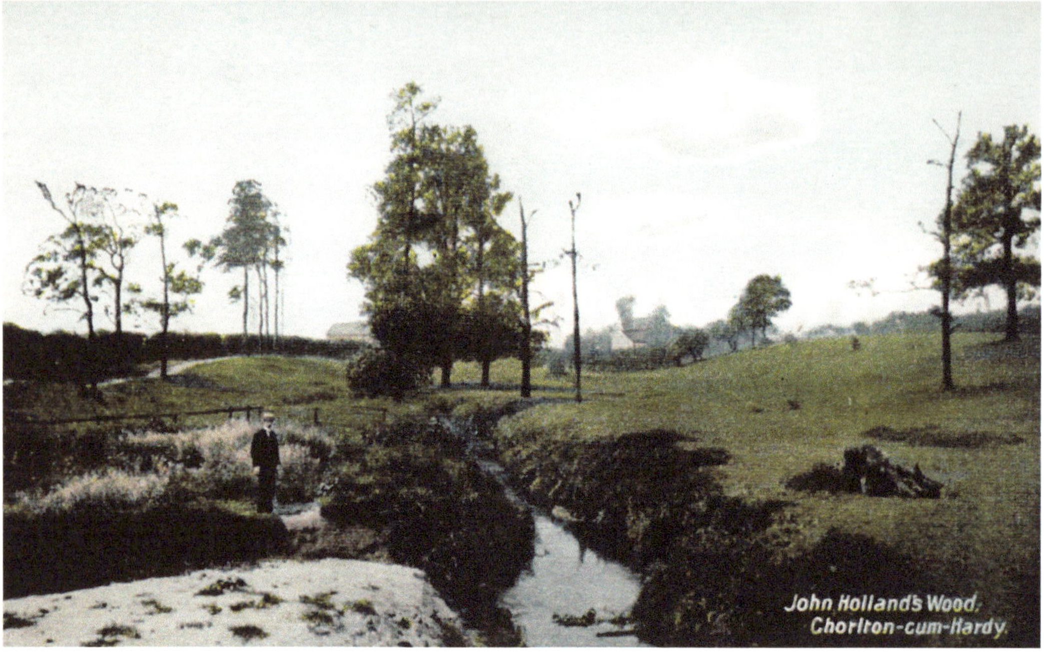

John Holland's Wood, Chorlton Meadows, *c.* 1905

The wood was located on Chorlton Brook, which here runs between Claude Road and Brook(burn) Road. The image above looks from what is today Brook(burn) Road bridge (*below* and *inset*).To the left is Brook(burn) Road, with Brook Farm in the distance. Here Chorlton Brook was known as the Cliffs and was at one time (and today) a heavily wooded area, although it was less so at the time of this image. Chorlton Brook, fed by Red Lion Brook, runs through Chorlton Park, eventually feeding into the River Mersey.

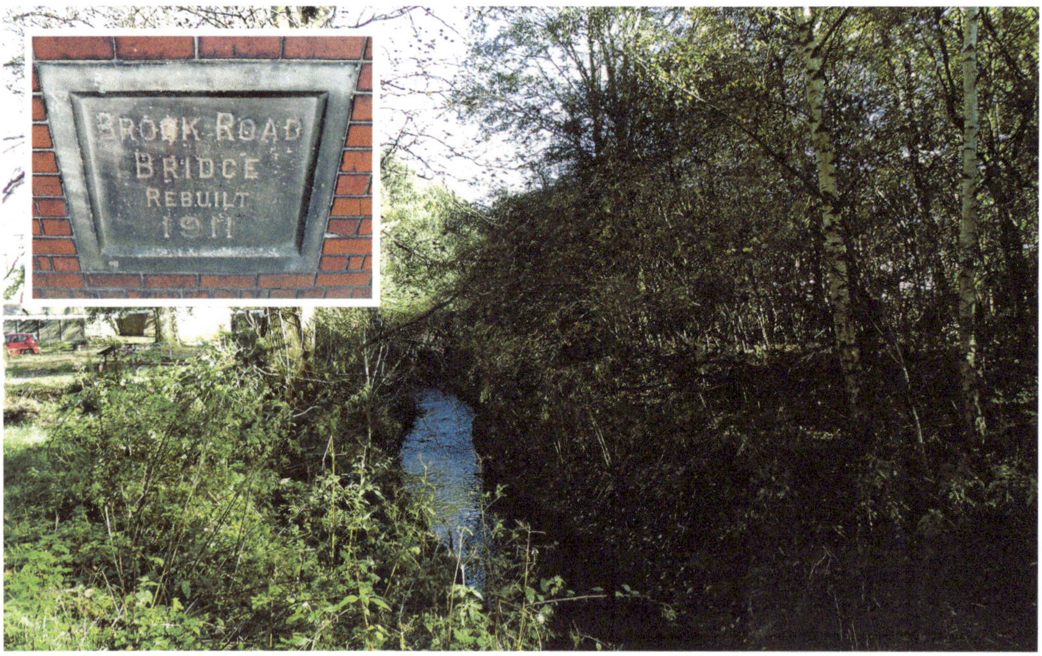

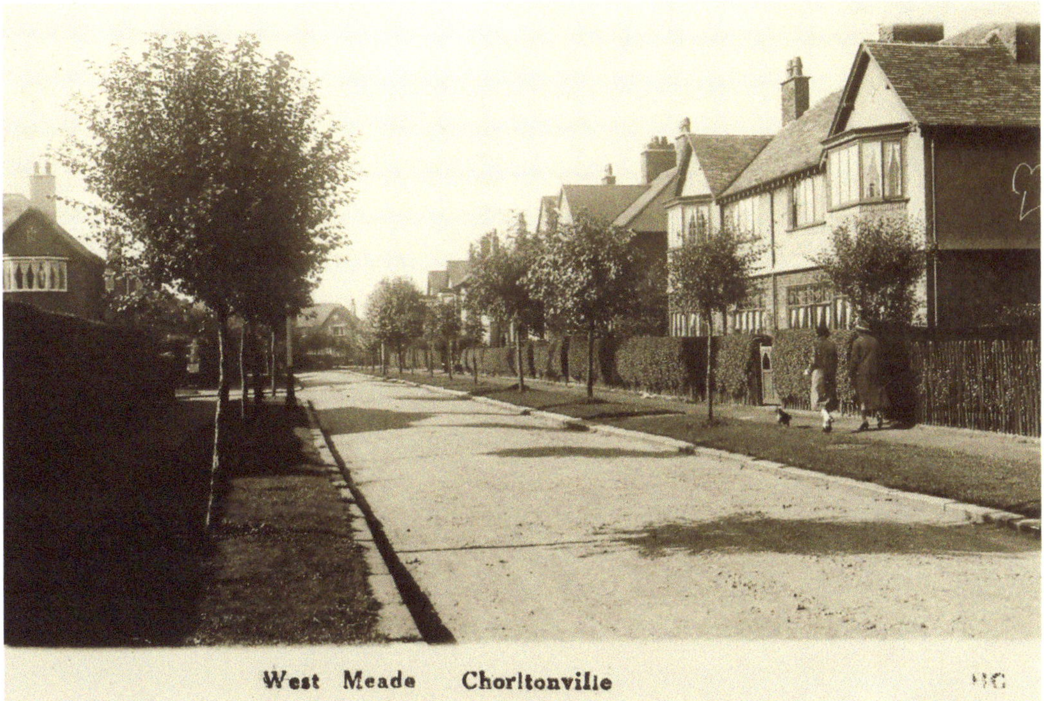

West Meade, Chorltonville, 1927

Chorltonville is an estate of 262 houses, built in 1910–11 as part of the garden village movement of affordable rental housing for skilled artisans. Today most are owner-occupied, with a Board of Trustees responsible for maintenance, meaning that much of the estate's original character has been maintained. Over 350 trees in public areas, grass verges, central greens and winding roads all give the estate a village appearance. Houses are mainly semi-detached and built in the Arts and Crafts style to many different designs.

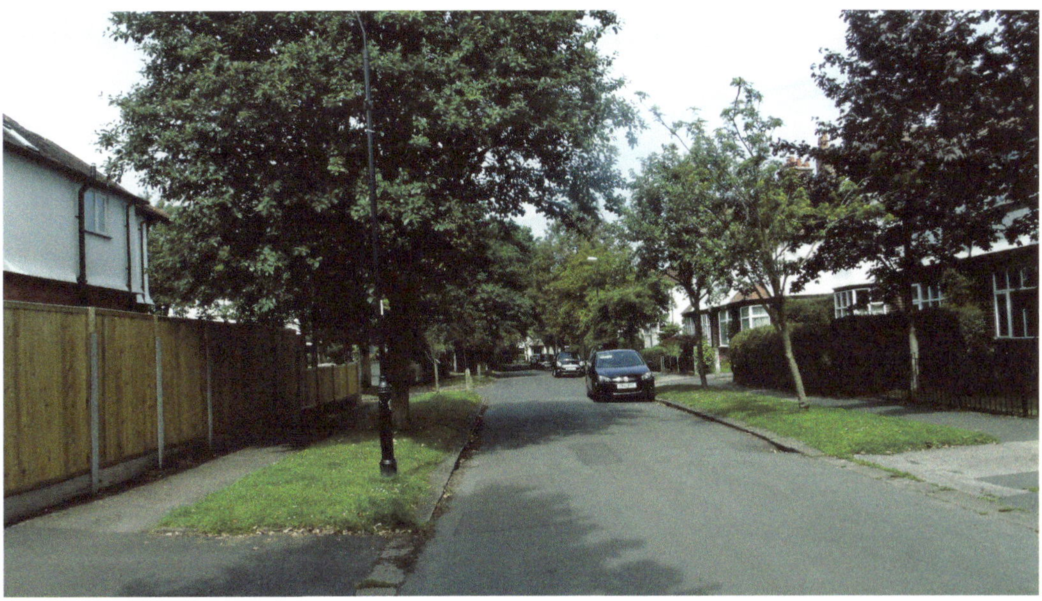

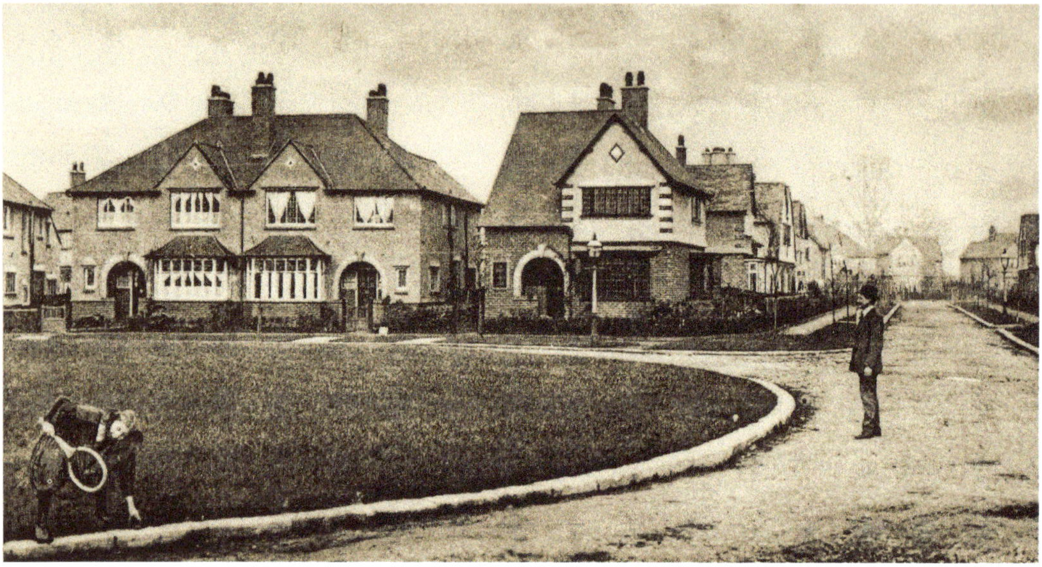

The Meade, Chorltonville, 1912

Detailing on the frontage of each pair of houses makes them unique to the estate. The Meade also has a fine example of a 'village green', with a mature horse chestnut tree as its centrepiece (*inset*). The twelve roads of the estate, which opened on 7 October 1911, converge on The Meade. Chorltonville is one of Manchester City Council's thirty-two Conservation Areas (since 1991) and covers around 26 acres. It was the idea of two local businessmen, James Herbert Dawson and William John Vowles.

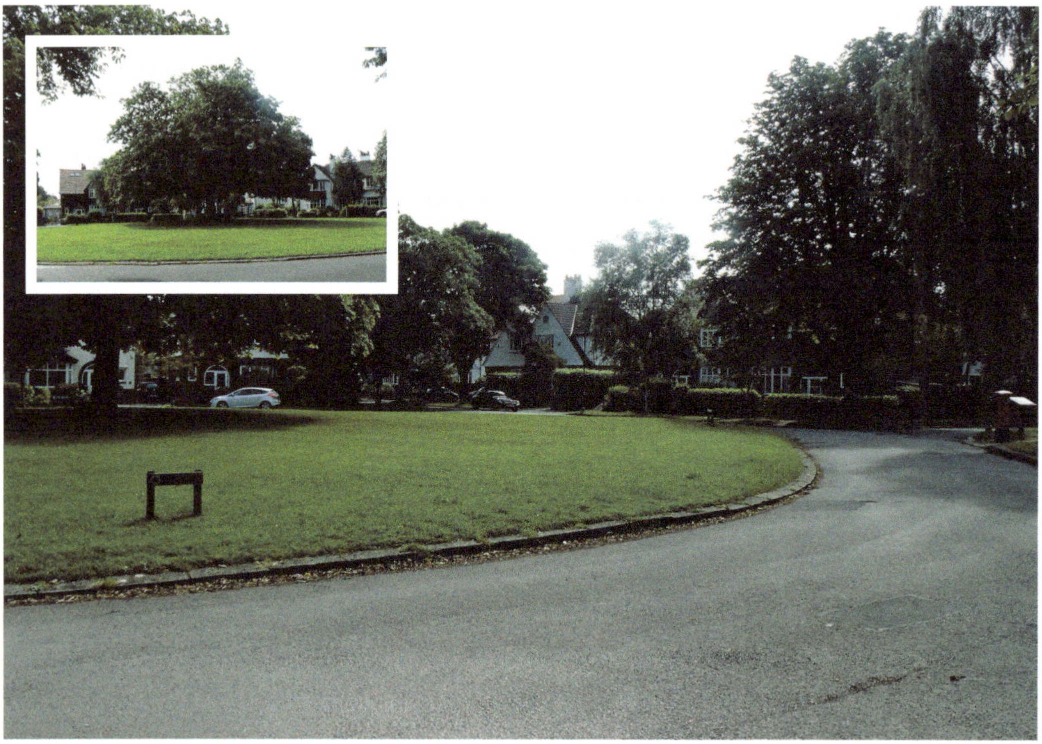

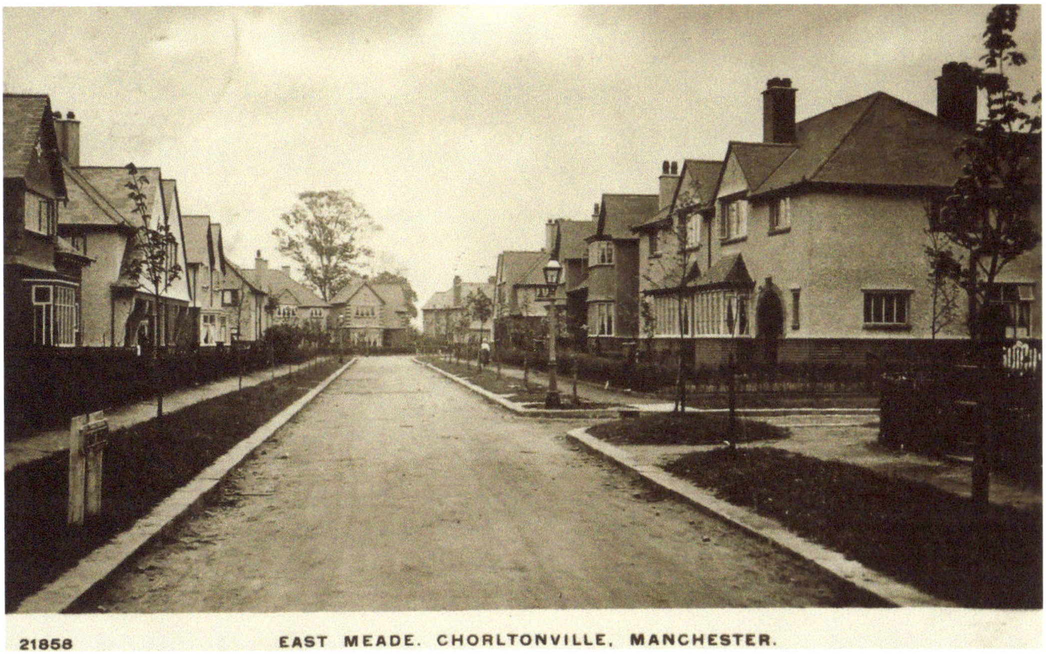

East Meade, Chorltonville, 1912

Chorltonville's houses were well planned in order to maximise light and fresh air for good health, and at affordable rents. Open spaces would encourage healthy recreation, and the houses themselves were supplied with both gas and electricity. The houses and estate were designed by Albert Cuneo and constructed by Thomas Whiteley. Harry Nuttall, MP for Stretford, officially opened Chorltonville. Annual rents started at £24, and although they were originally intended for skilled artisans, houses were quickly occupied by professional families.

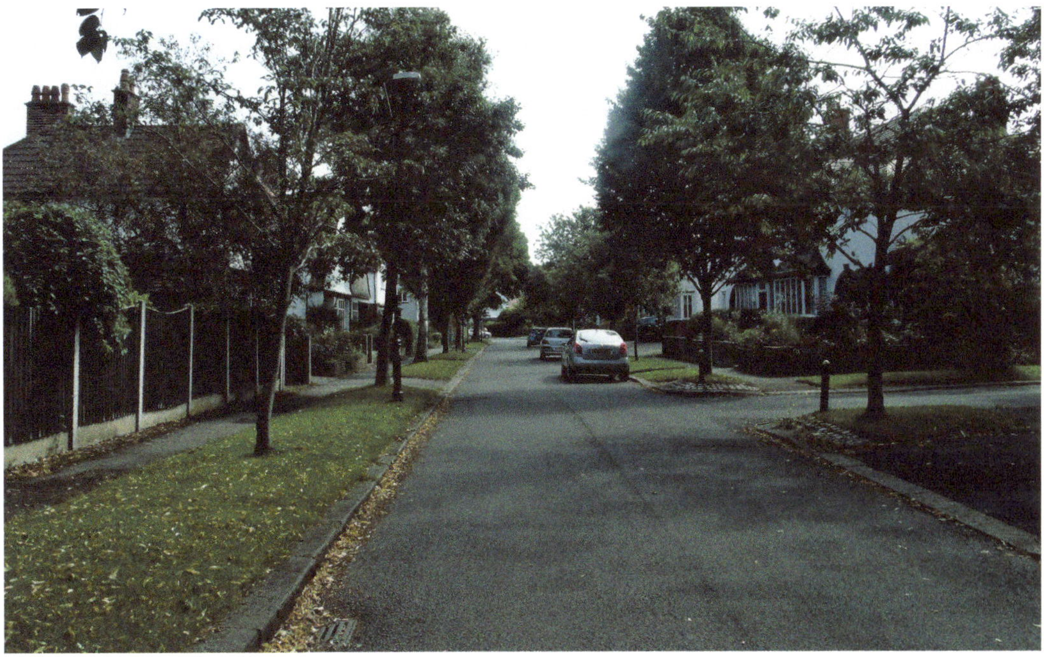

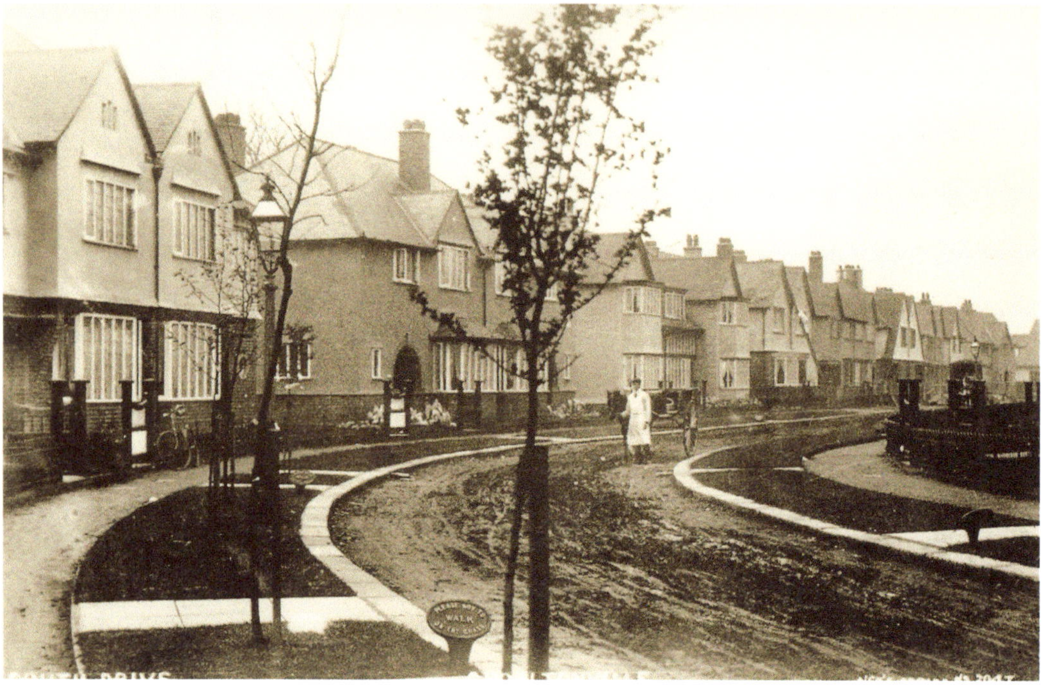

South Drive, Chorltonville, *c.* 1920

Here we can see South Drive curving away to the right, as the designers attempt to emulate winding country lanes. Grass verges typically butt onto roadways throughout Chorltonville, and extensive tree planting adds to the rural theme. There are two 'village greens' and the majority of houses retain most of their architecturally unique features, although most have lost their stained glass. A committee of volunteers undertakes maintenance of the estate, funded by a levy above the local council tax.

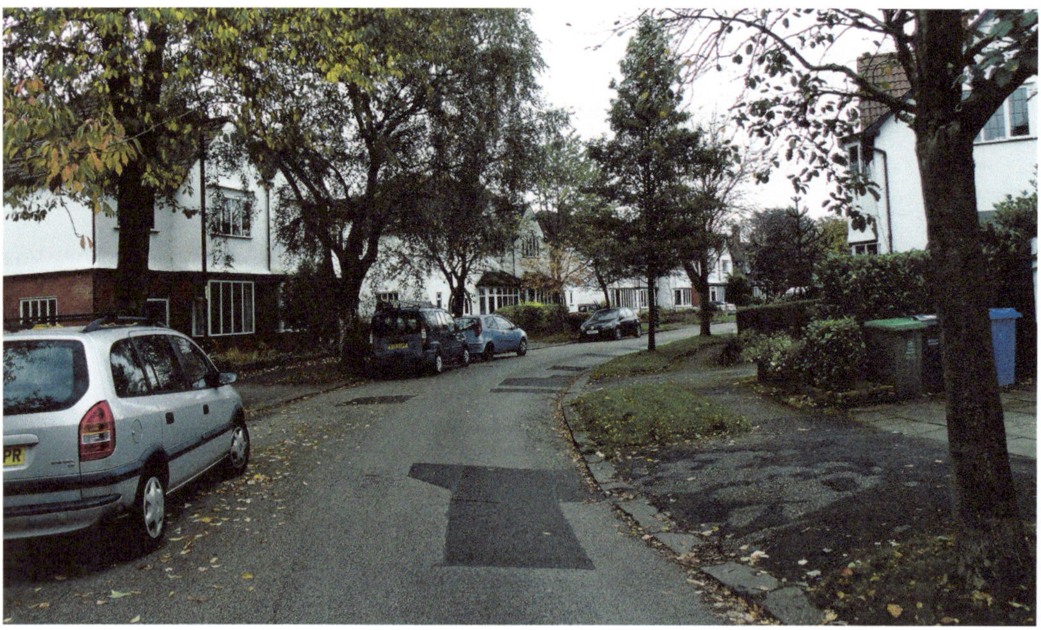

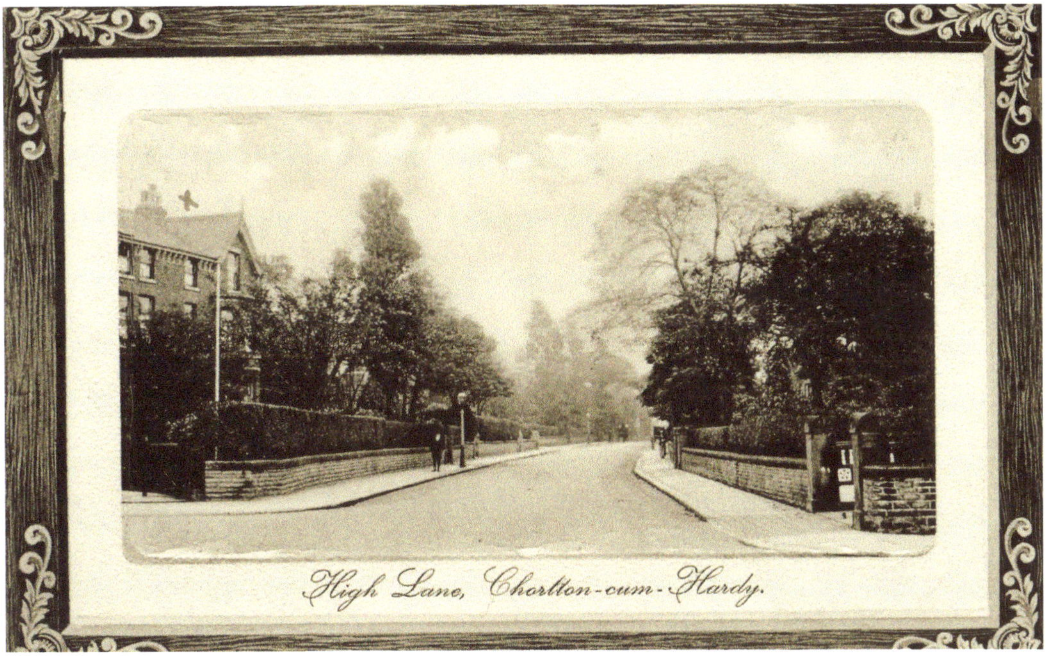

High Lane, Junction with Whitelow Road and St John's Church, Chorlton-cum-Hardy, *c.* 1910

It was 250 years after the martyrdom of St Ambrose that the Roman Catholic Church established a presence in Chorlton. In 1892 St Peter's Chapel was opened on Barlow Moor Road and St Augustine's was begun on High Lane, which St John's was built to replace, in 1926–27 (*inset*). St John's now includes a school and parish centre. Other places of worship on High Lane include the former Primitive Methodist chapel, founded in 1896 and closing in 1967, part of which is situated next to the Buddhist centre.

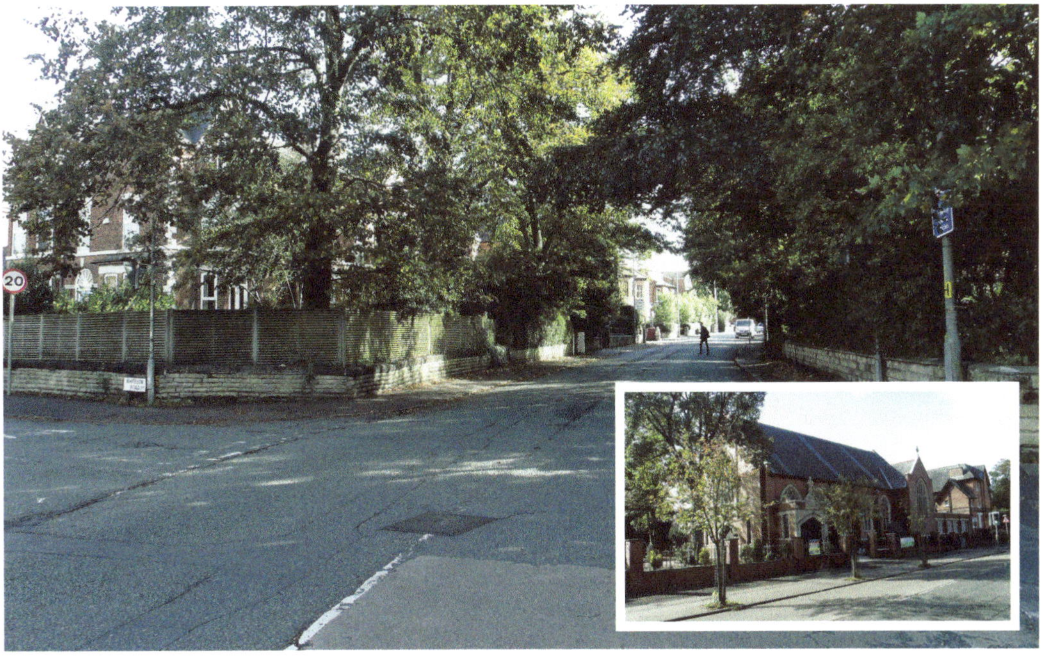

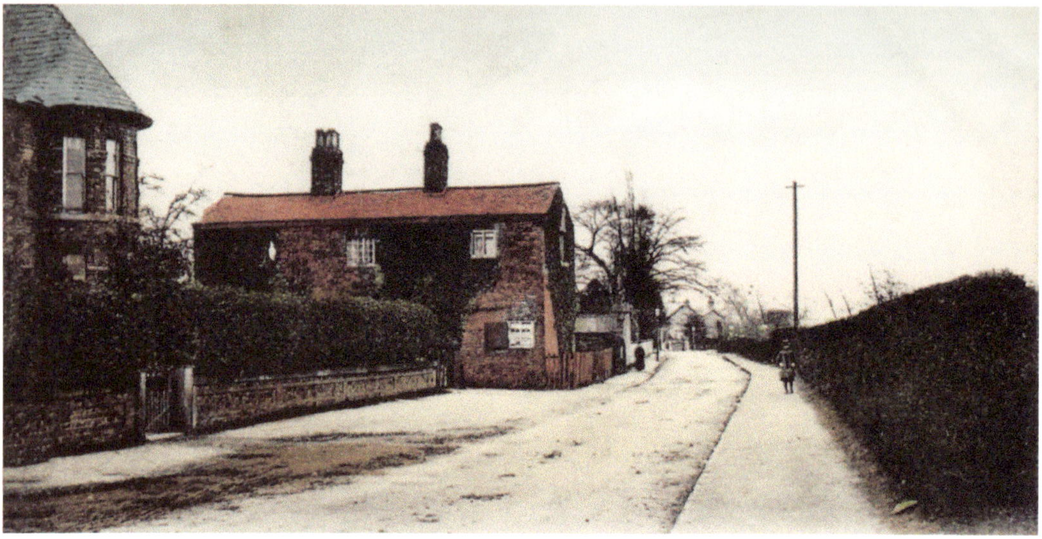

Beech Road from the Recreation Ground, Chorlton-cum-Hardy, *c.* 1905

This view looks towards Acres Road, where there was a footpath leading from Beech Road to High Lane, known as 'The Acre'. This was due to the fact that the fields in this vicinity, bounded by High Lane, Barlow Moor Lane and Beech Road, were one Lancashire acre in measurement. The footpath then ran from High Lane to Manchester Road, a portion being known as 'Scotshill', after the Scottish rebels of 1745. The rest was known as the 'Winnick', after an adjoining field.

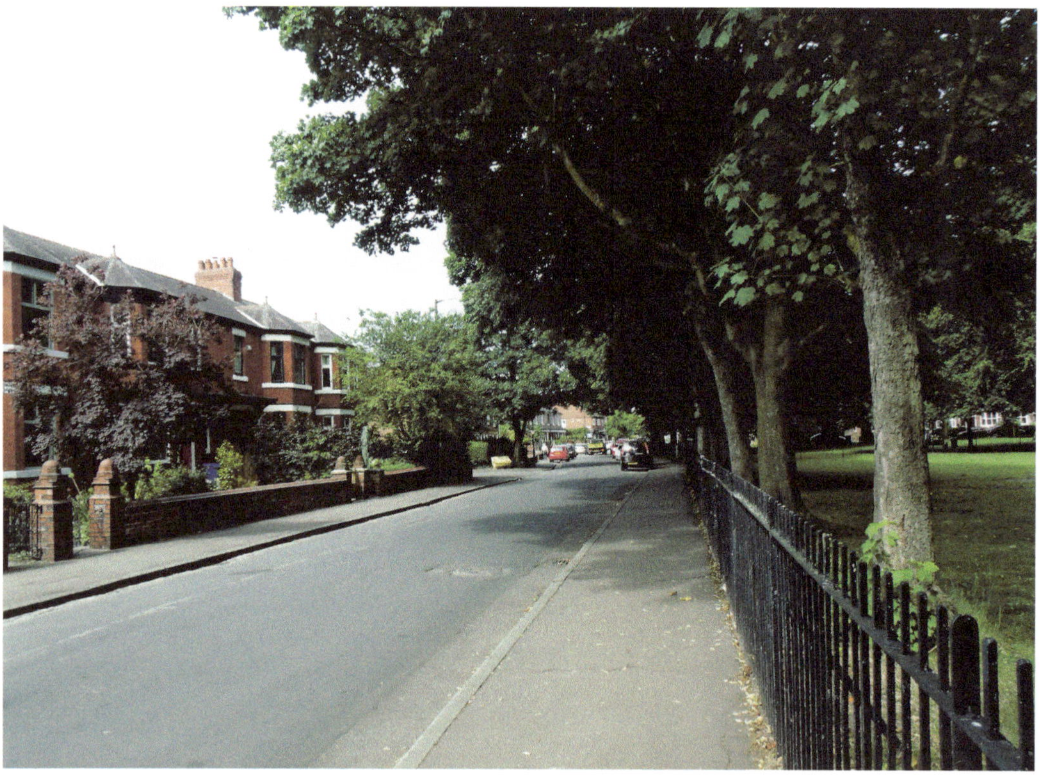

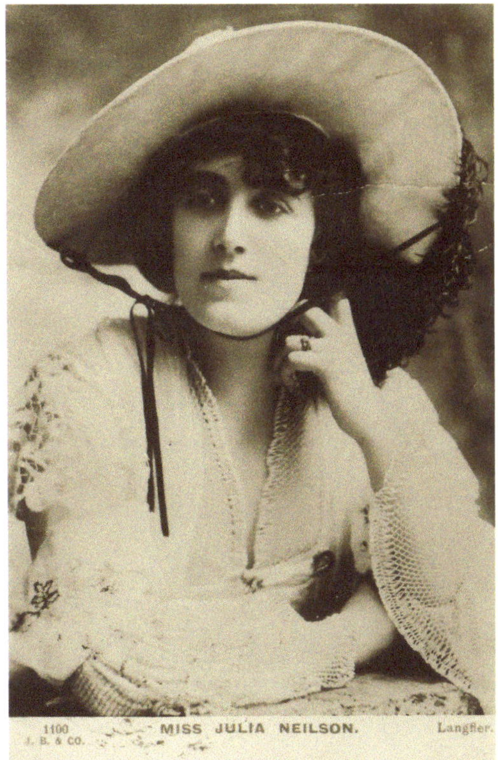

Miss Julia Nielsen and No. 31 Church (now Chequers) Road, Chorlton-cum-Hardy, 1914

Julia Emilie Nielsen (1868–1957) was an English actress who performed in many tragedies and historical romances. With her husband, Fred Terry, she played in London and on tour for nearly three decades. At the time of the photograph (1914) they were preparing to star in and produce *Mistress Wilful* by Ernest Hendrie (1915). The theatres of Manchester would have been very familiar to her, in what was a popular entertainment of the time. Entertainment in Chorlton was also growing in popularity at this time.

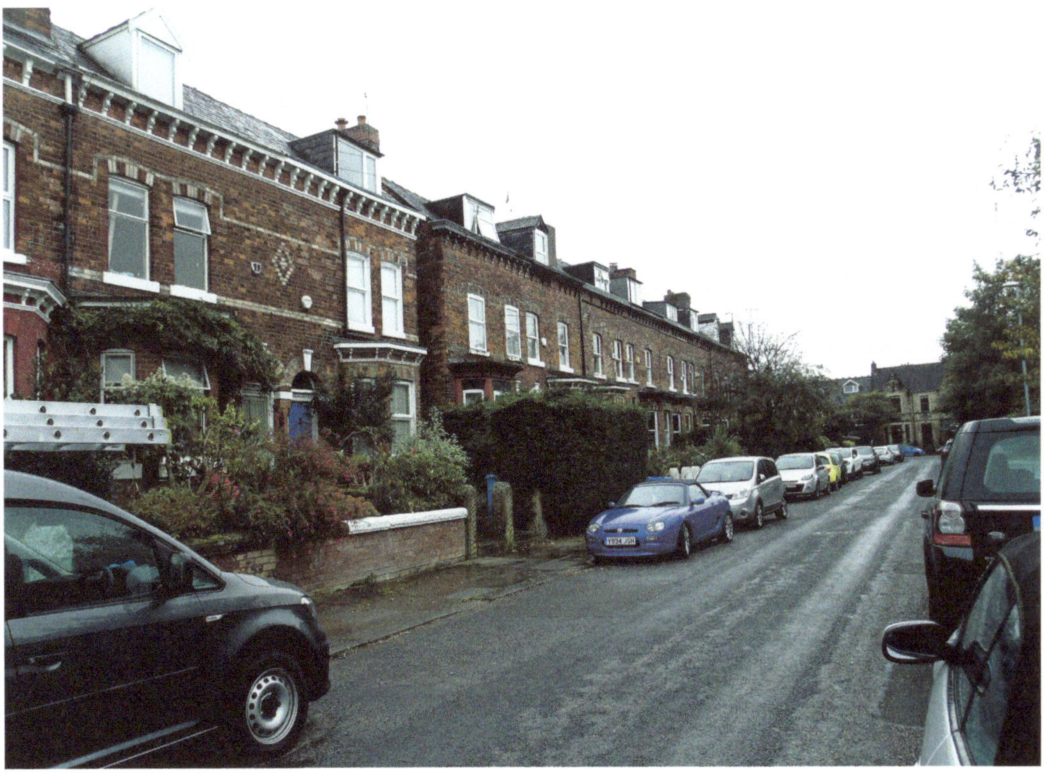

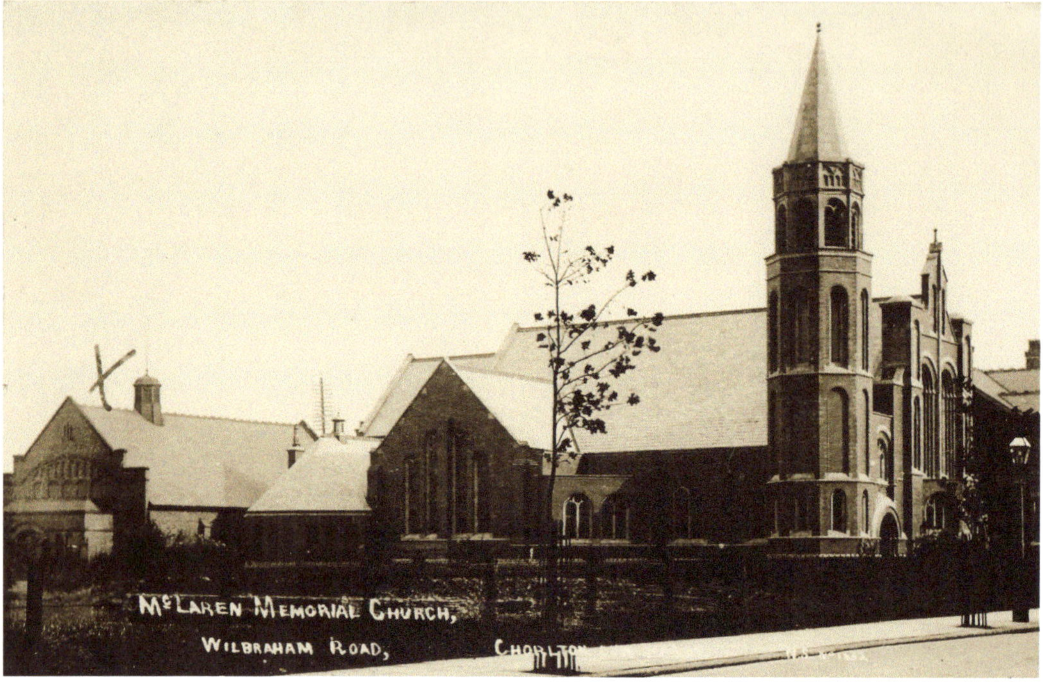

Mclaren Memorial Church, Wilbraham Road, Chorlton-cum-Hardy, *c.* 1915

The Mclaren Baptist Church was established in 1907. In the photograph of *c.* 1915 there is a cross above the Baptist Sunday school, immediately behind the church, with the reverse of the photograph stating that 'this is the hospital'. This refers to the time when it was used as an auxiliary hospital during the First World War. Local people served as voluntary nurses, orderlies, kitchen staff and administrators, and its cost was partly met by the public. Now demolished, the site is occupied by flats.

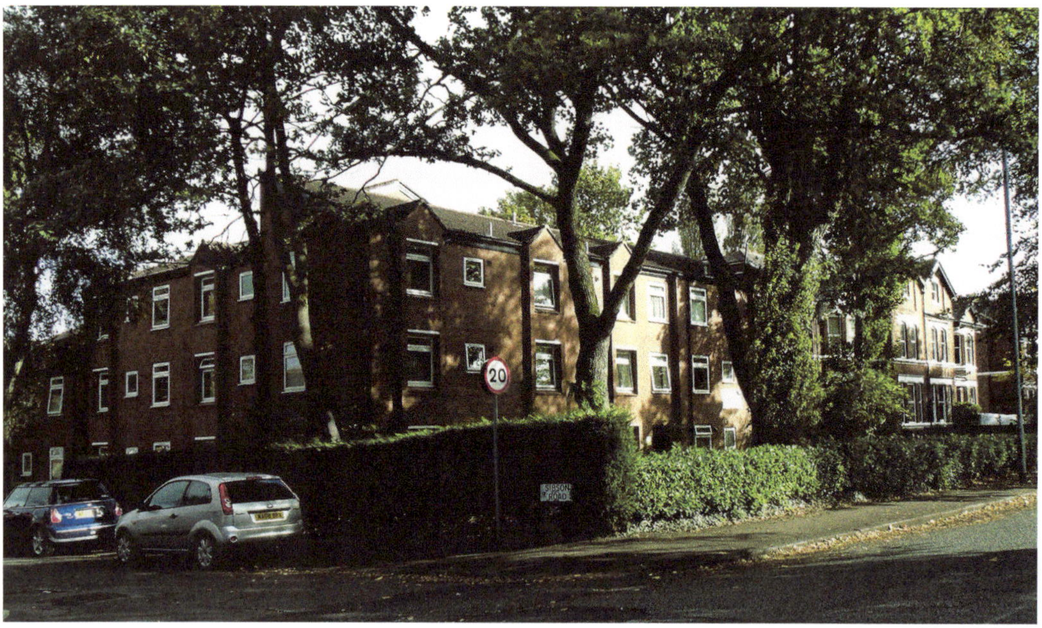

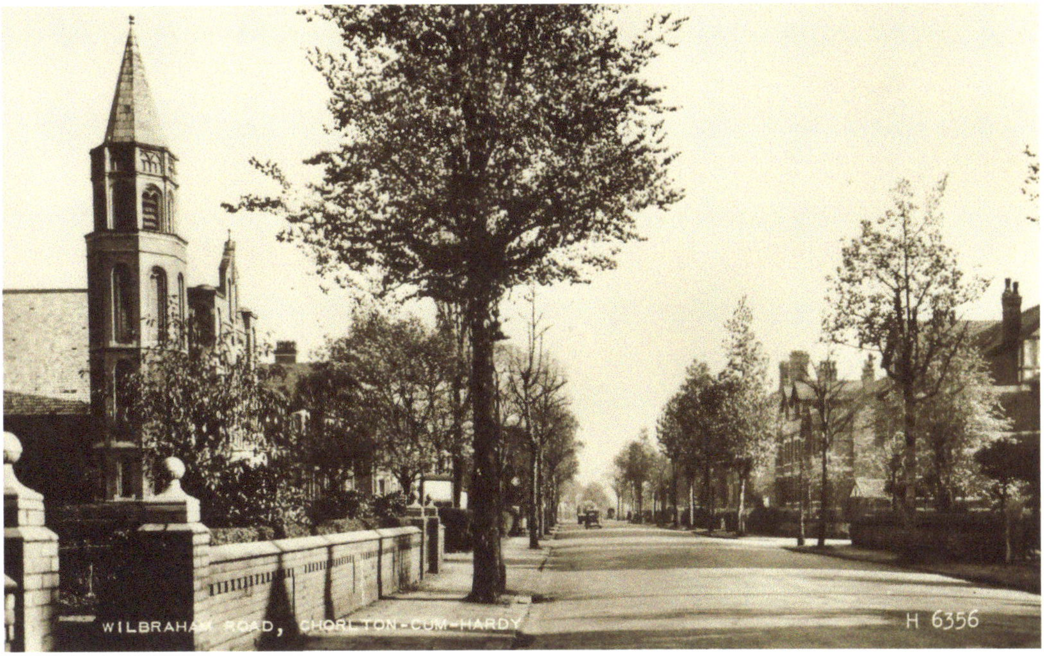

Wilbraham Road, Chorlton-cum-Hardy, *c.* 1950

On the left is the Mclaren Baptist Church and Wilbraham Road's junction with Sibson Road. Today this is the site of Mclaren Court flats. On the right is the junction of Hastings Avenue and Wilbraham Road and beyond this is the former Public Hall (Conservative Club) building. This view looks towards the centre of Chorlton-cum-Hardy, and takes into account the fact that today the road is both extremely busy at times, and obstructed with parked motor vehicles.

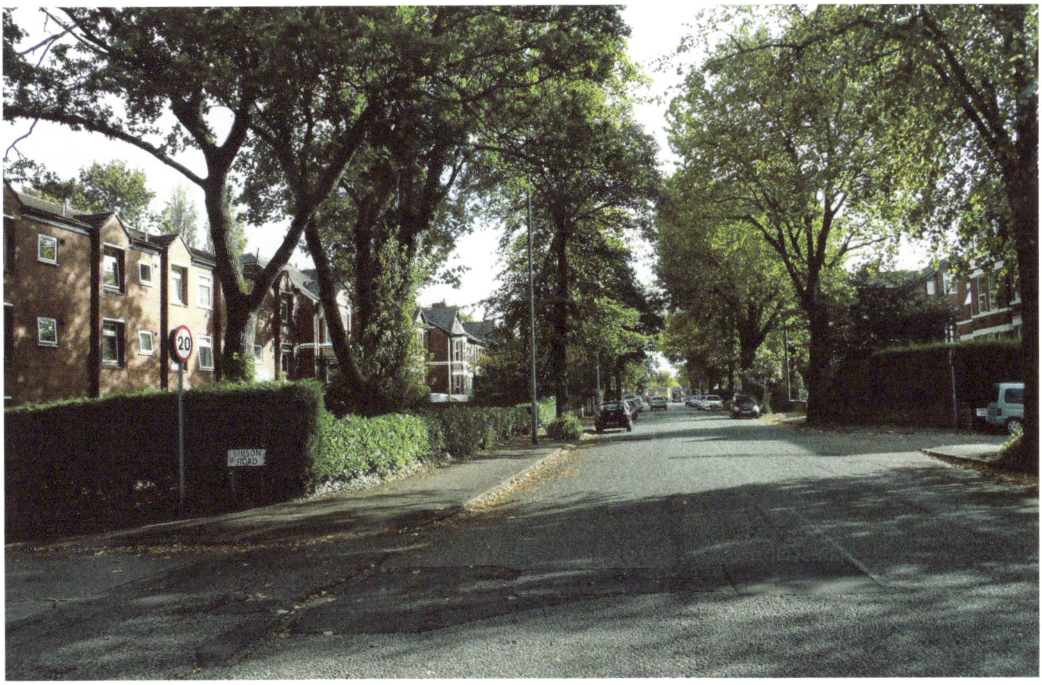

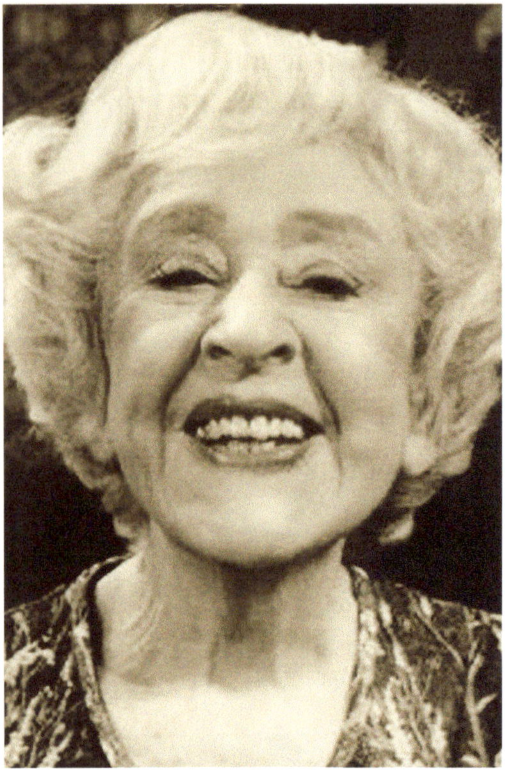

Doris Speed and No. 13 Sibson Road (below, left), Chorlton-cum-Hardy, 2017

No. 13 Sibson Road is the site of a plaque commemorating former Coronation Street actress Doris Speed, who lived at this address while appearing in the long-running soap opera. The plaque reads 'Doris Speed actress 1899–1994 lived in this house whilst appearing as Annie Walker in Coronation Street.' Sibson Road forms a junction with Wilbraham Road, where the old Mclaren Baptist Church once stood, on the corner. The properties here are of the semi-detached type, along wide, tree-lined roads.

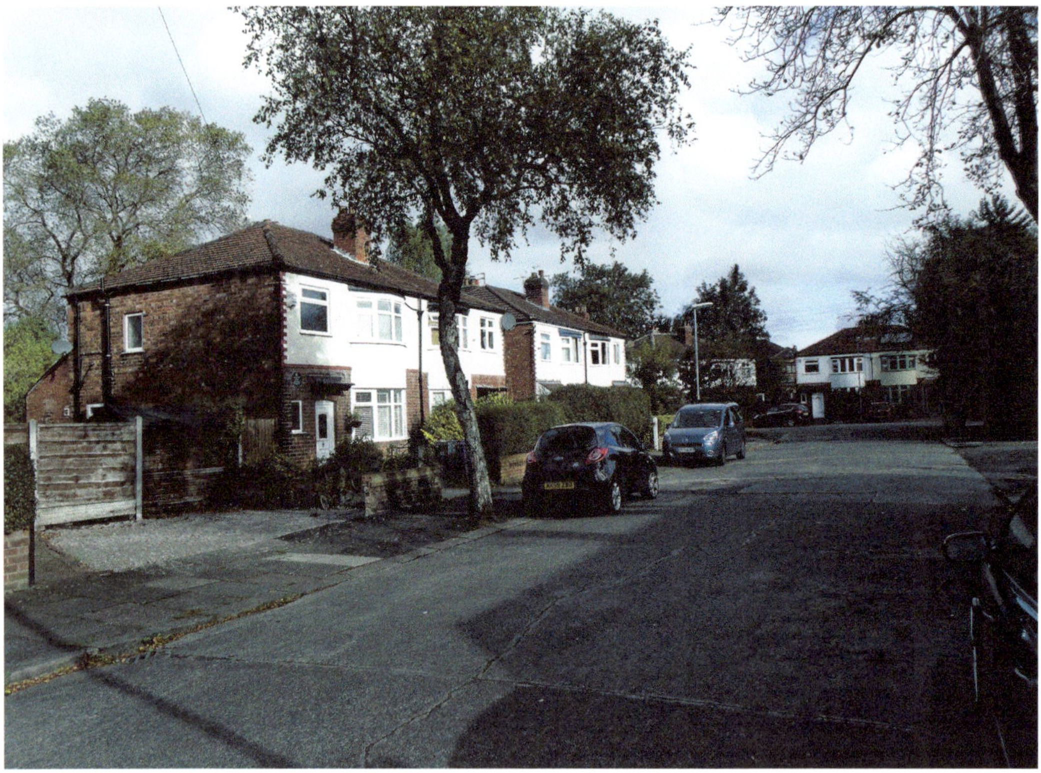

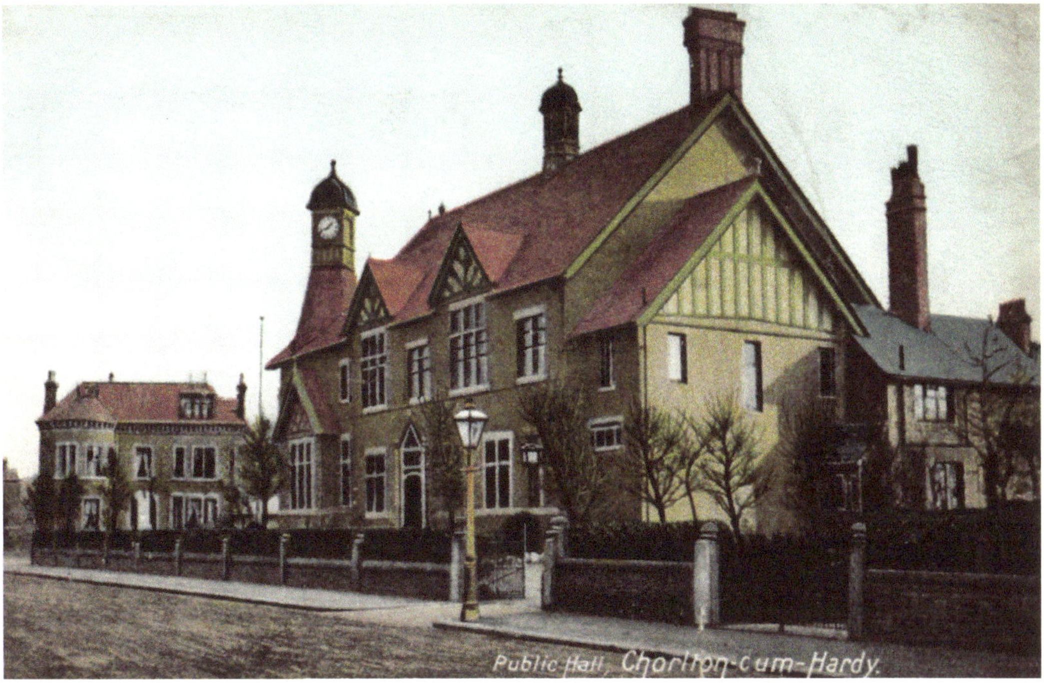

Public Hall, Looking Towards the Lloyds Hotel, Chorlton-cum-Hardy, 1907

On the right of the above 1907 image is Wilbraham Road's junction with Manchester Road, which forms a crossroads with Oswald Road and the Spread Eagle, to the left. Beyond the Public Hall can be seen the site of the Lloyds Hotel, and the clock tower of the Public Hall – or Conservative Club – can also be clearly seen. It remains a landmark in Chorlton-cum-Hardy to this day, although the influence of the political party the club represented has declined locally in recent years.

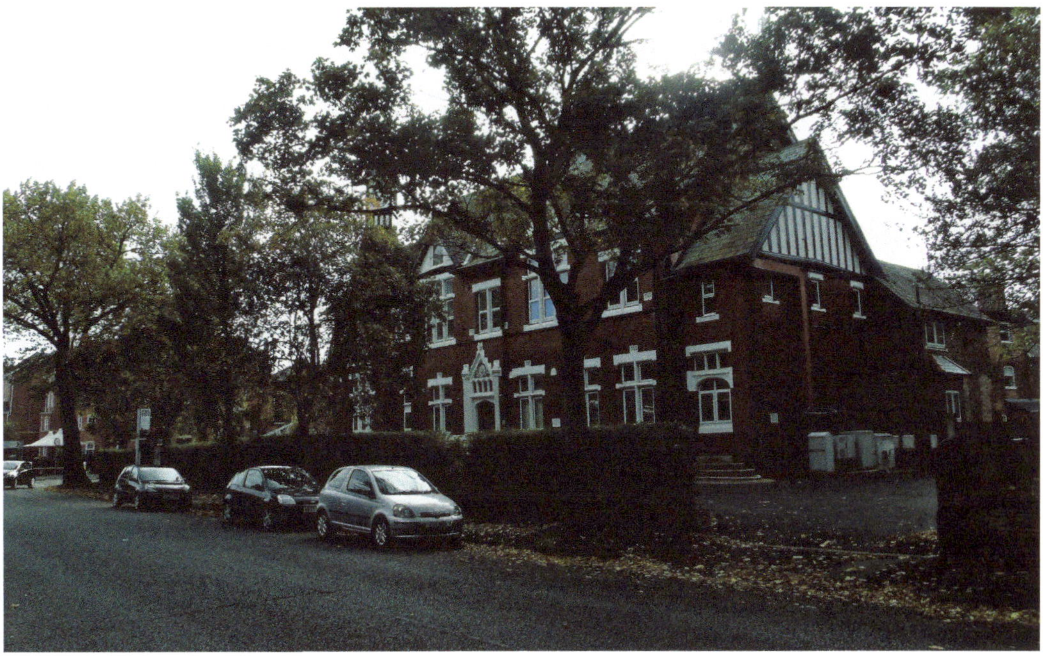

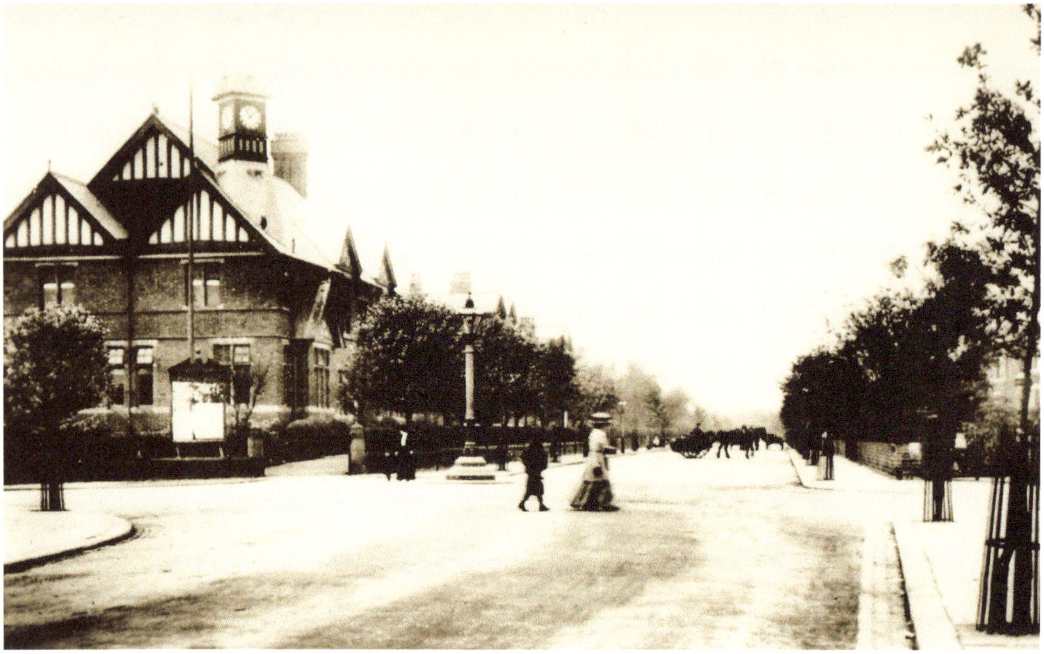

Wilbraham Road Conservative Club, Looking Towards Edge Lane, Chorlton-cum-Hardy, c. 1900

In 1883 the Conservative Association of Chorlton met at the Lloyds Hotel and came to an agreement to seek permission from the Egerton Estate for land to construct a club. From the Conservative Club's opening in 1892 it was known as the Public Hall. It was the centre for many activities – not all of them political – as it was the base for an amateur dramatics group which performed there at one time. Chorlton-cum-Hardy returned mainly Tory MPs until the mid-1980s.

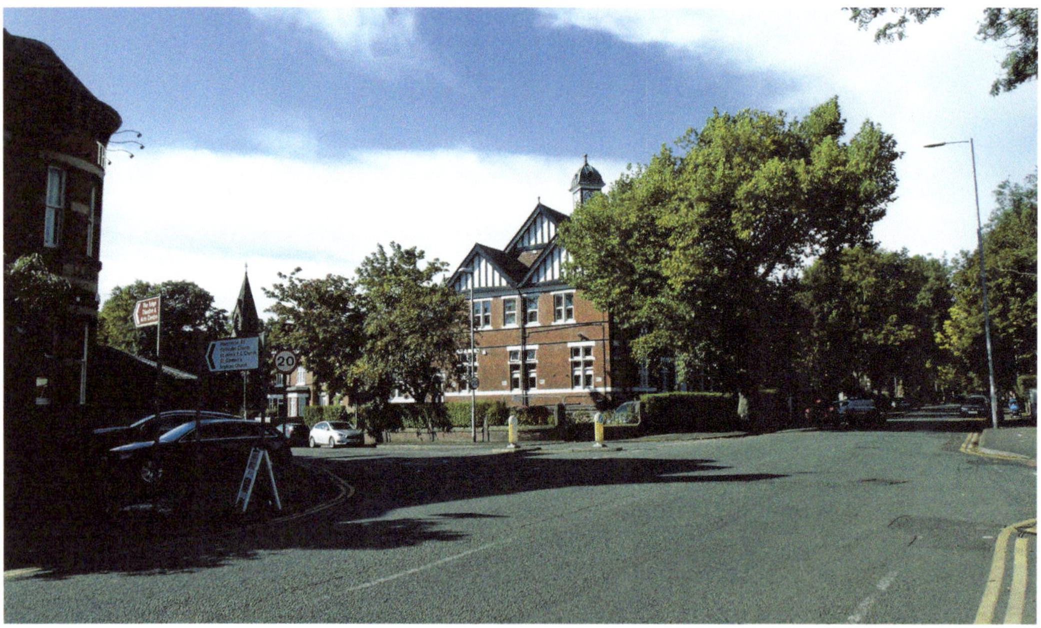

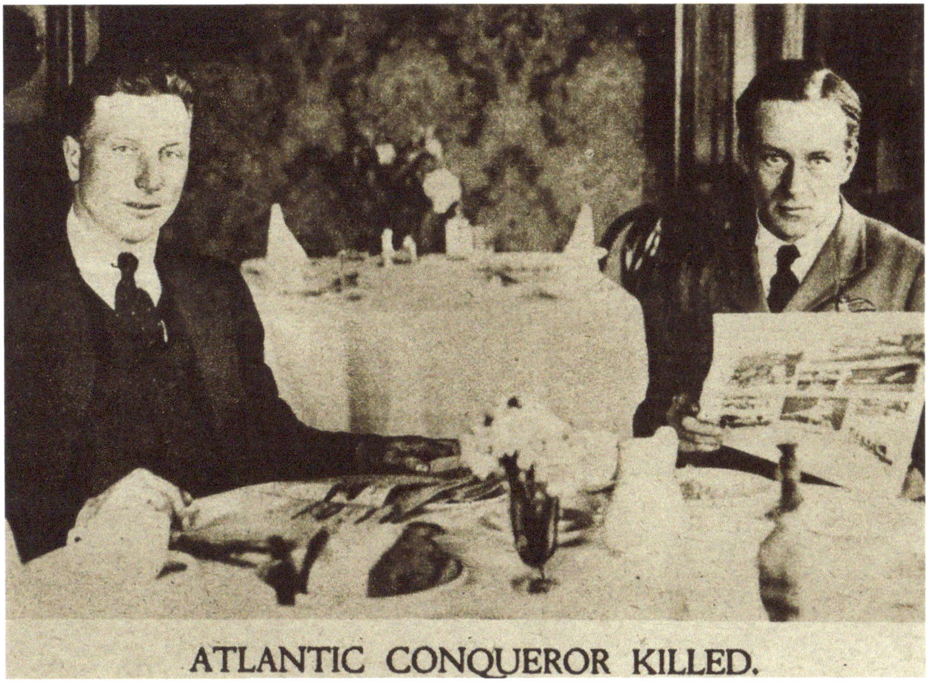

Alcock (left) and Brown (right), 1919, and No. 6 Oswald Road, Chorlton-cum-Hardy, 2017
Sir John Alcock was born at Basford House, Seymour Grove, Old Trafford (*inset*), in 1892. He became a military pilot, and after the First World War continued to fly. Sir Arthur Whitten Brown was born in Glasgow, in 1886, to American parents, and before the First World War became an engineer at the Westinghouse factory, Trafford Park, Stretford. He continued as an aerial navigator after the end of the war. Their flight across the Atlantic, from Newfoundland to Ireland, took sixteen hours.

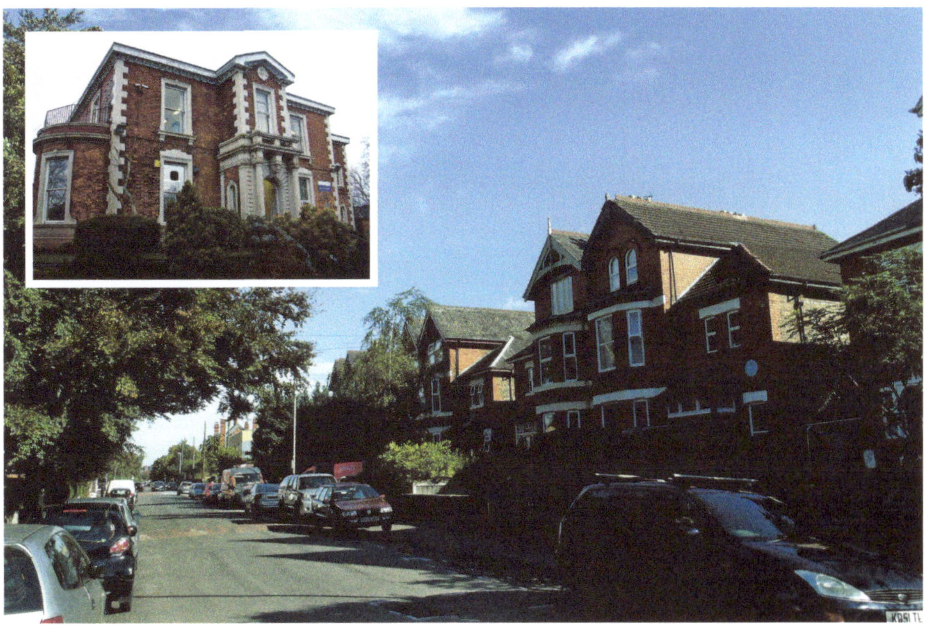

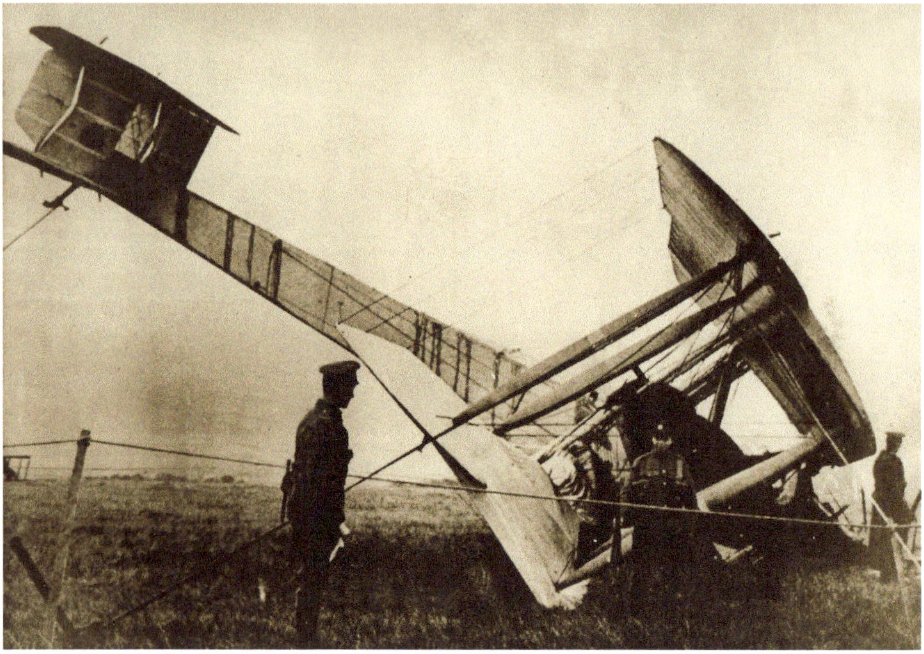

Alcock and Brown's Aeroplane, 1919, and Blue Plaque, No. 6 Oswald Road, Chorlton-cum-Hardy, 2017

The blue plaque at Oswald Road reads 'Lieut. Sir Arthur Whitten Brown KBE (1886–1948) who with Capt. Sir John Alcock made the first non-stop aeroplane crossing of the Atlantic 14–15 June 1919 lived here'. Sir John Alcock was killed on 18 December 1919, when he crashed near Rouen while flying the new Vickers Viking amphibian to the Paris air show. Sir Arthur Whitten Brown, who was born in Glasgow and moved to Chorlton as a boy, died on 4 October 1948, of an accidental overdose.

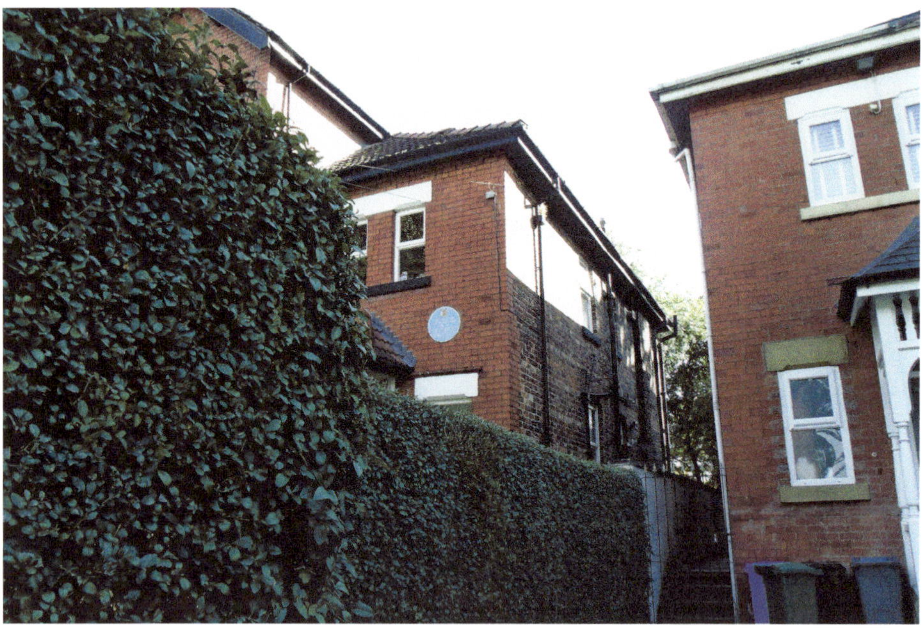

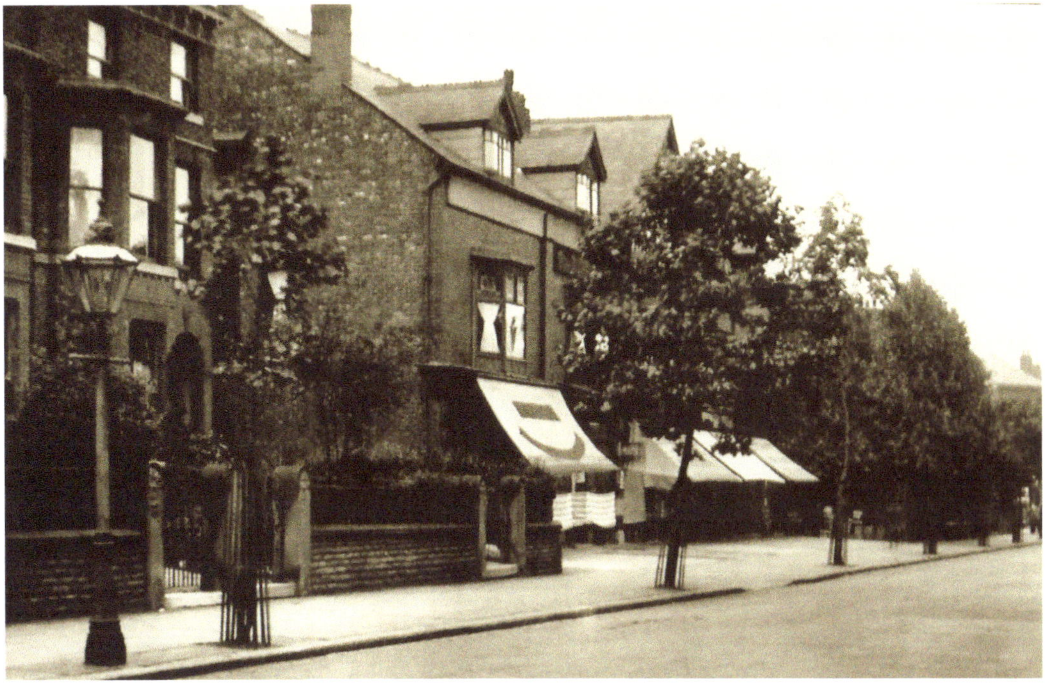

Wilbraham Road, Chorlton-cum-Hardy, *c.* 1910

Wilbraham Road is one of the main shopping districts of Chorlton-cum-Hardy. Typically small-shop owners plied their trade here. The photograph shows a row of terraced residential properties (extreme left), which are now retail premises that have also had their frontages extended across former gardens and the pavement. The shops in the centre of the image, with blinds drawn against the sun, are now a Costa coffee shop, with Wilbraham Road here (on both sides) heavily redeveloped over the decades.

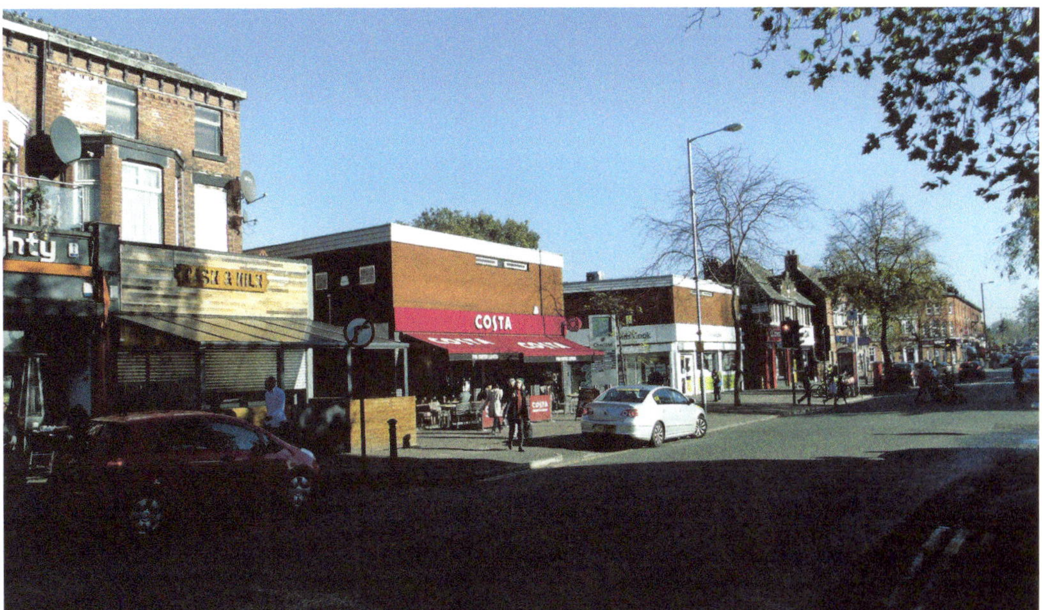

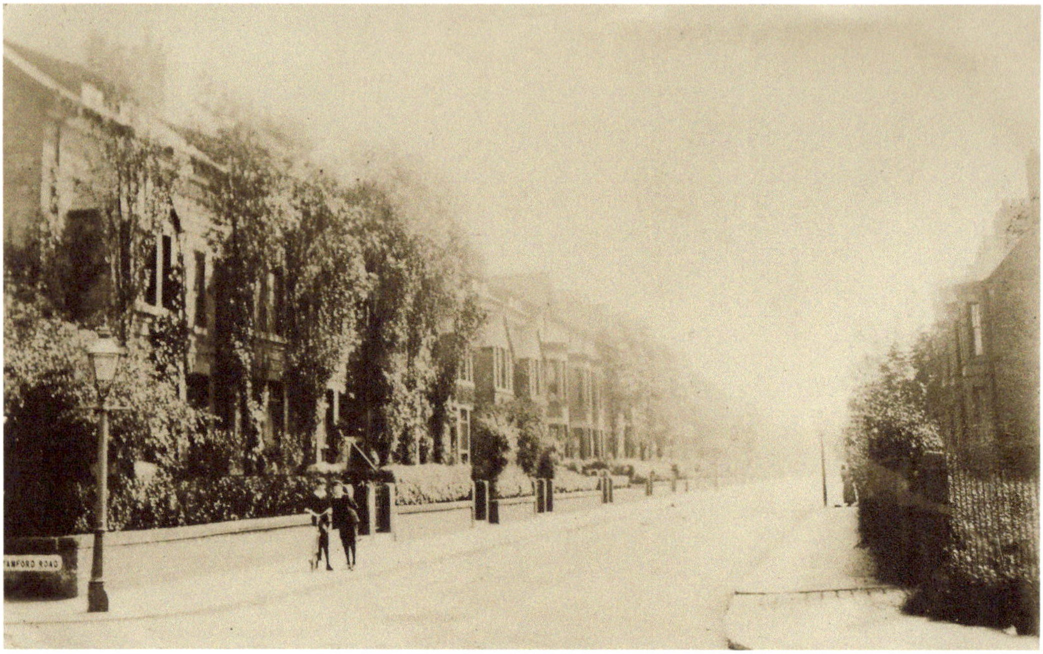

Keppel Road from Stamford Road Junction, Chorlton-cum-Hardy, *c.* 1910

Keppel Road is shown here at its junction with Stamford Road, which was renamed Brantingham Road sometime after the First World War, when the area was developed. Brothers Barry, Robin and Maurice Gibb, members of world-famous pop group The Bee Gees, spent their childhood at Keppel Road before emigration to Brisbane, Australia. The brothers were born on the Isle of Man but moved to Manchester in the 1950s, living in Keppel Road until they emigrated in 1958. Maurice died in 2003, and Robin in 2012.

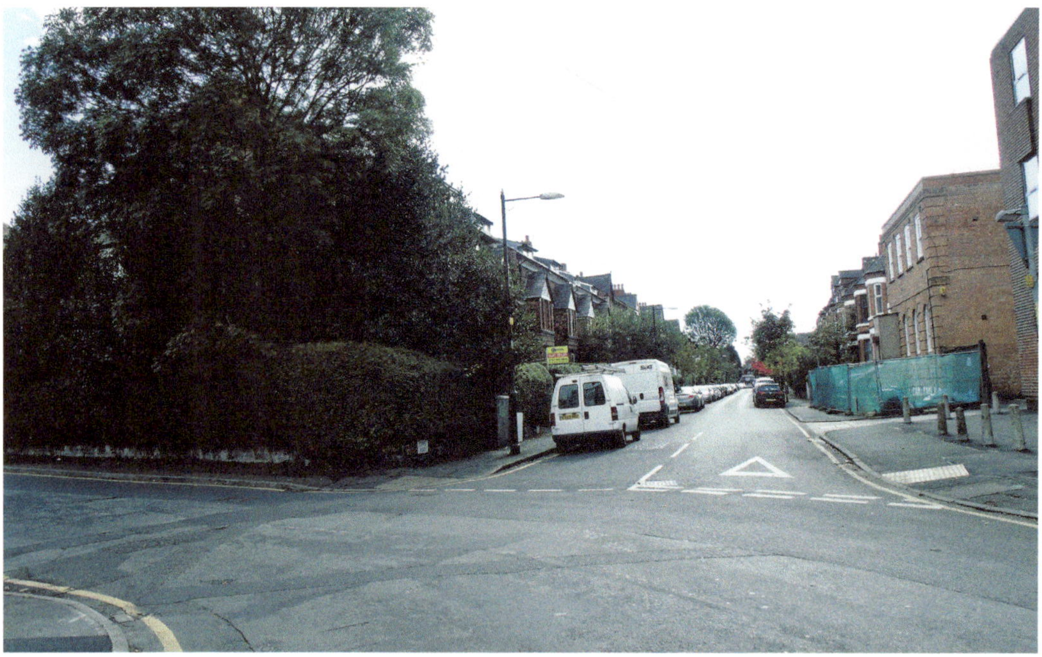

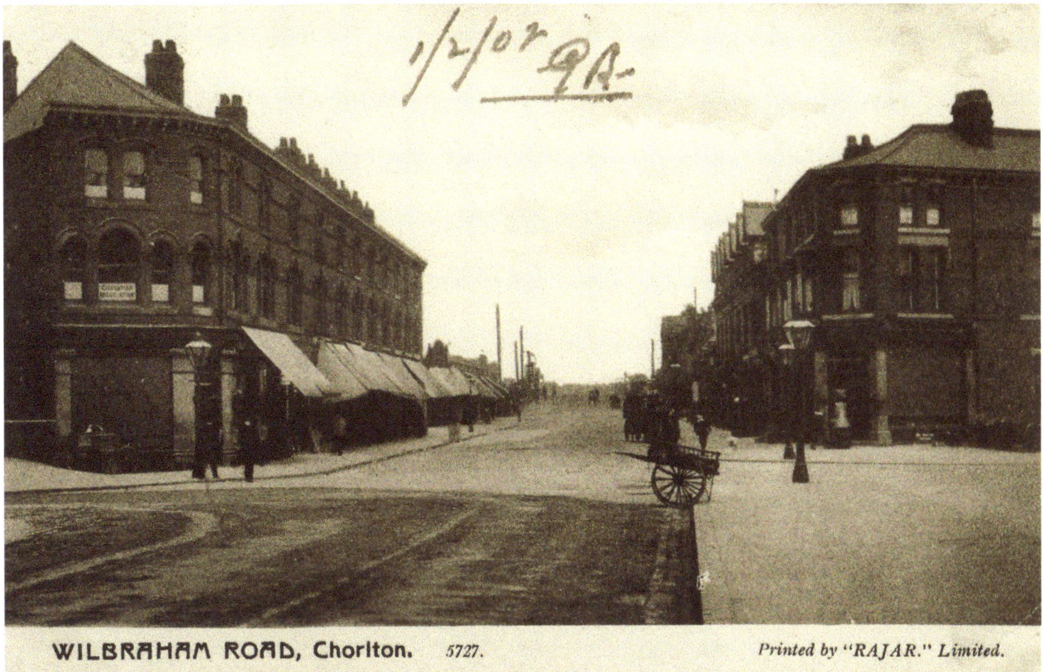

Wilbraham Road, Chorlton-cum-Hardy, 1907

Wilbraham Road was built by Lord Egerton and extended from Wilmslow Road at Fallowfield to Edge Lane, heading into Stretford. With the construction of Wilbraham Road came the building of a main sewer along its length. Close to the former railway bridge (photographed here), at Chorlton station, which is now a part of the Metrolink system, the sewer runs to Barlow Moor Road, Cross Road and Beech Road. Eventually it empties into Chorlton Brook, around 200 yards from the bridge leading to Jackson's Boat.

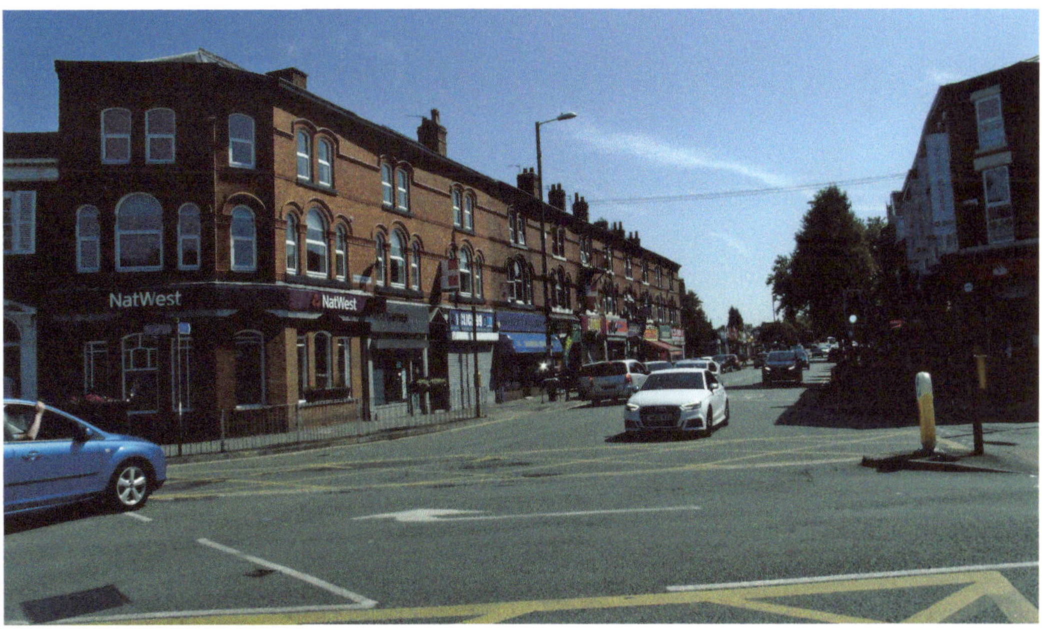

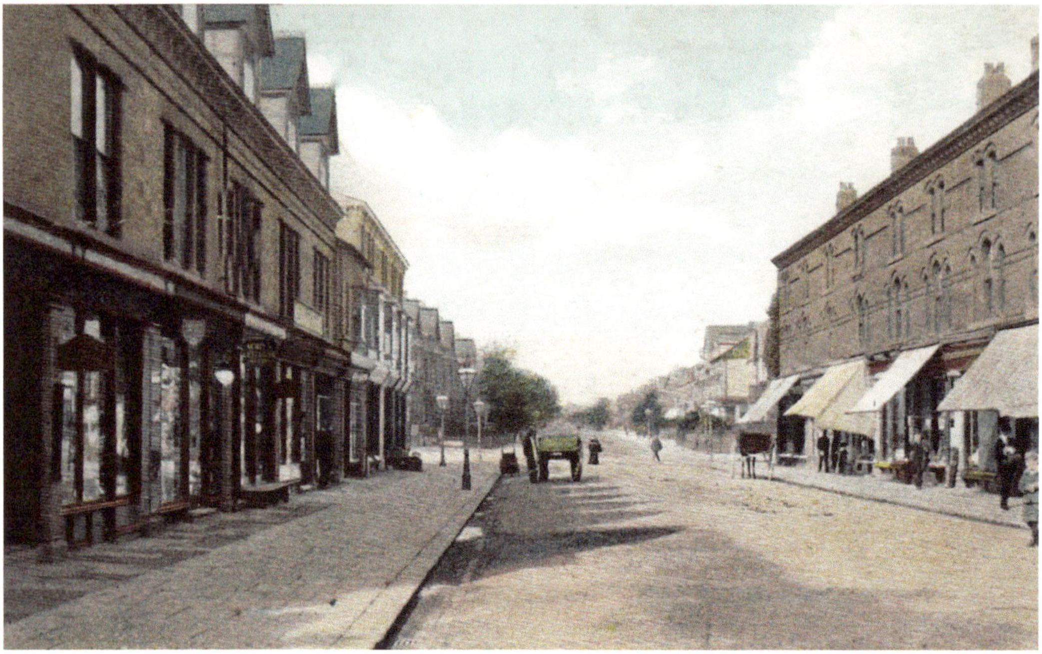

Wilbraham Road, Chorlton-cum-Hardy, *c.* 1910

This view of Wilbraham Road looks towards Edge Lane and Stretford. The railway station, now a Metrolink line, is behind the photographer, as is a set of traffic lights controlling traffic towards the supermarket in 2017. Around 1910 the retail establishments were serviced by horses and carts, whereas today the scene is busy with modern motor traffic. Beyond the terraces Wilbraham Road crosses Barlow Moor Road at Kemp's Corner (later Bank Corner), named after the chemist's shop located here at the time.

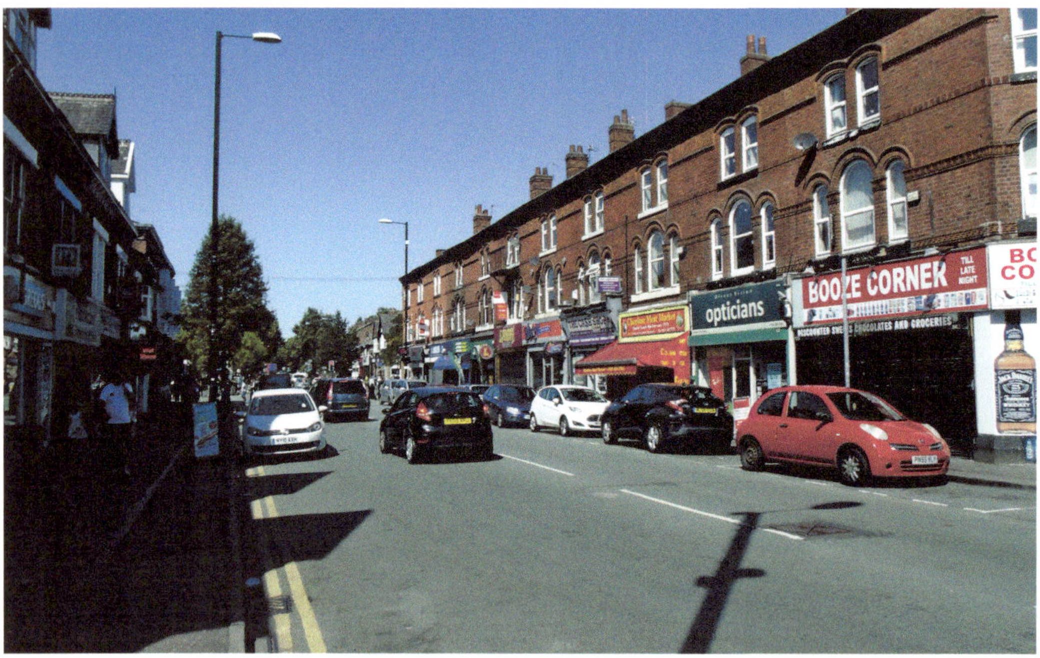

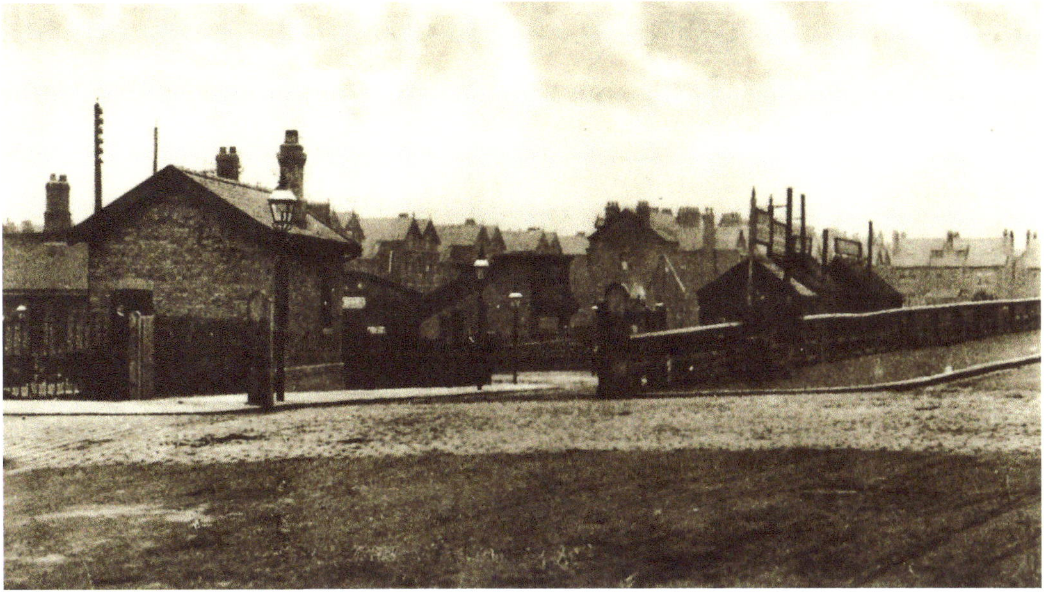

Chorlton Railway Station, Wilbraham Road, Chorlton-cum-Hardy, *c.* 1900

The station buildings were opened in 1880, together with two platforms. The northbound platform to Manchester Central saw the construction of the station building and a two-storey stationmaster's house. It was built to the same design as the Cheshire Lines Committee buildings, constructed on their main line between Manchester and Liverpool. In contrast, the southbound platform was provided with a large wooden waiting shelter. There was also a footbridge linking the two platforms and extensive goods yard facilities.

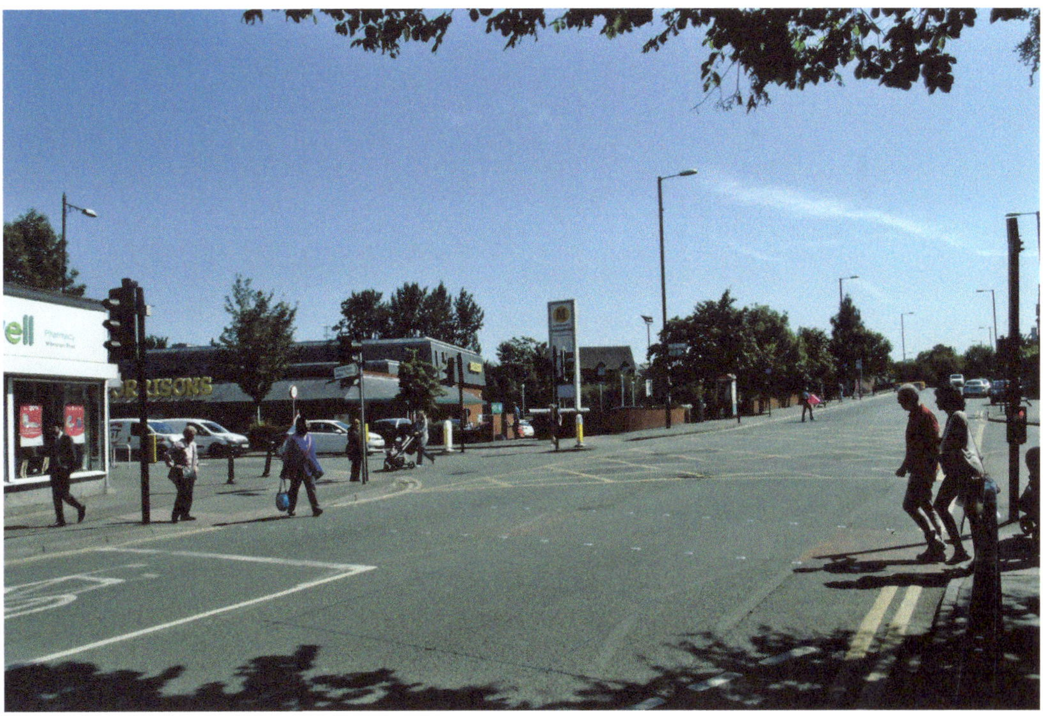

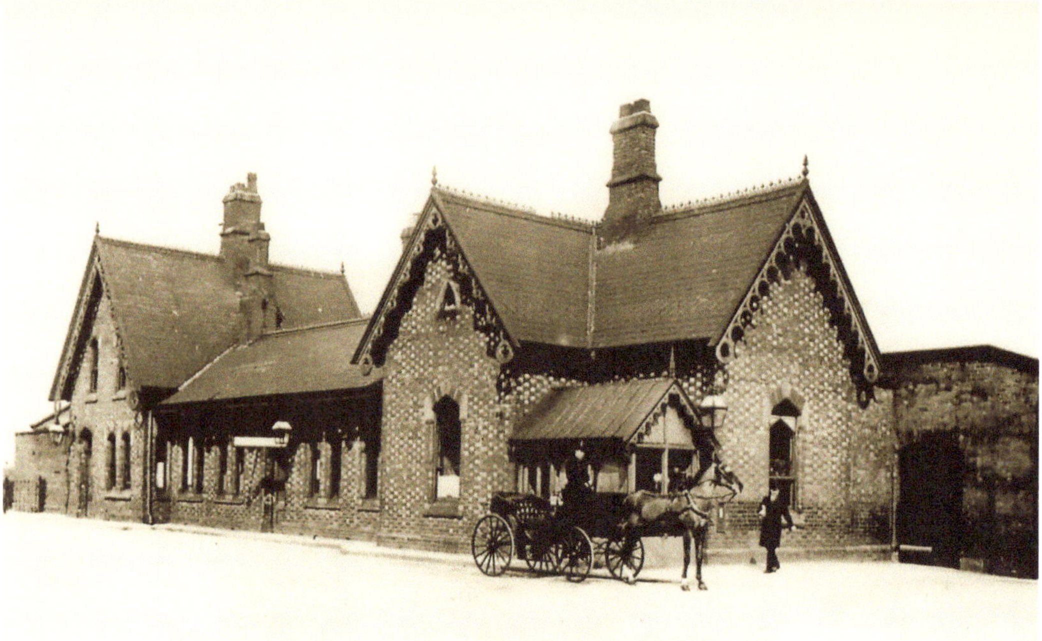

Chorlton Railway Station, Wilbraham Road, Chorlton-cum-Hardy, 1890

Chorlton-cum-Hardy railway station was opened in 1880 by the Midland Railway on the north side of Wilbraham Road, and was closed on 2 January 1967. The station was demolished, and part of the site is now beneath a supermarket. The trackbed through the former railway station is now the route of a Metrolink extension, which opened on 7 July 2011. The station was originally opened as part of the Manchester South District Railway between Manchester Central and Stockport Tiviot Dale.

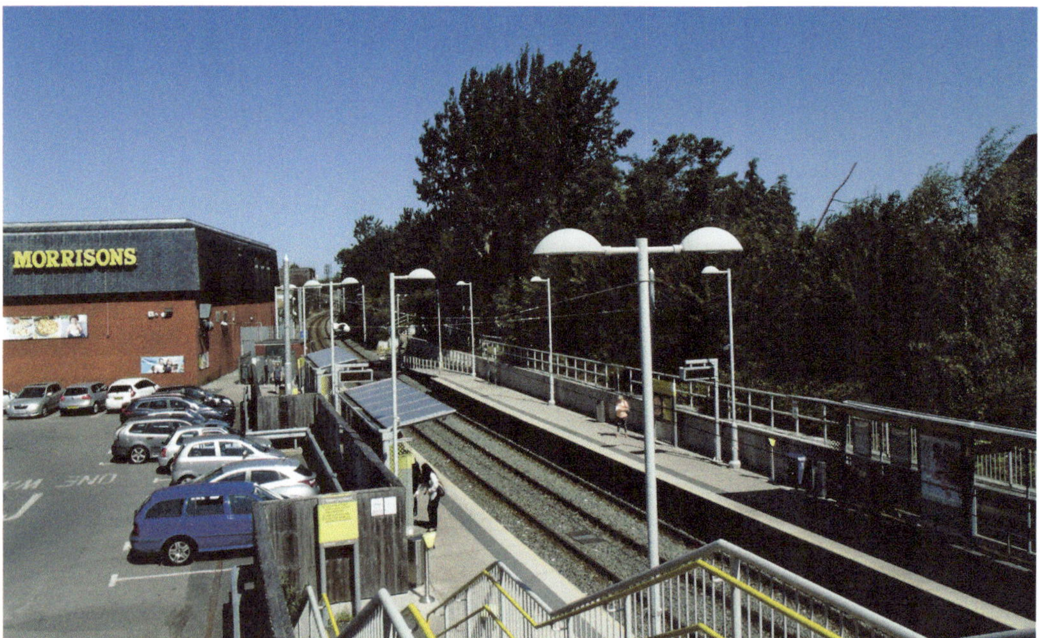

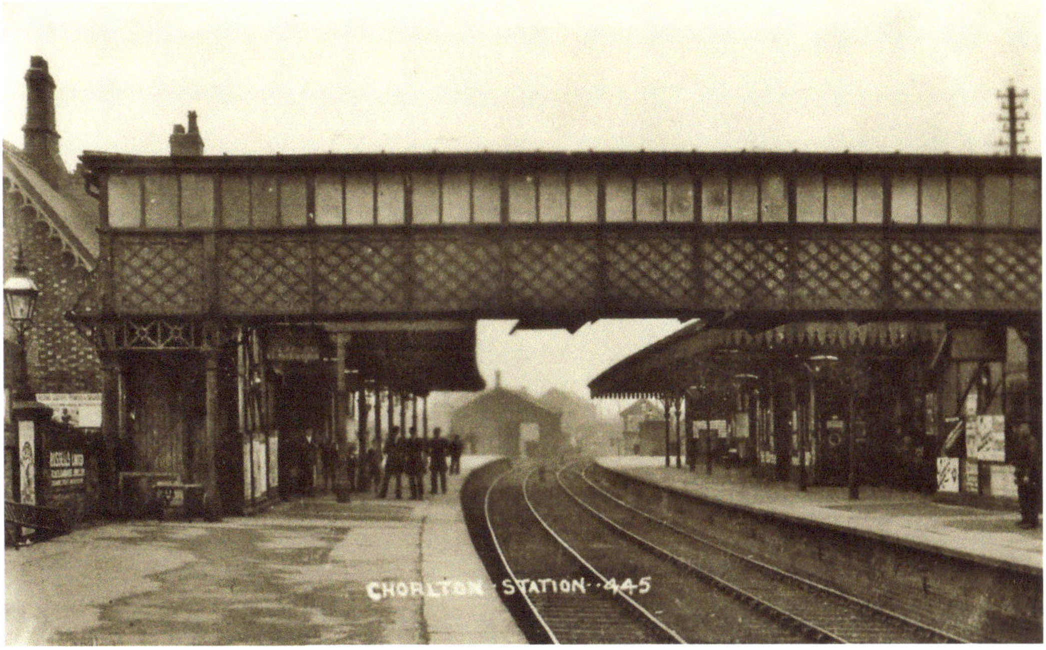

Chorlton Railway Station Footbridge, *c.* 1910

The footbridge was provided to link the two platforms at the time of the station's opening, and was later removed – passengers used ramps up to Wilbraham Road in order to cross the line. The station's goods yard was located on the west side of the main line, to the north of the station, and included a goods shed and a 5-ton crane; it was closed on 30 November 1964. Trains continued to pass through the station until 1989, after which the line was closed and lifted.

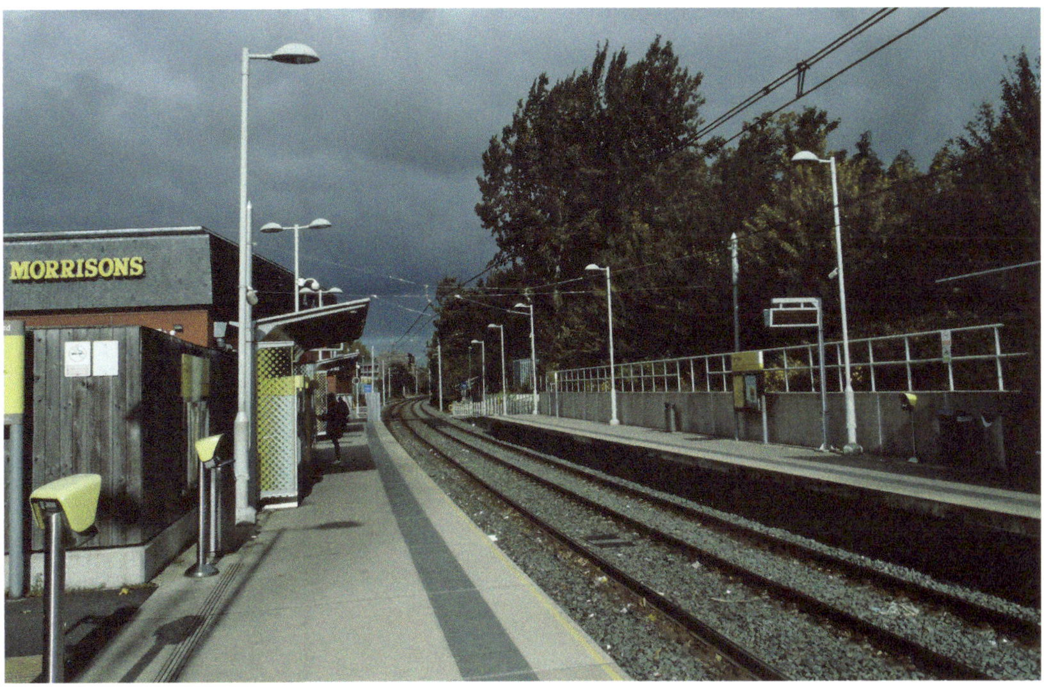

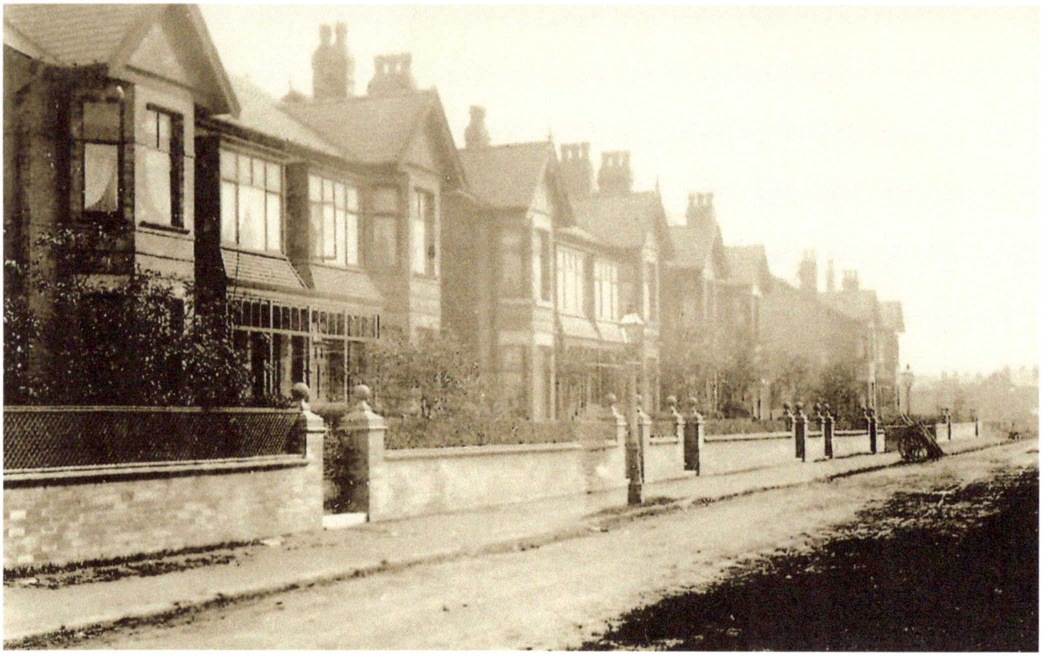

Ellesmere Road South, Chorlton-cum-Hardy, *c.* 1910

Ellesmere Road South is a typical suburban development, emphasising Chorlton-cum-Hardy's expansion. It was constructed as the 'new' village began to extend along Wilbraham Road towards Withington, where there had been little development before 1911. As many Victorian/Edwardian terraced properties were constructed without substantial drives, it is not uncommon to see rows of motor vehicles parked by the kerbside, as a by-product of the twenty-first century! However, tree development and growth provides some welcome shade from the summer sun.

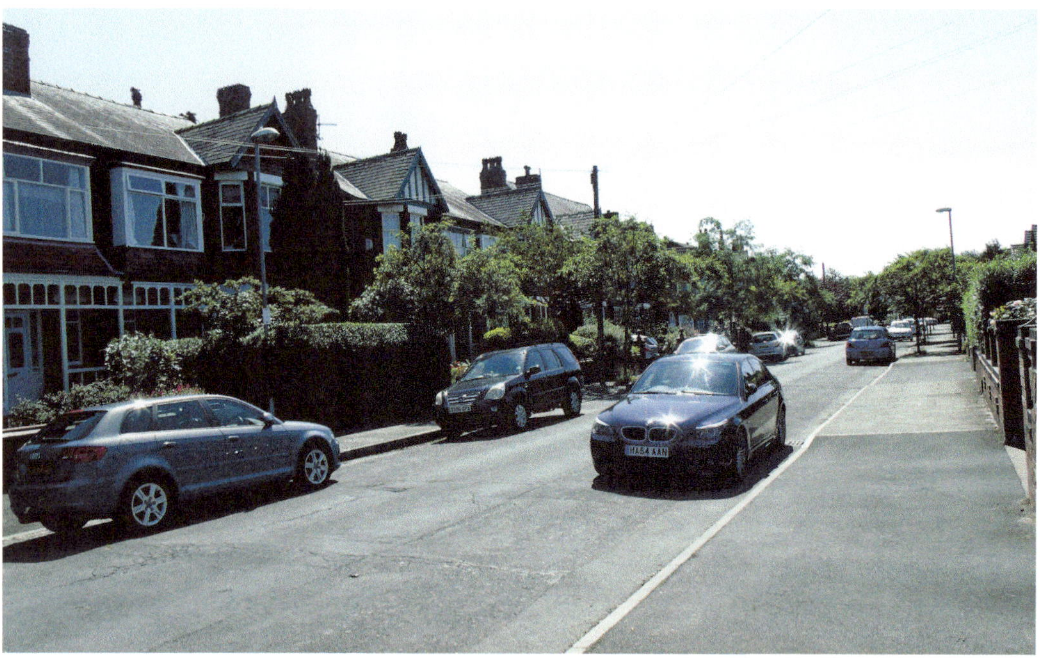

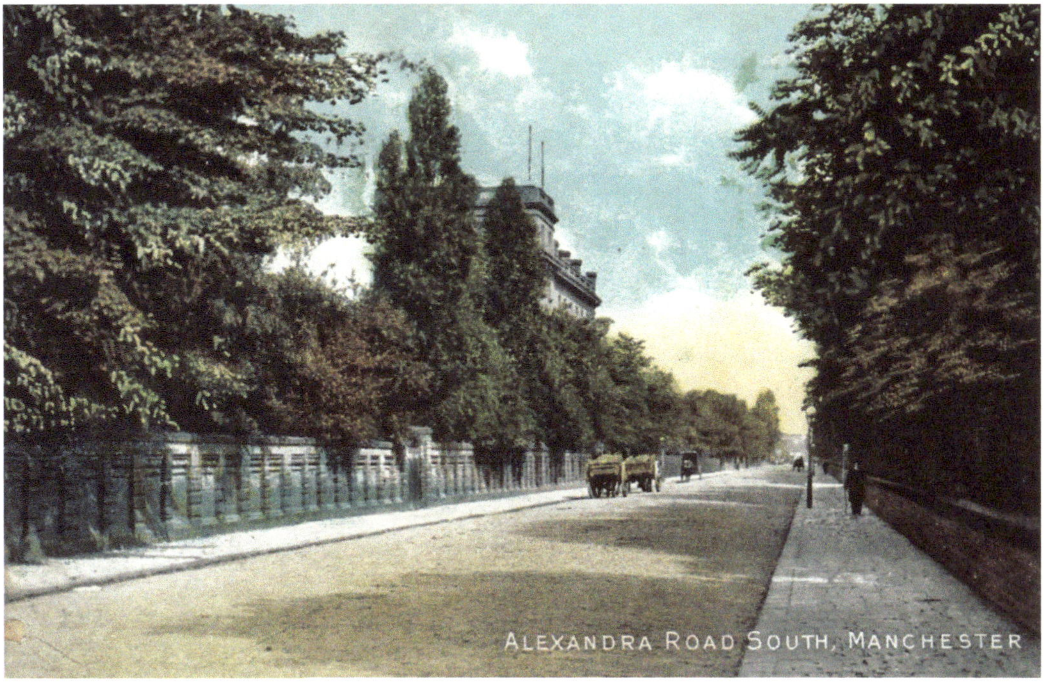

St Bede's College, Alexandra Road South, 1905

Alexandra Road South forms a junction with Wilbraham Road, although this image of 1905 shows St Bede's College on the left and is in neighbouring Whalley Range. It is included here because St Bede's is an independent college and its student intake is from the wider Catholic community across Greater Manchester; therefore the college has an extensive history and influence, particularly across south Manchester. St Bede's, which was opened in 1877, also has many architectural features that are worthy of note.

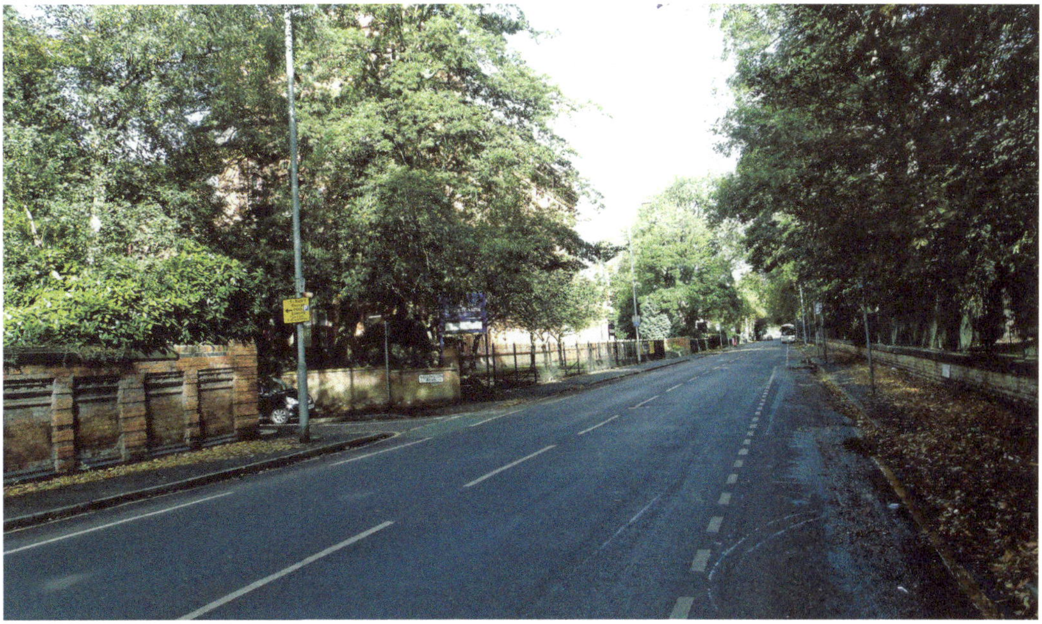

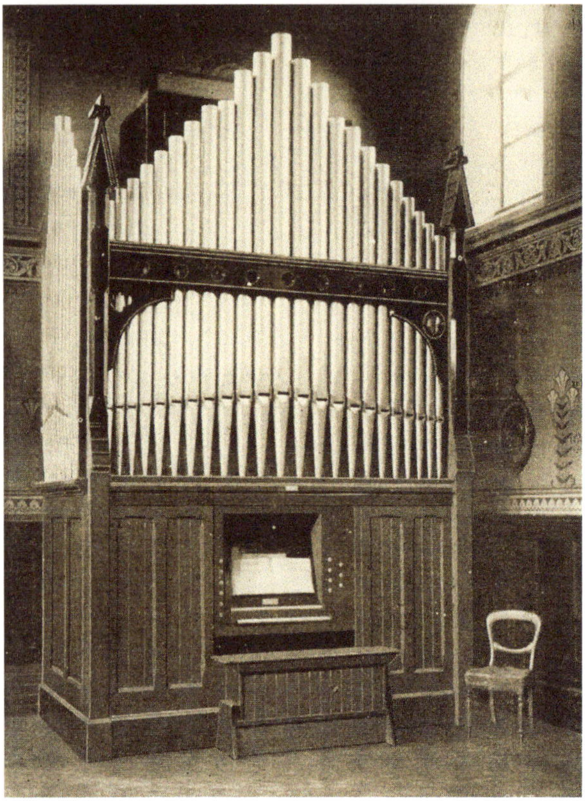

Organ at St Bede's College, Alexandra Road South, 1917

The original school was established by Cardinal Vaughan at Devonshire Street, off Oxford Road, in 1875 and opened in 1876. In August 1877, the Manchester Aquarium on Alexandra Road and the plot of land surrounding it was purchased for the college. St Bede's reopened on 10 September 1877. Then, in the late 1870s and early 1880s, the Grade I-listed Vaughan Building was constructed, with the college becoming a seminary for the education of priests. The college chapel was built in 1898.

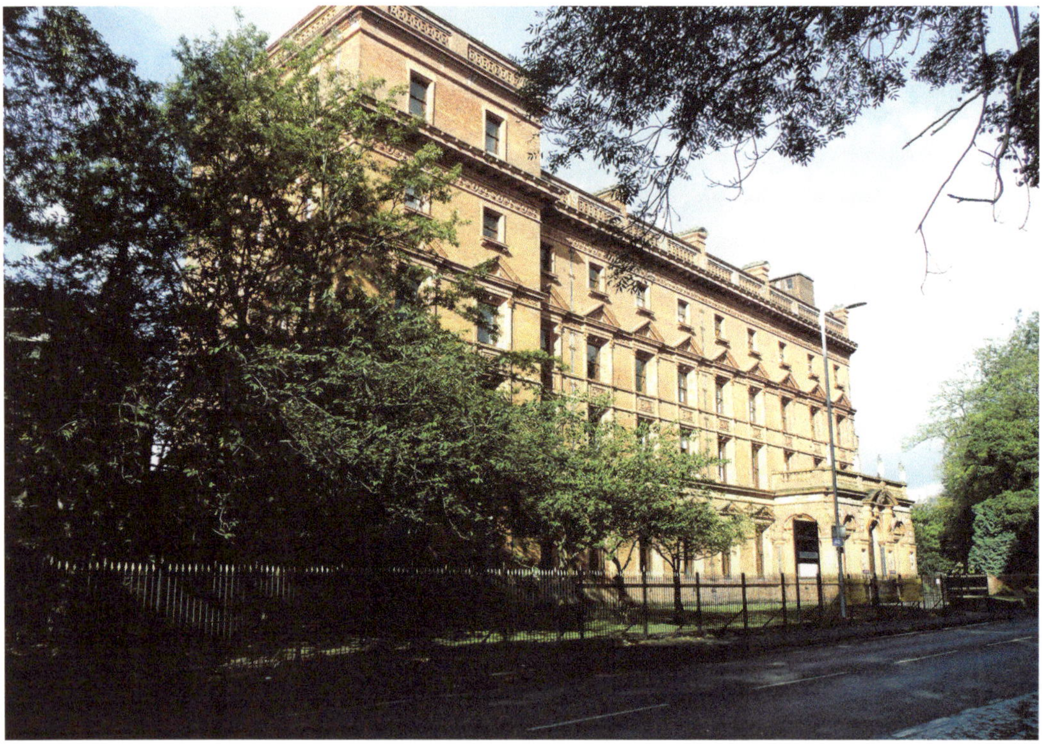

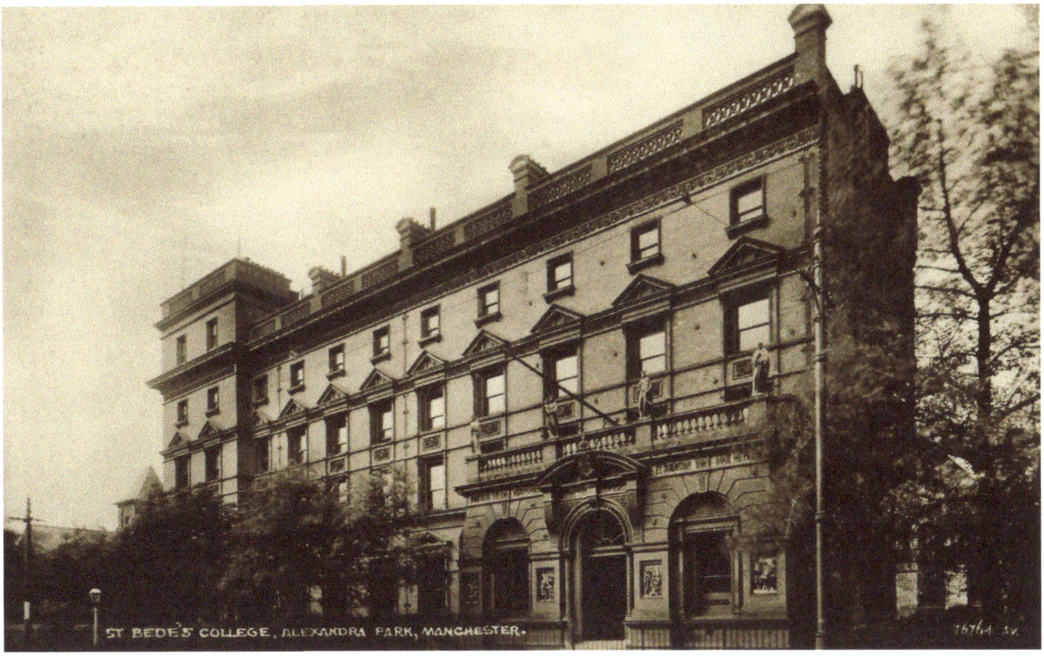

St Bede's College, Alexandra Road South, *c.* 1905

The college continued to expand, with the Henshaw Building opening in 1932 and the college becoming co-educational in 1984. After 140 years of development, nearly 800 boys and girls attend St Bede's. Originally built as the Manchester Aquarium in 1874, it is now located within the Whalley Range Conservation Area, and is a Grade II-listed building in the Italian Renaissance style. The 'Venerable Bede' is regarded as the greatest Anglo-Saxon scholar, writing around forty books, notably *The Ecclesiastical History of the English People*.

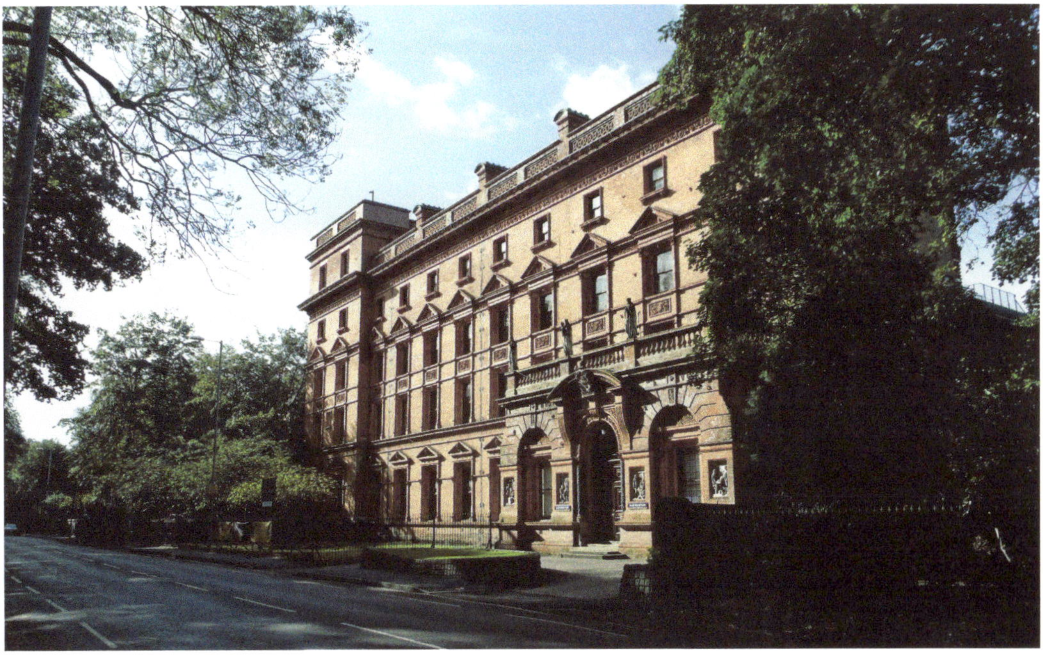

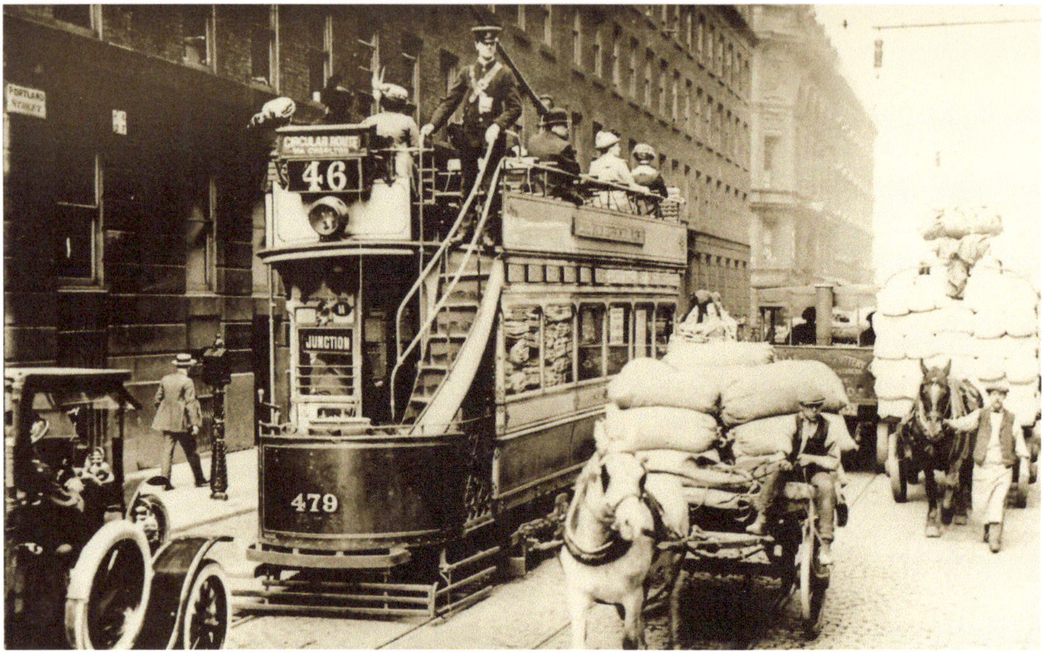

No. 46 Tram Circular Route via Chorlton, *c.* 1920, and Metrolink Station at Chorlton, 2017

In 1913 the tram route from Chorlton was extended into West Didsbury, meaning that there was now a circular route from Manchester to Chorlton, on through Didsbury, and back into the city of Manchester. This was known as the 'Circular Route', which is clearly displayed on the destination board of the tram in the above image. It offered two routes into Chorlton: the short route from Princess Street, or the long one down Oxford Road, through Rusholme, Fallowfield and Withington, before heading into Chorlton.

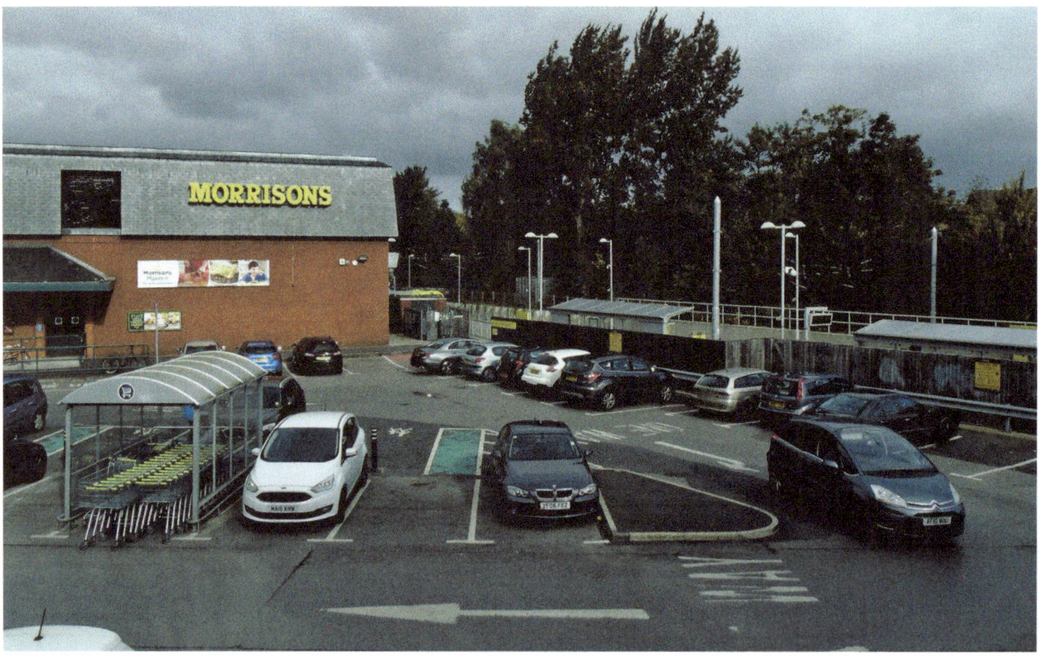

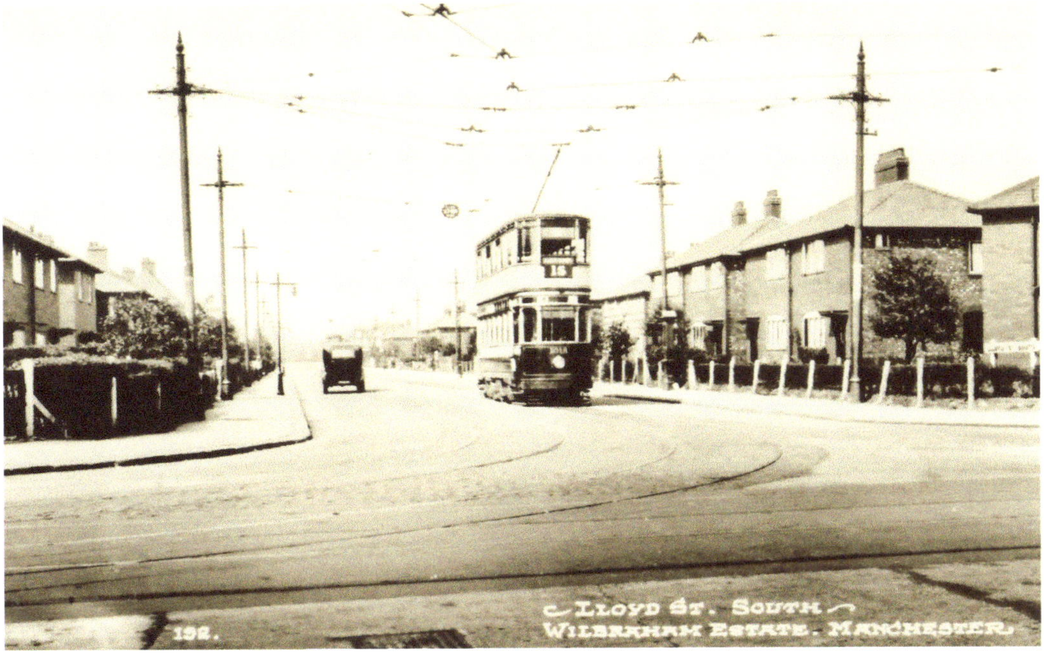

Lloyd Street South, Wilbraham Estate, *c.* 1920

A slight diversion with this image, as Lloyd Street South is located just outside the district in neighbouring Fallowfield. However, it is worth showing this view of Lloyd Street South's junction with Wilbraham Road, as it clearly emphasises the changes in transportation that have taken place across the decades. Gone are the tramlines, with tram services ceasing in Manchester around 1949, to be replaced by traffic lights to control motor vehicles at this busy junction. However, Lloyd Street South remains a residential district.

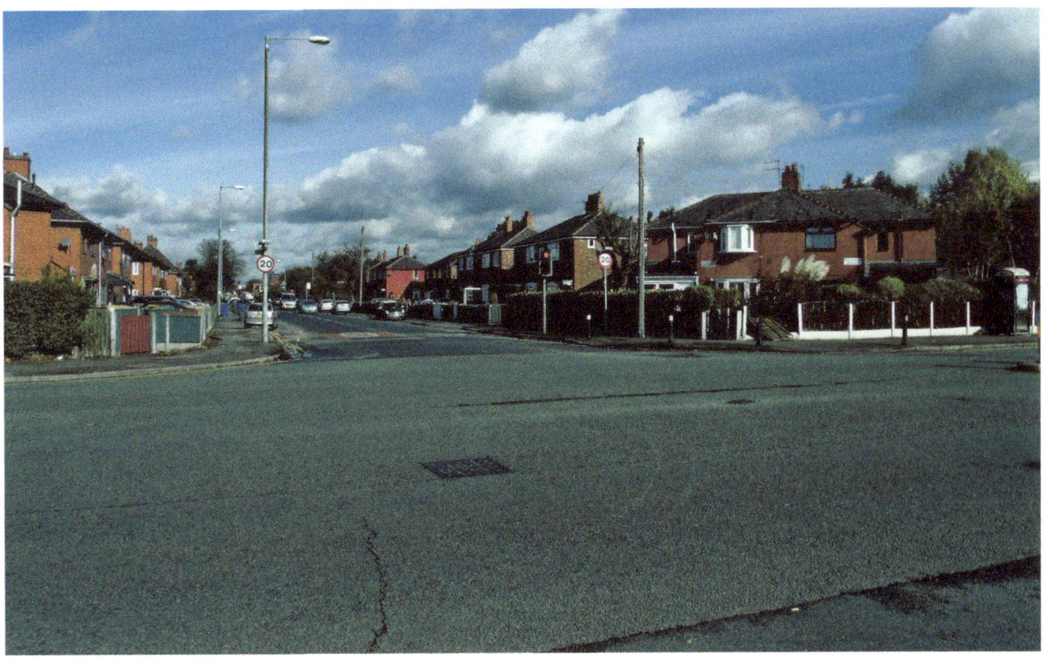

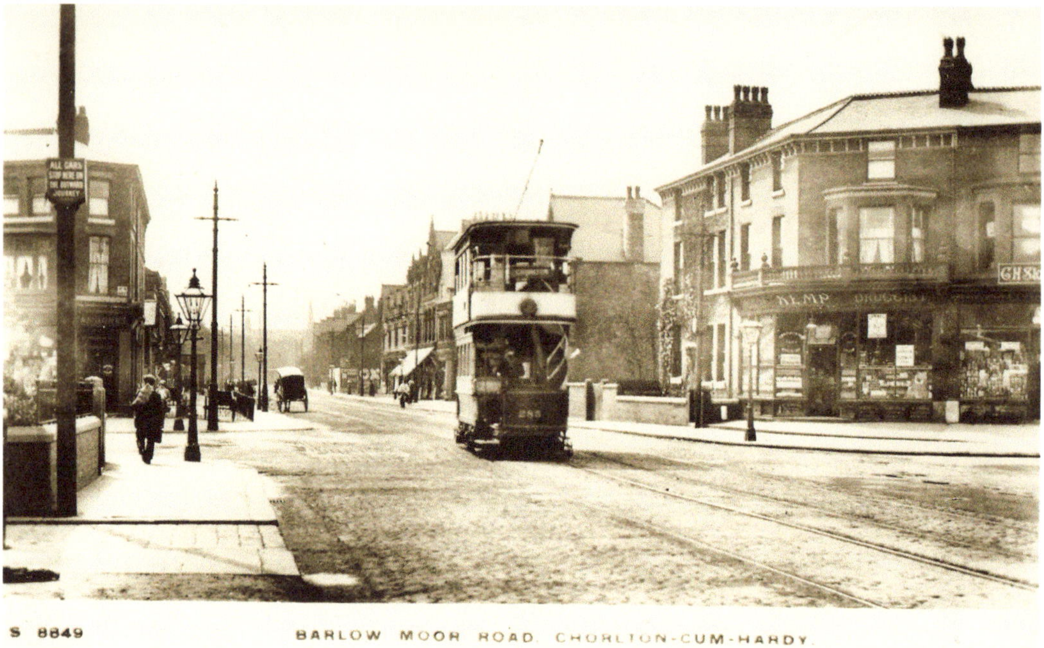

Barlow Moor Road, next to the Royal Oak Hotel, Chorlton-cum-Hardy, *c*. 1913

This is Barlow Moor Road where it crosses Wilbraham Road. Known at this time as Kemp's Corner, due to the chemist's shop located on the right of this image. Later, it was known as Bank Corner, with a bank on each corner of the crossroads. Within the last decade it has been renamed Chorlton Cross. In the distance is the spire of the Macfadyen Memorial Church, at the junction of Barlow Moor Road and Zetland (Holland) Road. Beyond the crossroads, the Arcade is on the left.

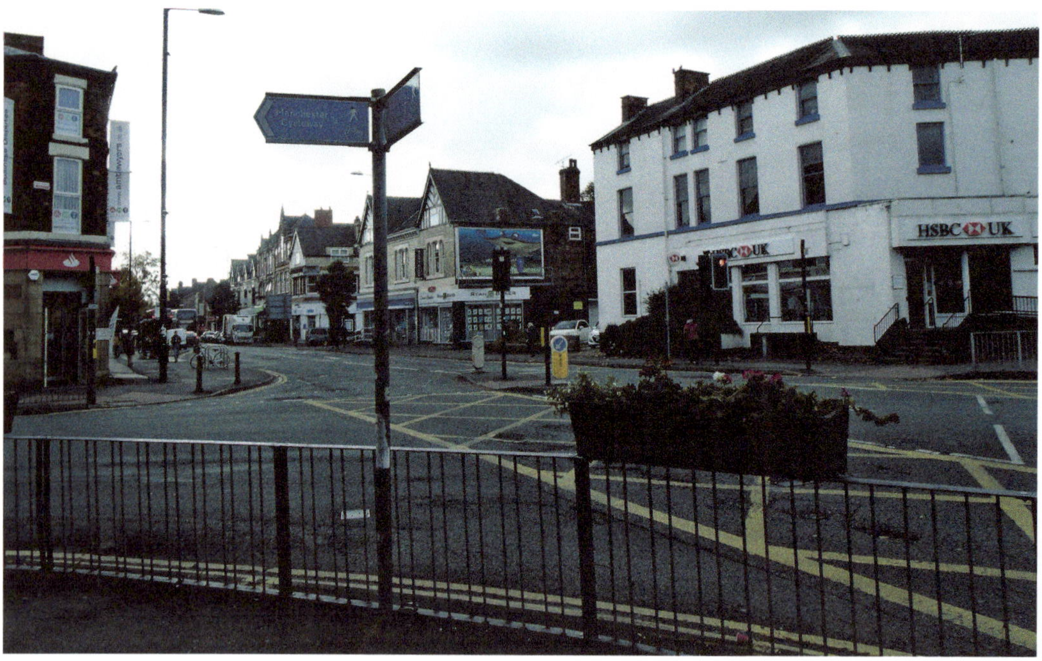

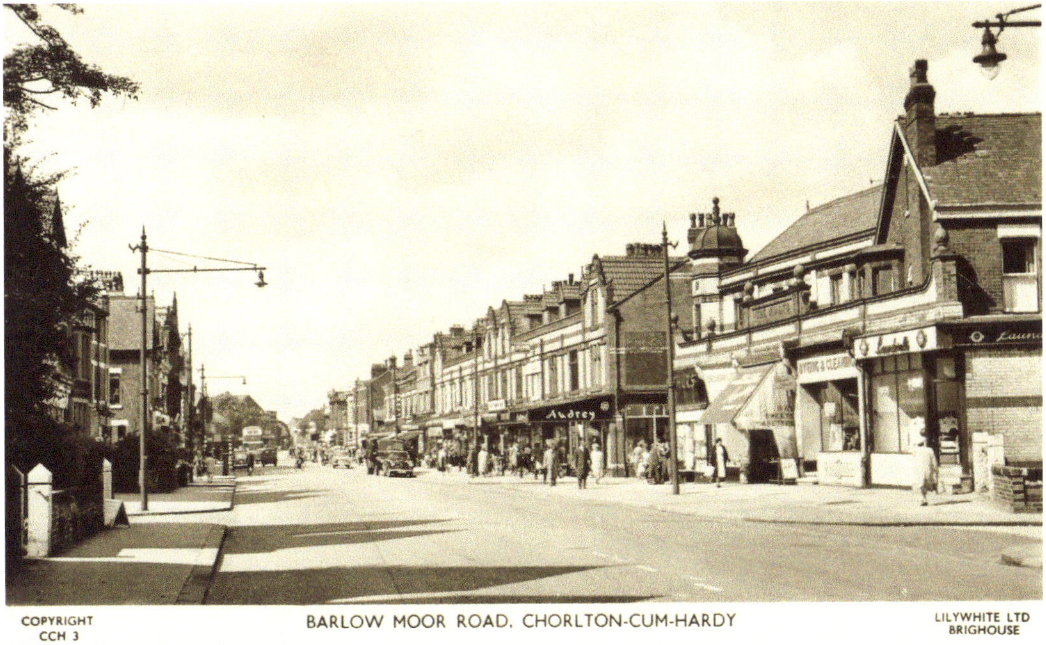

Barlow Moor Road, Chorlton-cum-Hardy, *c.* 1960

This view looks towards Wilbraham Road and Bank Corner, with the outline of the former Savoy/Gaumont cinema and temperance billiard hall visible in the distance (centre of the image). On the right the Rialto has been utilised as commercial premises, a situation which continues today; the modern image clearly shows the outline of the building. The Arcade, also on the right, remains intact despite some building work being undertaken. In 1960 motor traffic is beginning to make its presence felt.

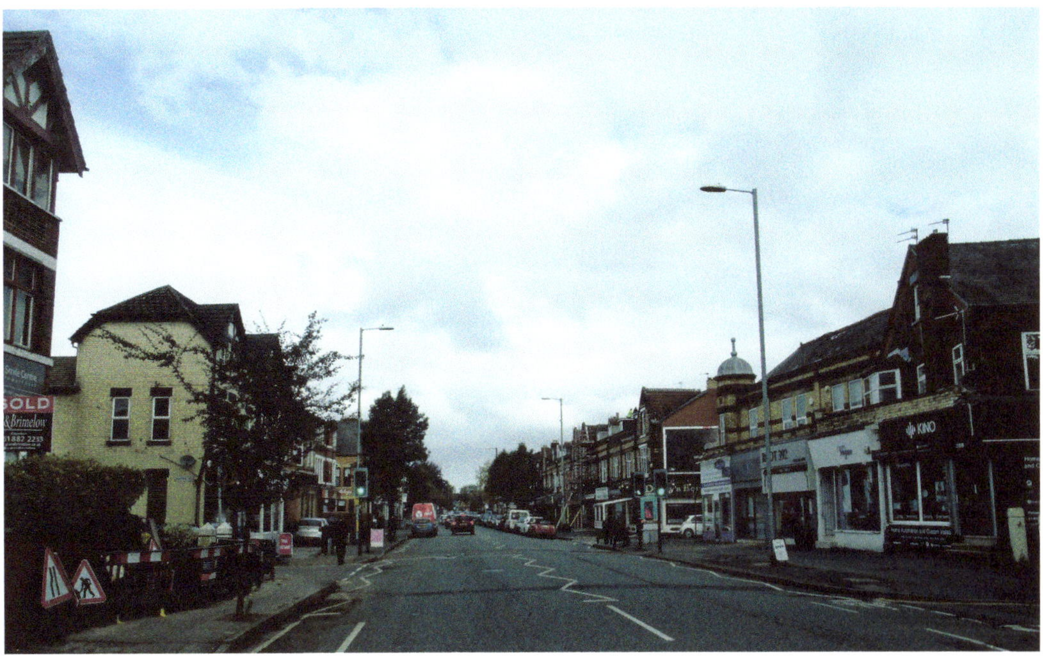

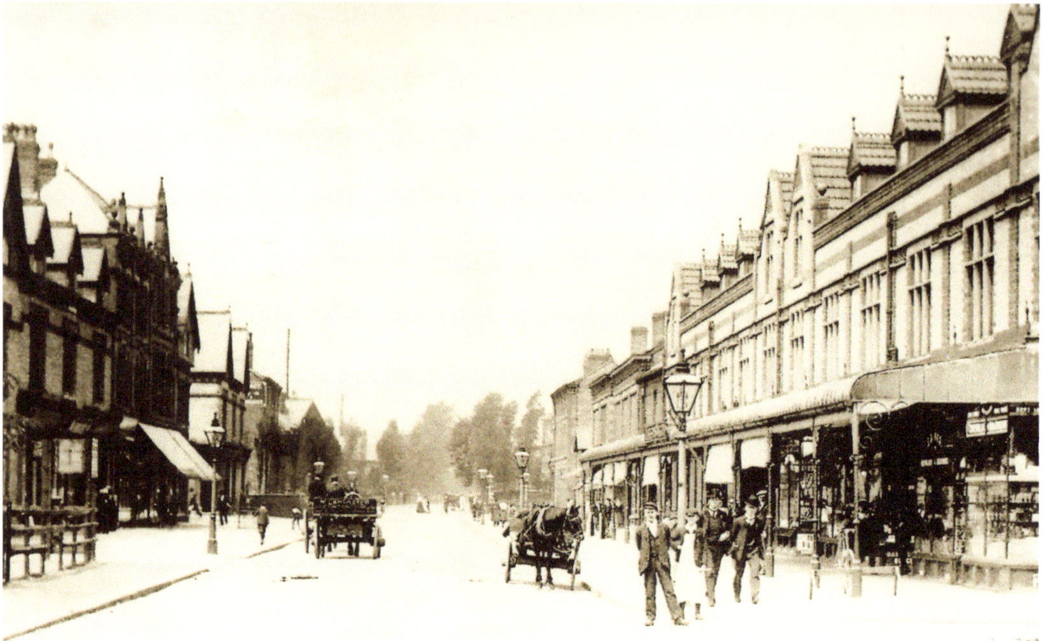

The Arcade, Barlow Moor Road, Chorlton-cum-Hardy, *c.* 1910

Moving slightly closer to the junction of Barlow Moor Road and Wilbraham Road, it can be noted that the Arcade has ornate wrought-iron supports clearly visible. There is no pedestrian crossing, of course, and the rather sparse traffic is of the horse and cart variety and distinctly more sedate than its modern counterpart – hence, the corresponding image of 2017 has been taken from the pavement. The buildings of around 1910, to the immediate left and right, remain intact today.

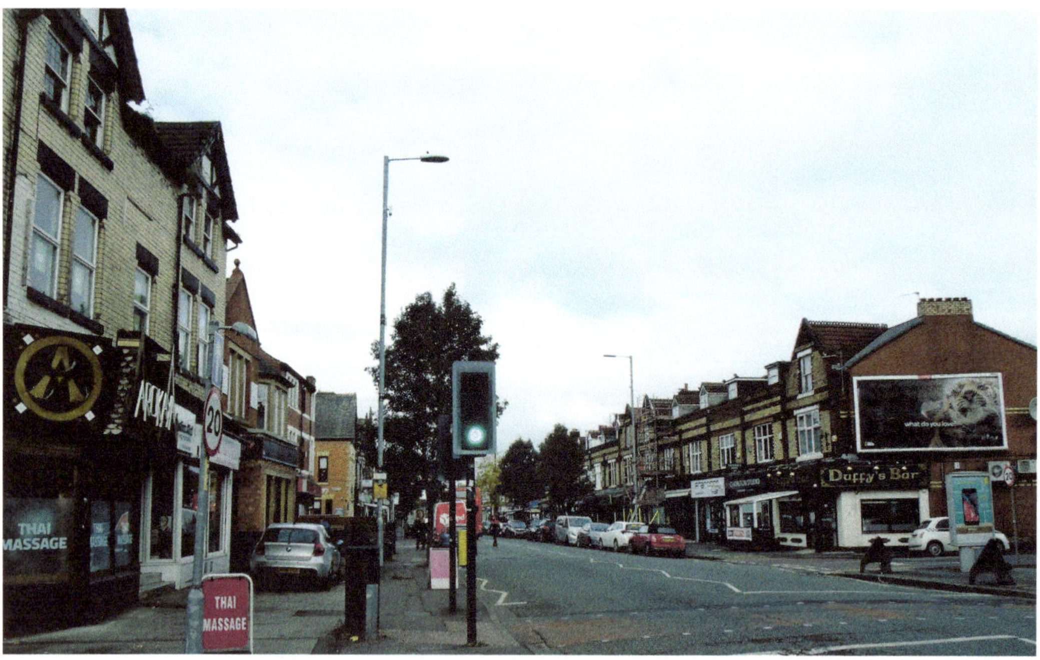

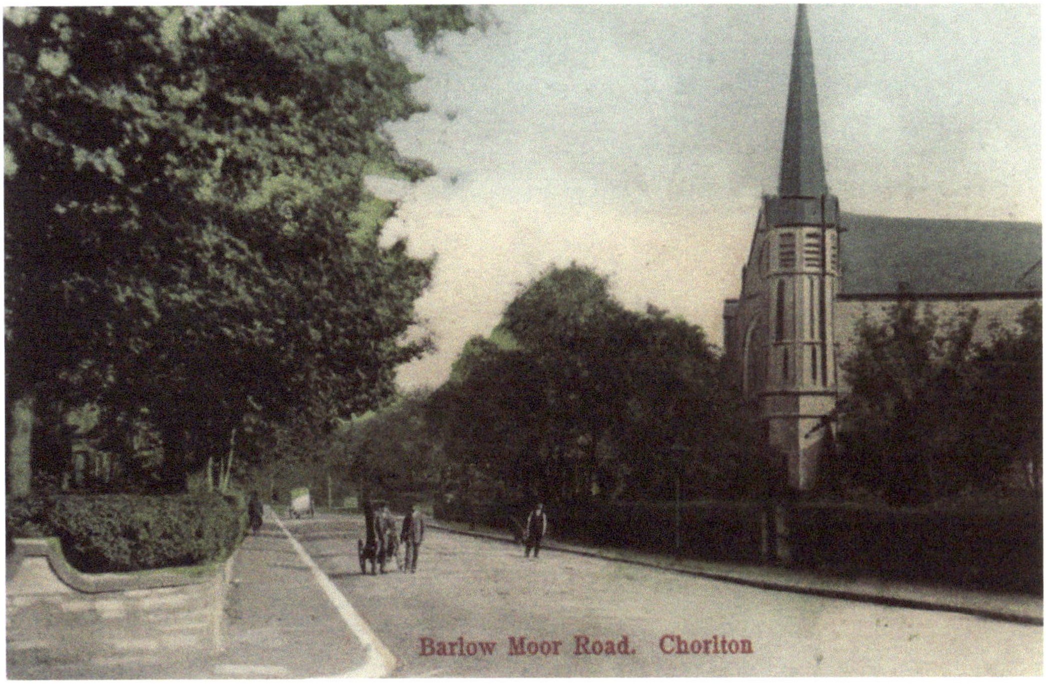

Barlow Moor Road, Chorlton-cum-Hardy, 1904

In 1904 we can see three workmen with their cart and a set of ladders posing for the camera in the middle of Barlow Moor Road, where there are now traffic lights in 2017. The Macfadyen Memorial Church can be clearly seen on the right. This building is now demolished, with the reconfigured Chorlton Central Church reforming in what was once the church hall. This was the original place of worship, before the Macfadyen Memorial Church opened in 1894.

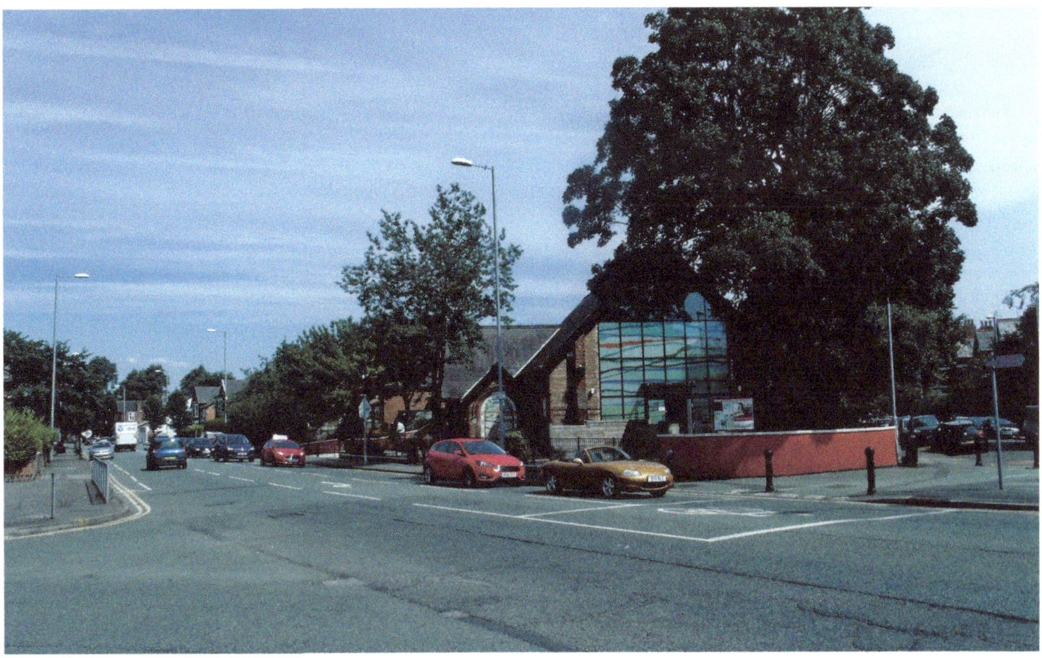

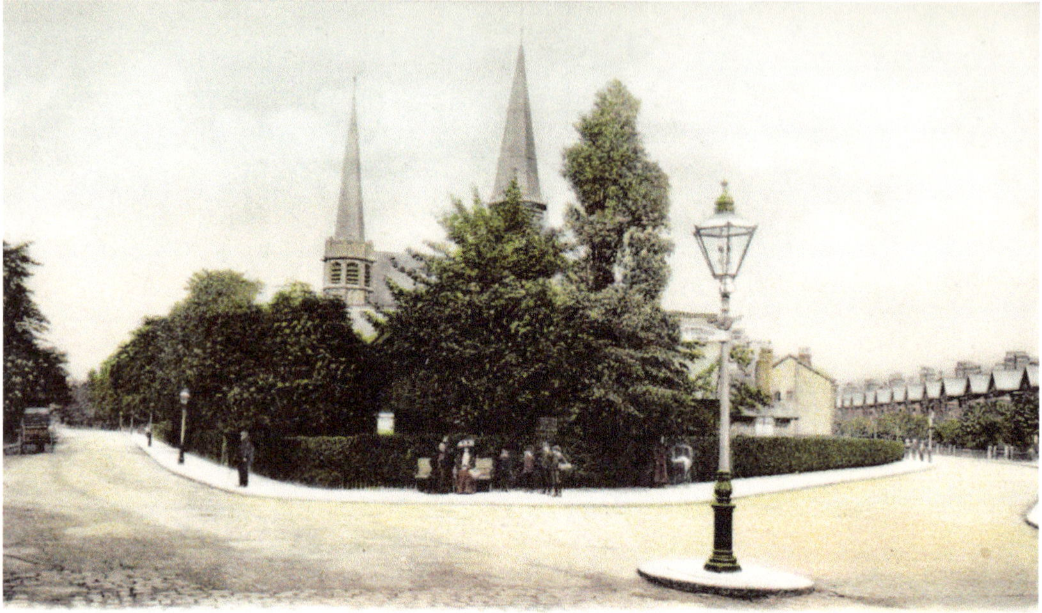

Macfadyen Church, Junction of Barlow Moor Road and Holland (Zetland) Road, *c.* 1905. *Inset*: Congregational Brotherhood, Brooks Bar, 1919

Revd J. A. Macfadyen of Chorlton Road Congregational Church, Brooks Bar, died in 1889. In 1890 a fund was started to build a new church in his memory. Although the new Congregational church was sponsored by Chorlton Road, the long-term plan was for it to be financially independent. The opening service of the new church was in October 1894. Dry rot in the roof led to its demolition, with the original church hall now used as a place of worship.

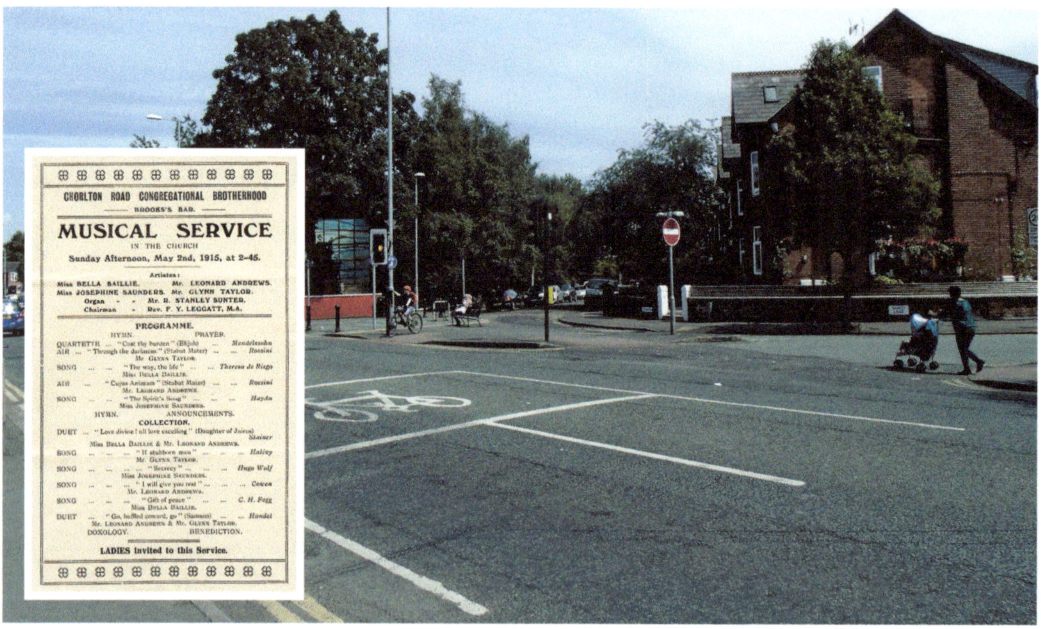

CHORLTON ROAD CONGREGATIONAL BROTHERHOOD

BROOKS'S BAR.

MUSICAL SERVICE

IN THE CHURCH

Sunday Afternoon, May 2nd, 1915, at 2–45.

Artistes:

Miss BELLA BAILLIE. Mr. LEONARD ANDREWS.
Miss JOSEPHINE SAUNDERS. Mr. GLYNN TAYLOR.
Organ - - Mr. R. STANLEY SUNTER.
Chairman - Rev. F. Y. LEGGATT, M.A.

PROGRAMME.

HYMN. PRAYER.

QUARTETTE ... "Cast thy burden" (Elijah) ... *Mendelssohn*
AIR ... "Through the darkness" (Stabat Mater) ... ... *Rossini*
Mr Glynn Taylor.
SONG ... ... "The way, the life" ... ... *Theresa de Riego*
Miss Bella Baillie.
AIR ... "Cujus Animam" (Stabat Mater) ... ... *Rossini*
Mr. Leonard Andrews.
SONG ... ... "The Spirit's Song" ... ... *Haydn*
Miss Josephine Saunders.

HYMN. ANNOUNCEMENTS.

COLLECTION.

DUET ... "Love divine! all love excelling" (Daughter of Jairus) *Stainer*
Miss Bella Baillie & Mr. Leonard Andrews.
SONG ... ... "If stubborn men" ... ... *Halley*
Mr. Glynn Taylor.
SONG ... ... "Secrecy" ... ... *Hugo Wolf*
Miss Josephine Saunders.
SONG ... ... "I will give you rest" ... ... *Cowen*
Mr. Leonard Andrews.
SONG ... ... "Gift of peace" ... ... *C. H. Fogg*
Miss Bella Baillie.
DUET ... "Go, baffled coward, go" (Samson) ... ... *Handel*
Mr. Leonard Andrews & Mr. Glynn Taylor.

DOXOLOGY. BENEDICTION.

LADIES invited to this Service.

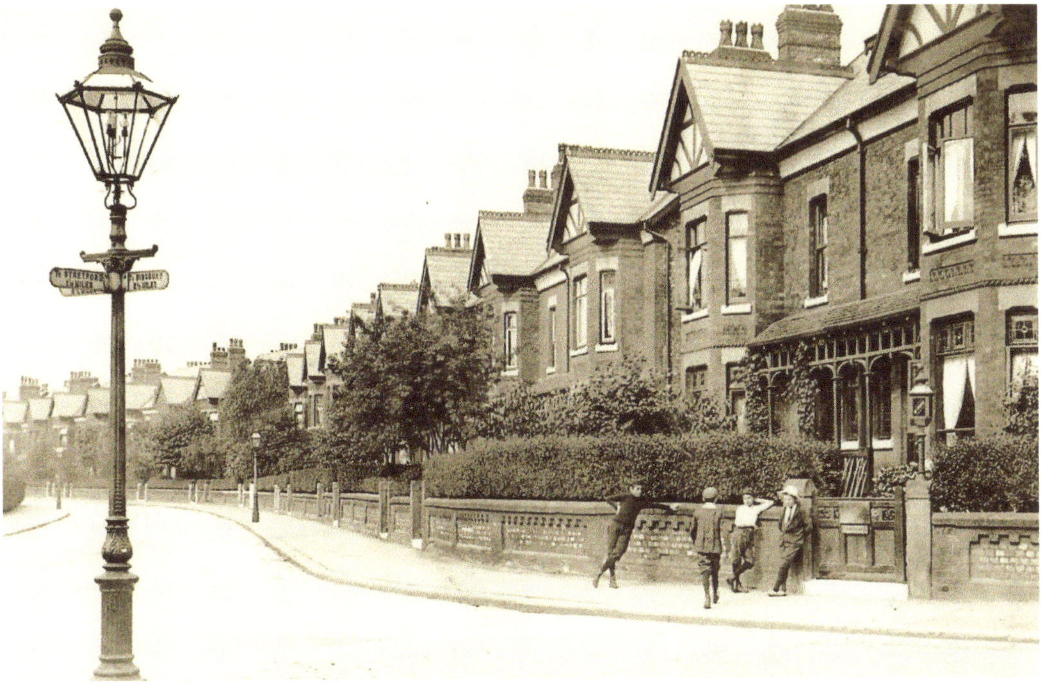

Holland Road, Chorlton-cum-Hardy, c. 1900

Today, Holland Road is known as Zetland Road (*inset*). The photograph of around 1900 shows Holland Road looking towards Corkland Road, with the photographer standing at the junction of Barlow Moor Road and Sandy Lane – High Lane junction is to the left of the photographer. Off-camera to the left is the Macfadyen Memorial Church. The rather imposing gas lamp tells us that Stretford is 1.5 miles away and Didsbury is 2.5 miles away. As with many photographs of this era, children gather to spectate.

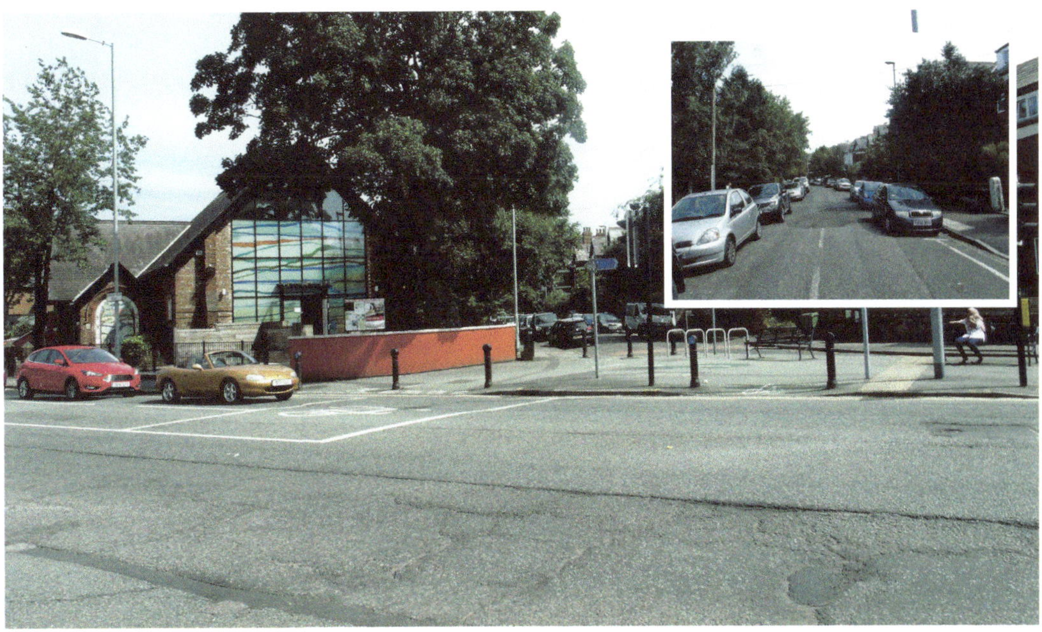

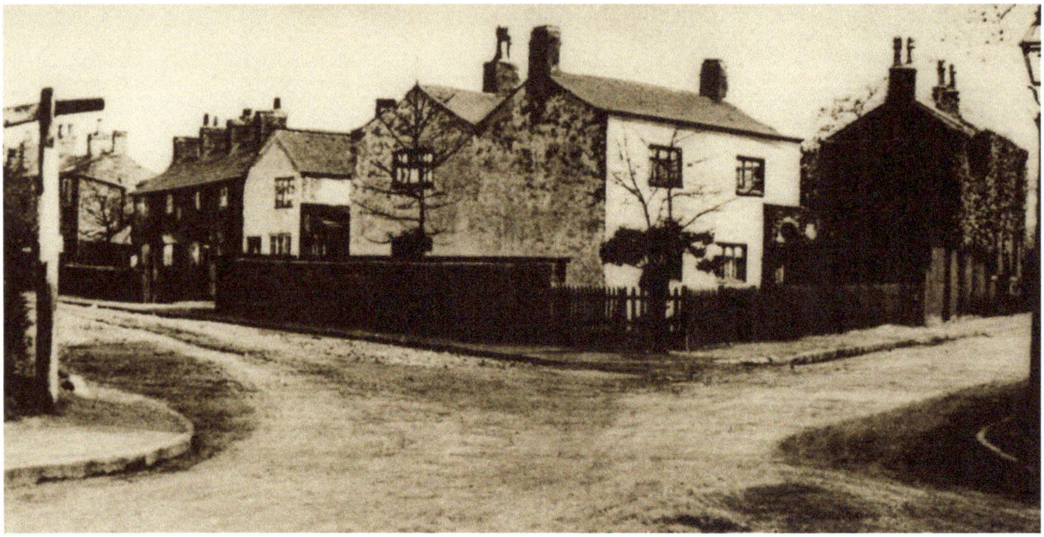

Brundrett's Cross, or Lane End, Barlow Moor Road, *c.* 1900

Barlow Moor Lane (Road) runs from left to right, with Sandy Lane/High Lane crossing it. This was another main route into Manchester – situated at the eastern end of the village – via Sandy Lane. The traveller would pass Sandy Brow, Moss Cottages and Dog House Farm, and would then head through the townships of Moss Side and Hulme, towards City Road and onto Chester Road. It was originally named Moss Lane and was also used by local people to gain access to places like Withington and Didsbury.

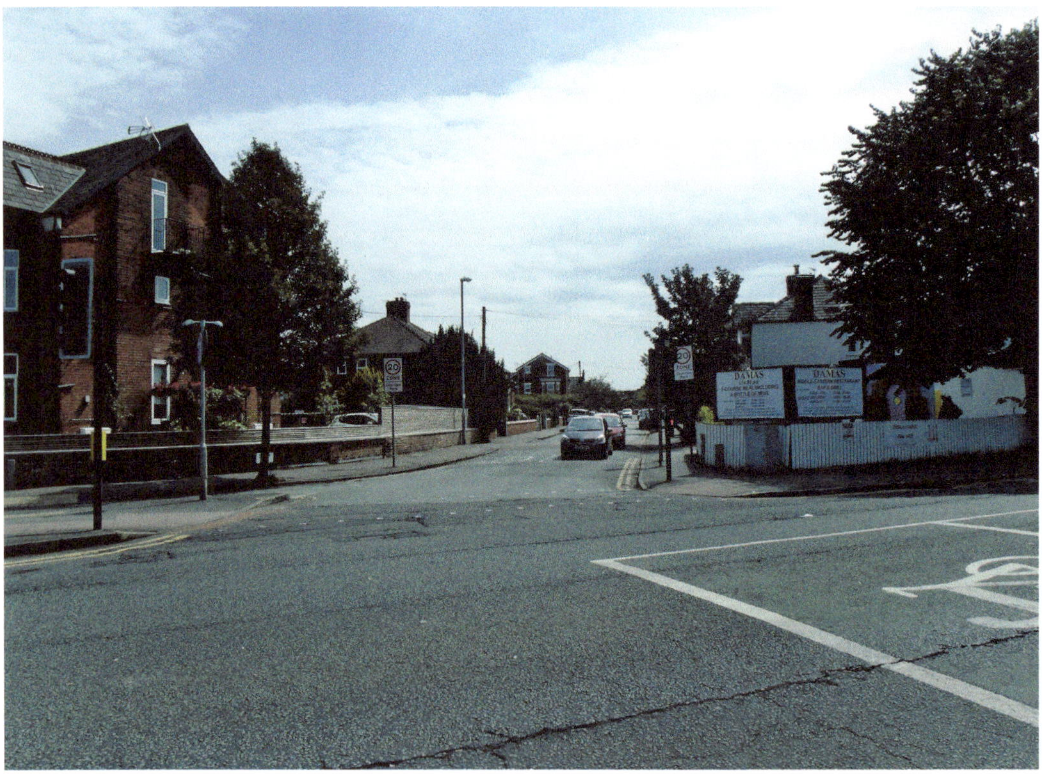

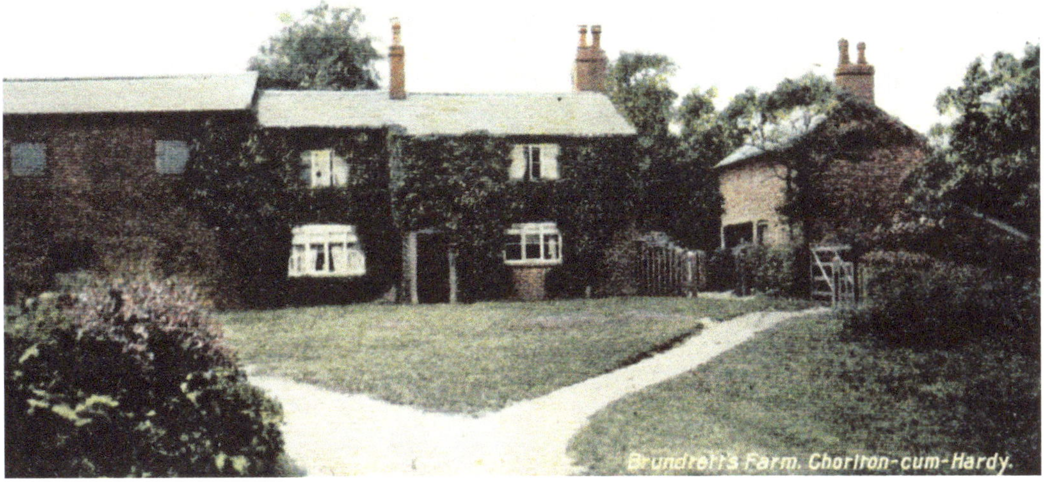

Brundrett's Farm, Chorlton-cum-Hardy, 1907, and the Site of Laburnum Farm, Chorlton Green, 2017

The junction of Barlow Moor Road, High Lane and Sandy Lane was known as Brundrett's Corner, as the Brundrett family owned a nearby cottage at the junction. The same family also owned Brundrett's Farm (above). This was one of many farms in the township that thrived before the suburban developers made their mark. There were many around the 'old' village at Chorlton Green, including two in the nineteenth century that dated back to the eighteenth century, Hardy Farm, and that of the Higginbotham family.

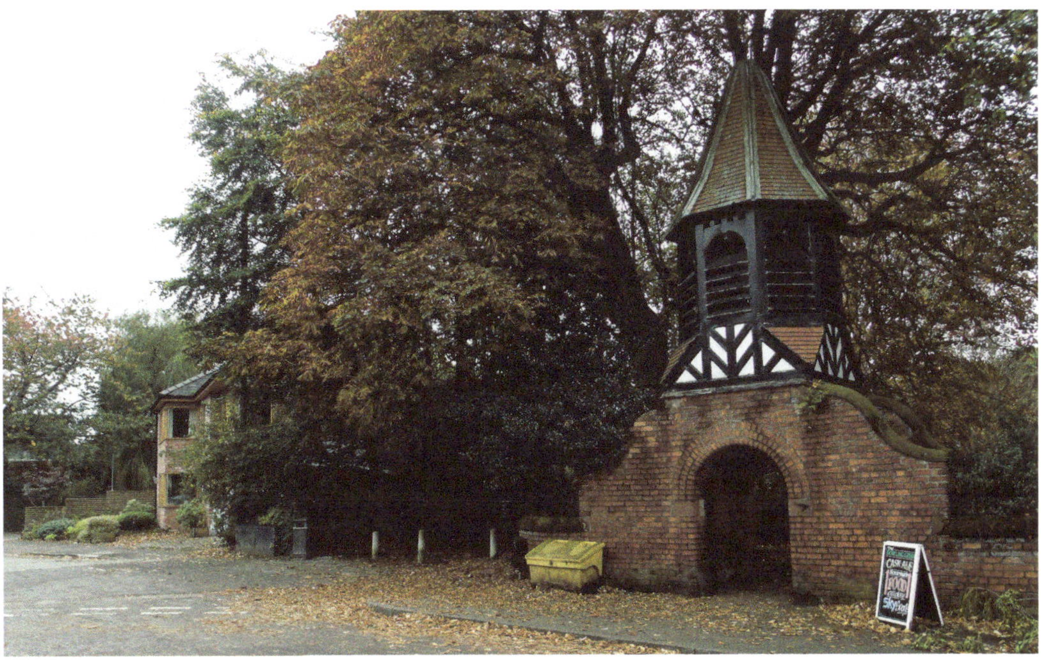

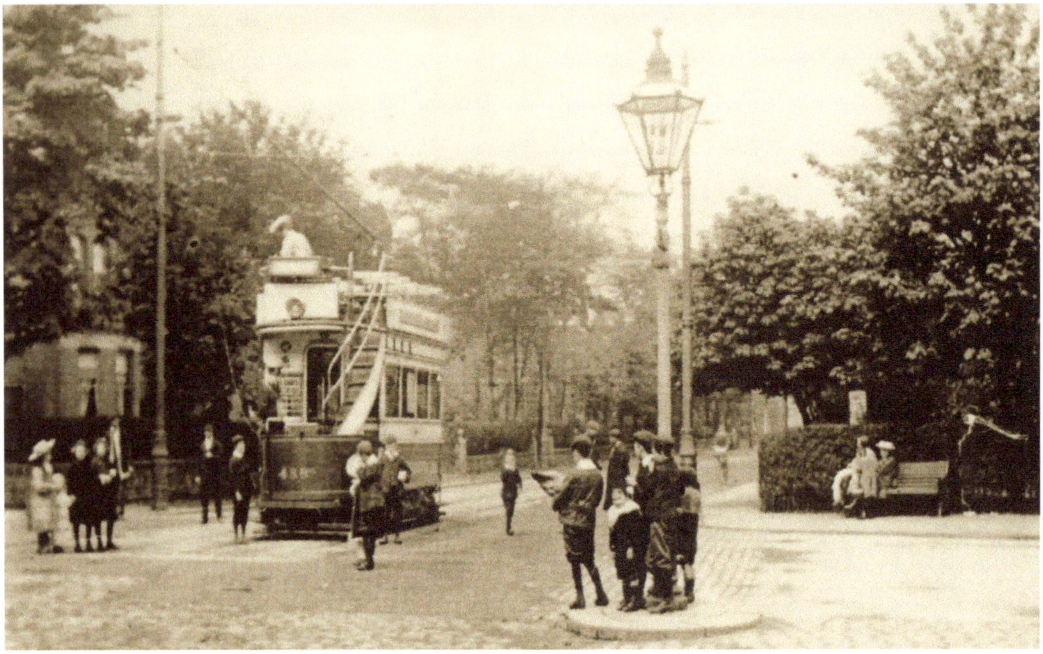

Tram Terminus, Barlow Moor Road, Chorlton-cum-Hardy, *c.* 1910

The tram terminus on Barlow Moor Road shows a tram outside the Macfadyen Memorial Church. The tram track extension from Whalley Range into Chorlton-cum-Hardy, along Barlow Moor Road, took place in 1911, with the last connection taking place in 1913. The last trams were withdrawn from service in Manchester in 1949. The electric tram first arrived in Chorlton-cum-Hardy on 9 May 1907 (the first car was at 5 a.m.) and the last tram through the district was on Sunday 22 November 1942.

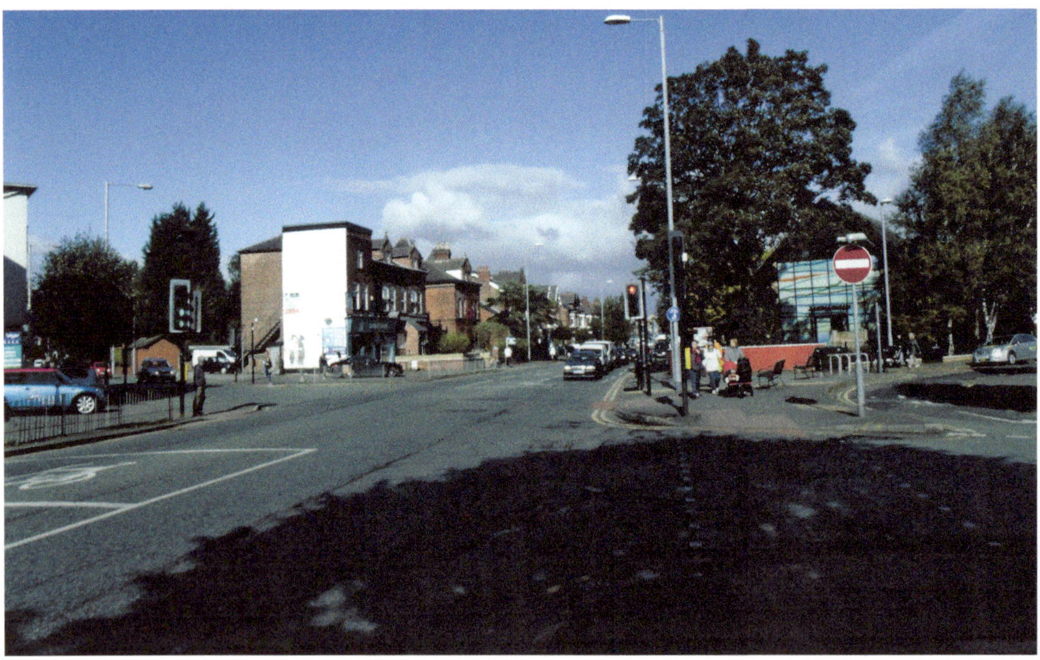

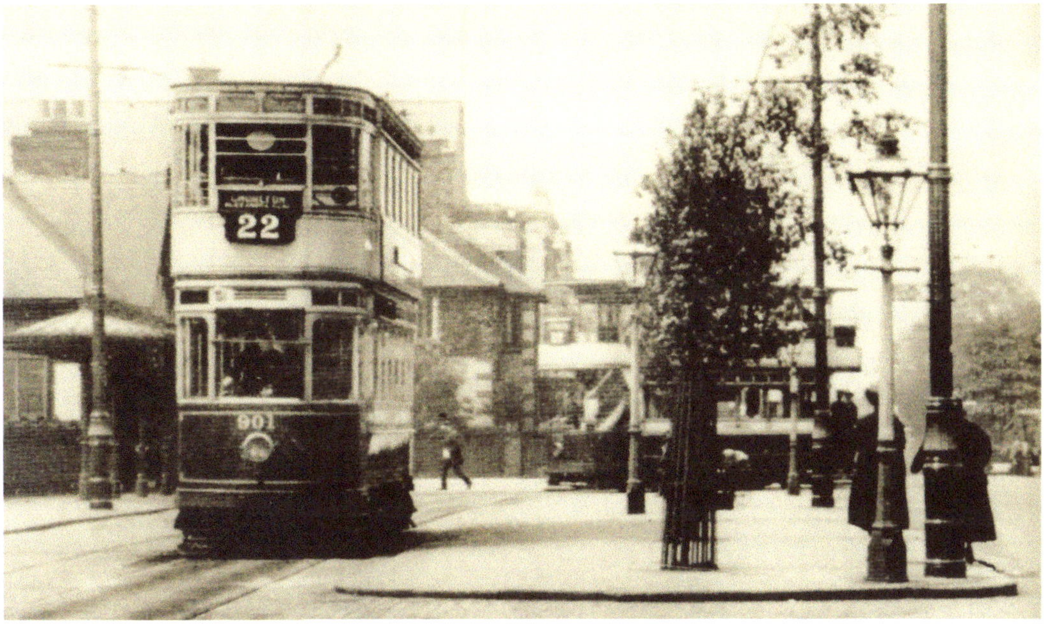

Chorlton Tram Siding, Barlow Moor Road, Chorlton-cum-Hardy, *c.* 1915

Opened on 14 May 1915 and originally a double-track tram siding. Passenger facilities included a shelter, toilets and an office building, located on the west side of Barlow Moor Road, between Malton Avenue and Beech Road. Trams used the north end of the siding until 1929, when the south end was linked. Today it is used by buses. On the same side, towards Chorlton, was the Palais de Luxe cinema, which opened in 1915 and closed late 1950s, becoming a supermarket.

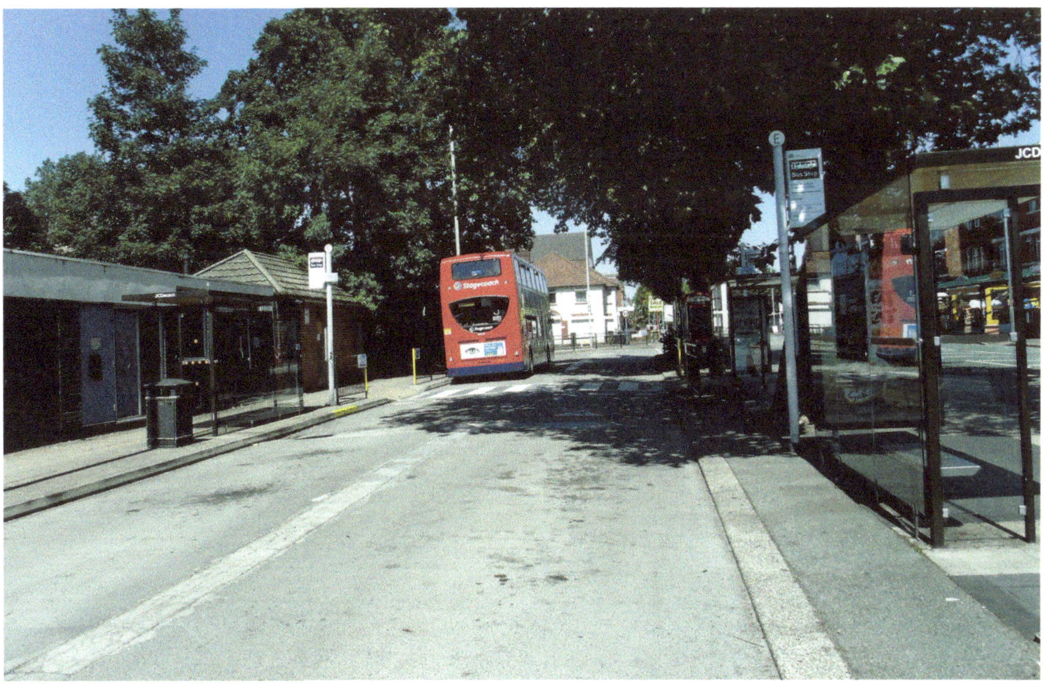

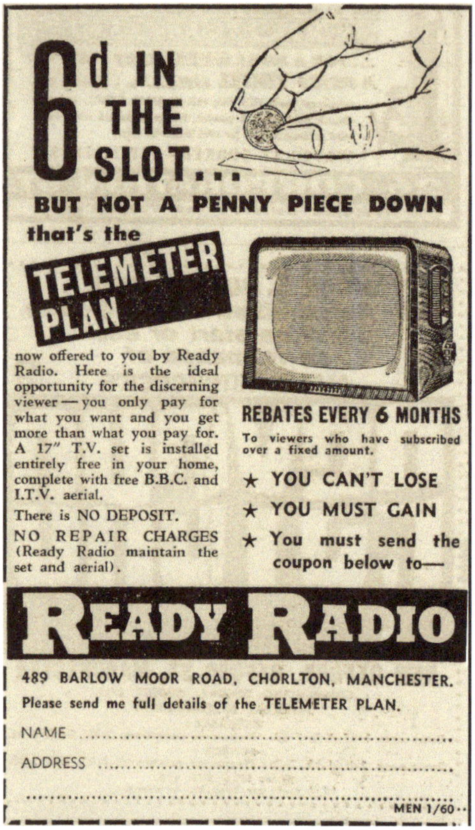

No. 489 Barlow Moor Road (centre), Chorlton-cum-Hardy, January 1960

Ready Radio are advertising the 'Telemeter Plan' in January 1960, where '6*d* in the slot' allows television viewers to rent a then 'state-of-the-art' television, in order to view the increasingly popular BBC and ITV programmes. Schemes like this allowed the massive expansion of popular media in the 1960s. Of course, the concept of 'pay as you go' is familiar to modern television viewers, although the choice and variety of programmes and channels have increased greatly in half a century.

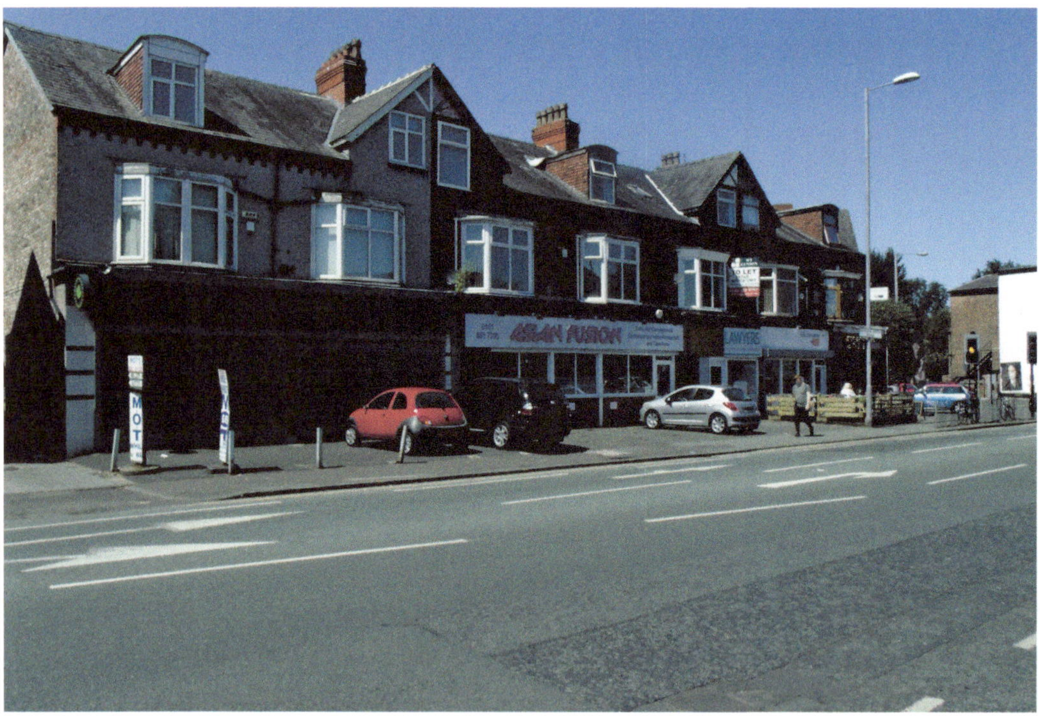

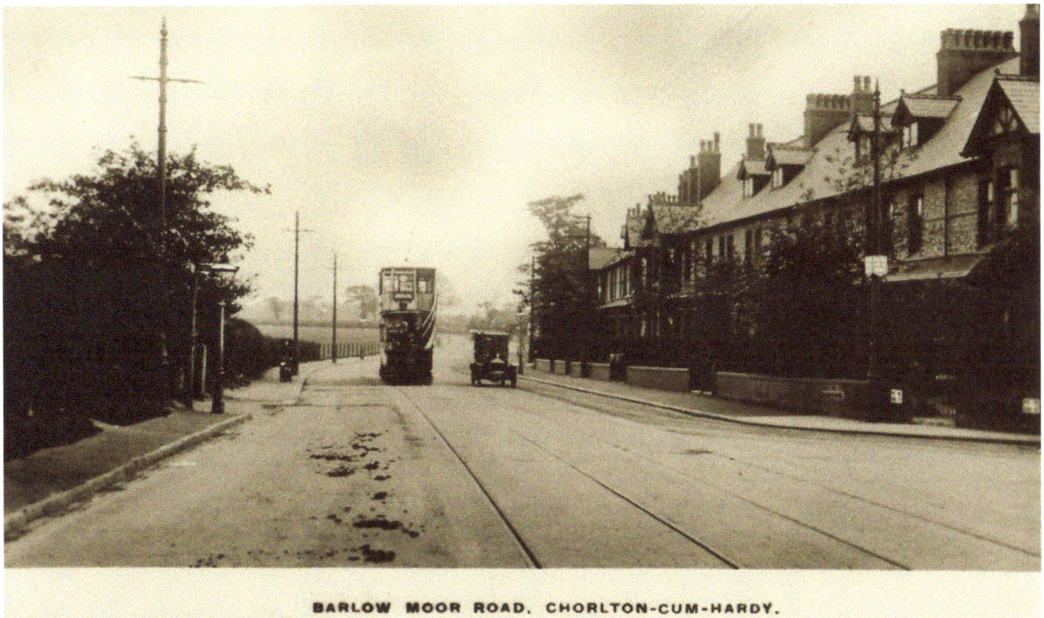

Barlow Moor Road, Chorlton-cum-Hardy, 1917

This view of Barlow Moor Road looks towards Didsbury and shows a row of terraced houses on the right in 1917 that have been transformed into commercial premises by 2017. In 1917, this section of Barlow Moor Road is still dominated by agricultural properties, but 100 years later the scene is overlooked by a popular fast-food establishment, whose logo is clearly visible along Barlow Moor Road. Today the trams have been replaced by the Metrolink system at Mauldeth Road West.

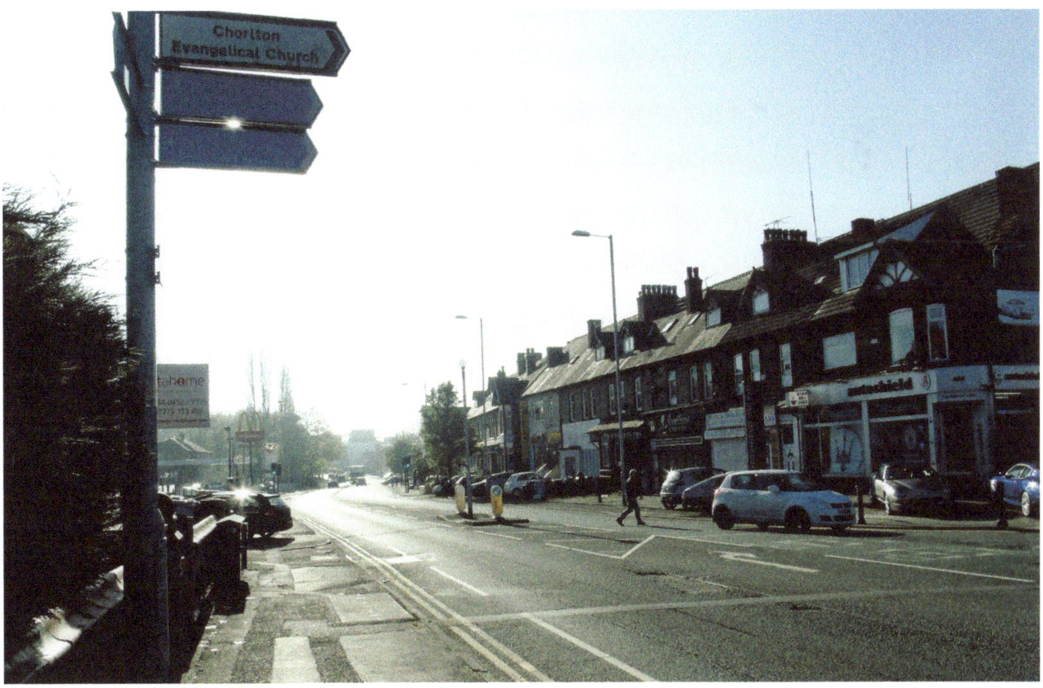

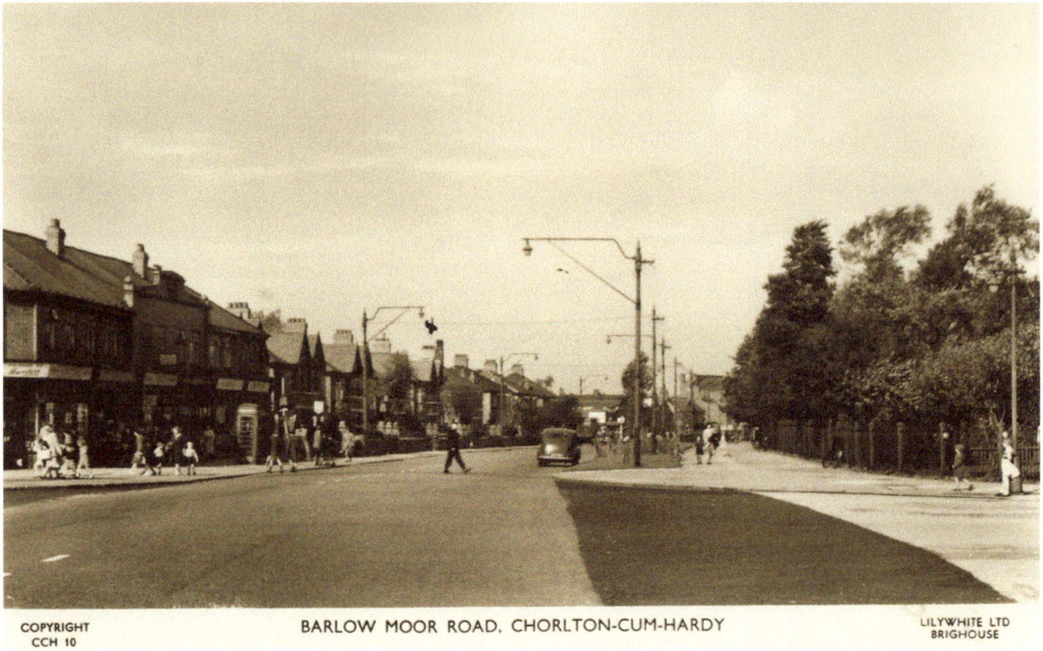

Barlow Moor Road, Chorlton-cum-Hardy, *c.* 1955

Beyond the right-hand extremity of the image is Chorlton Park (which opened in 1928), Nell Lane and Chorlton Park Primary School. The traffic policeman in the middle of Barlow Moor Road is escorting children across as they return home from school. The school remains today, as does the park. The main change here is the Metrolink tramway, which runs across the junction of Barlow Moor Road with Mauldeth Road West to the right and Hardy Lane to the left.

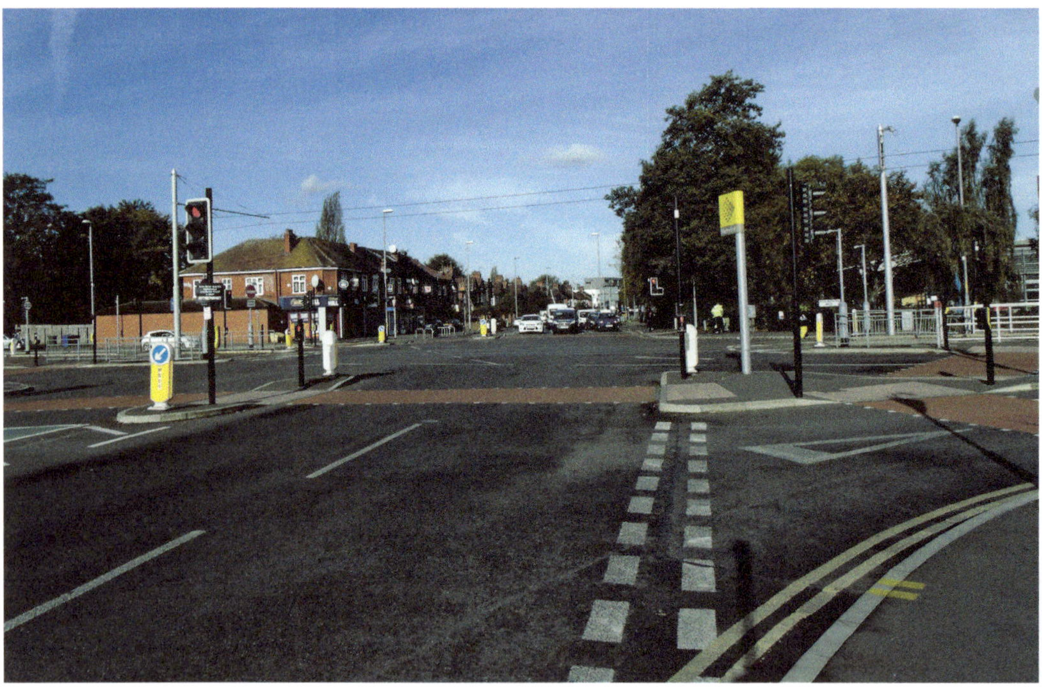

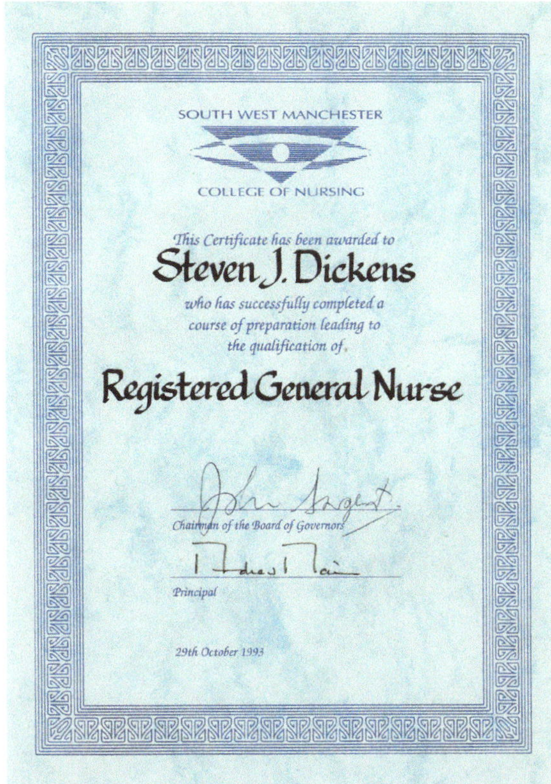
SOUTH WEST MANCHESTER

COLLEGE OF NURSING

This Certificate has been awarded to

Steven J. Dickens

who has successfully completed a course of preparation leading to the qualification of

Registered General Nurse

Chairman of the Board of Governors

Principal

29th October 1993

Mauldeth House, Mauldeth Road West and South West Manchester College of Nursing, 29 October 1993

Now offices, Mauldeth House was originally the administrative building and headquarters of the South Manchester School (later College) of Nursing, centred on Withington and Wythenshawe hospitals. My memory of it dates to May 1989, when I attended a nurse training interview here. By the time I qualified (see above), it had become the headquarters for South-West Manchester College of Nursing, when nurse training was in transition from the traditional nursing school format, towards Project 2000 and degree-level nursing.

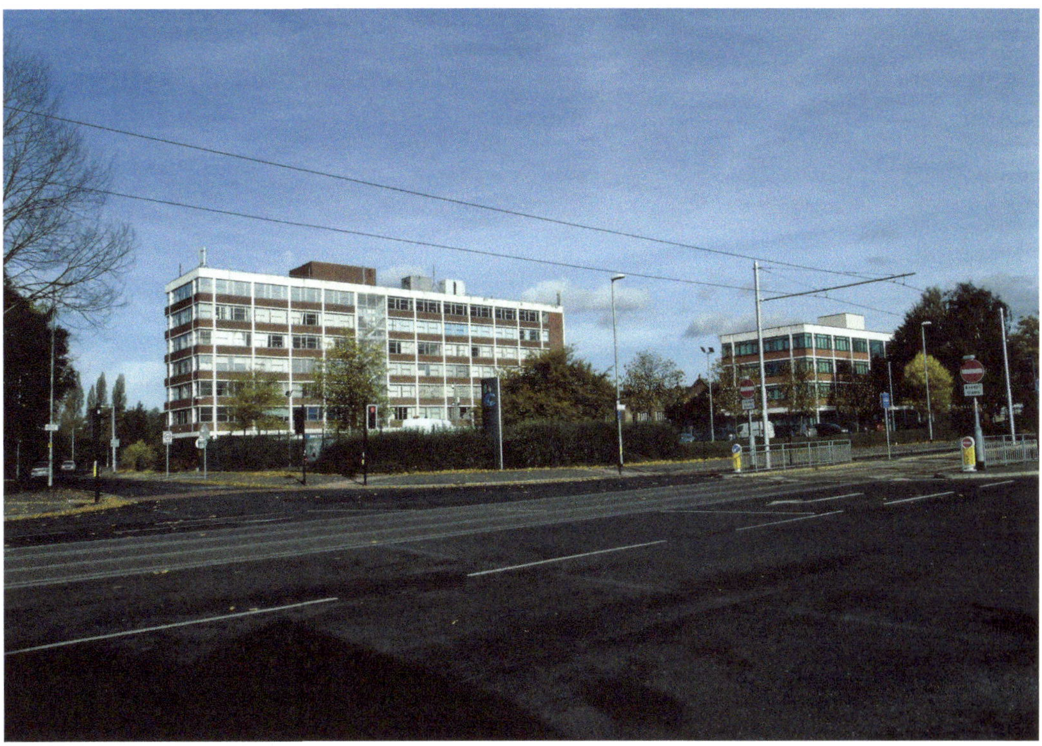

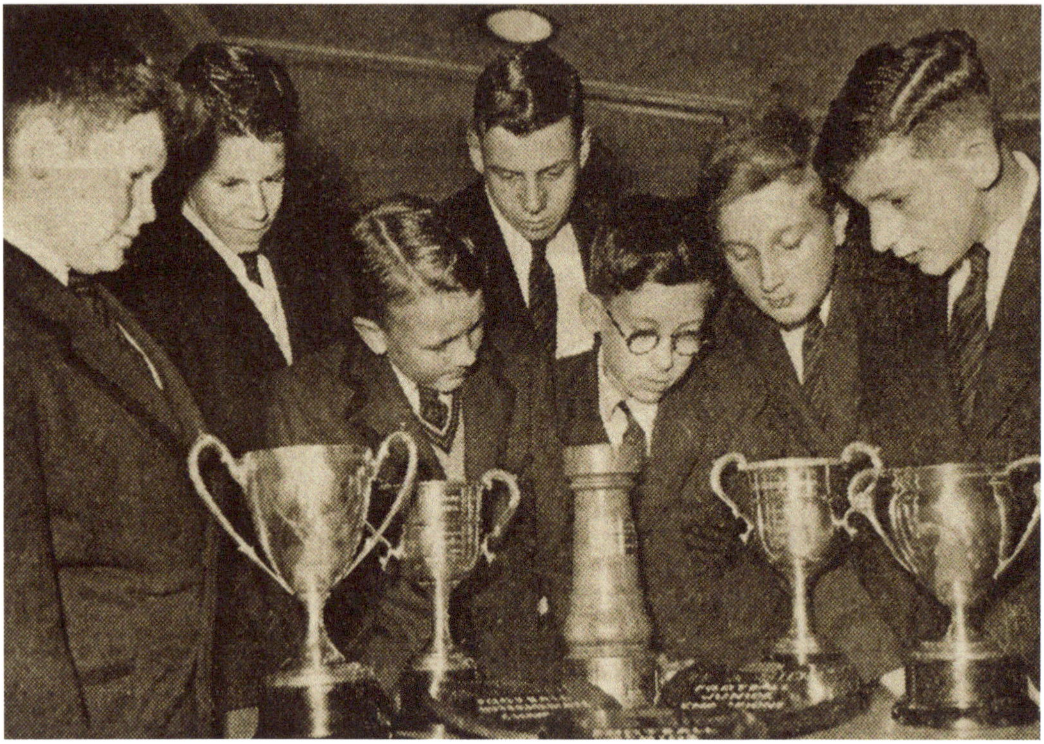

Chorlton Grammar School Pupils at the Free Trade Hall, 1959, and Corkland Road, 2017

The Grammar School began as Chorlton High School on 15 September 1924, becoming Chorlton Grammar School from 1952–67 (both at Corkland Road). The school initially opened with 110 boys, and by November 1927 had 420 registered. In September 1928 a sixth form was established, although there were just eight boys at first. The school continued to increase in size, until there were 500 boys and thirty in the sixth form by September 1944. In the 1950s the school underwent structural changes, reflecting its new status as a boys' grammar school.

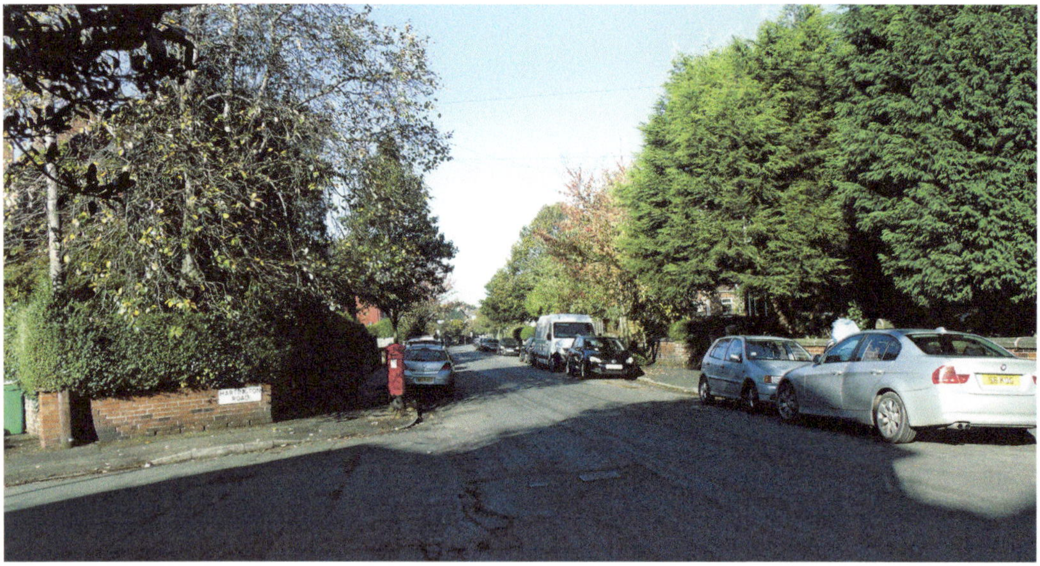

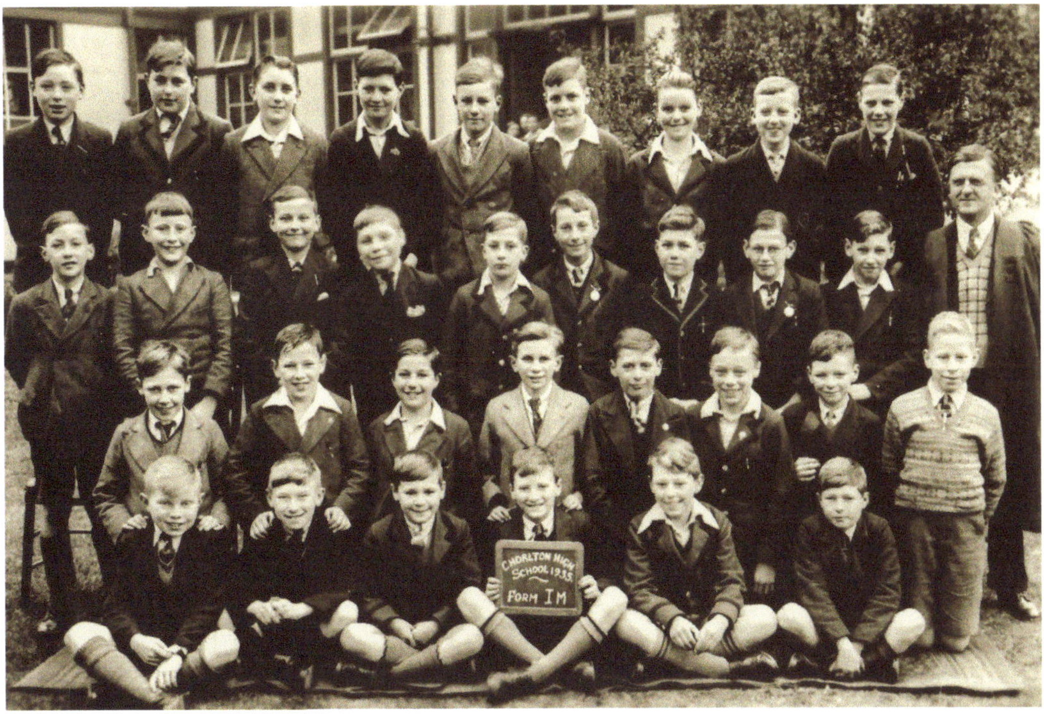

Chorlton High School for Boys, *c.* 1930, and School Entrance and Mauldeth House, Nell Lane, 2017
This image of students at Chorlton High School for Boys shows Form I M outside what looks like the central block. The school was established in 1924 to cater for demand in the education of older local boys. Once pupil numbers had increased sufficiently a lower school was established at Darley Avenue, which was at one time Barlow Hall School. When the school achieved grammar school status in 1952 construction work began, reflecting its new academic needs and the demands of the curriculum.

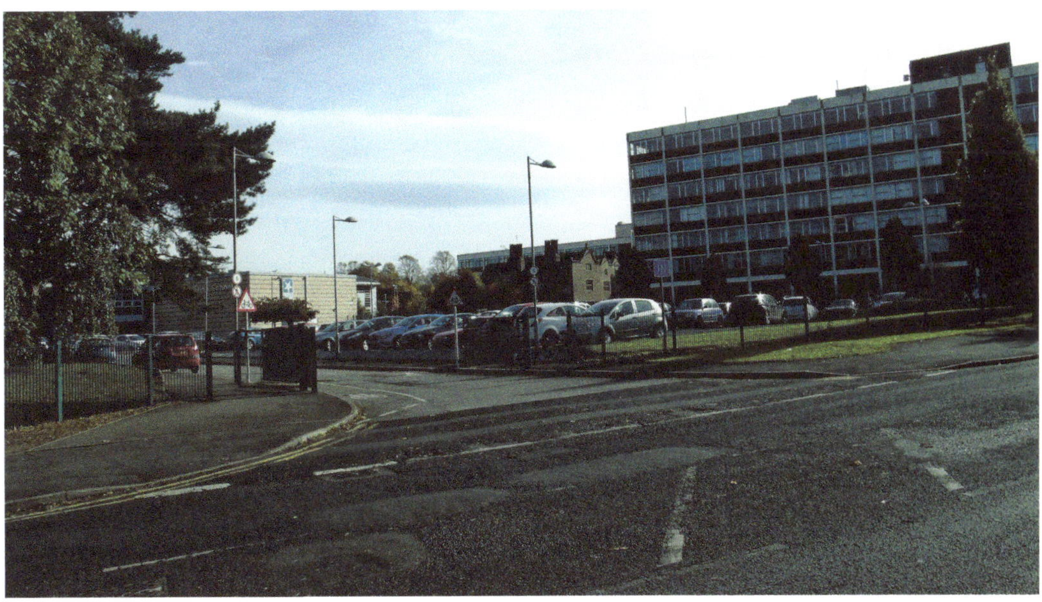

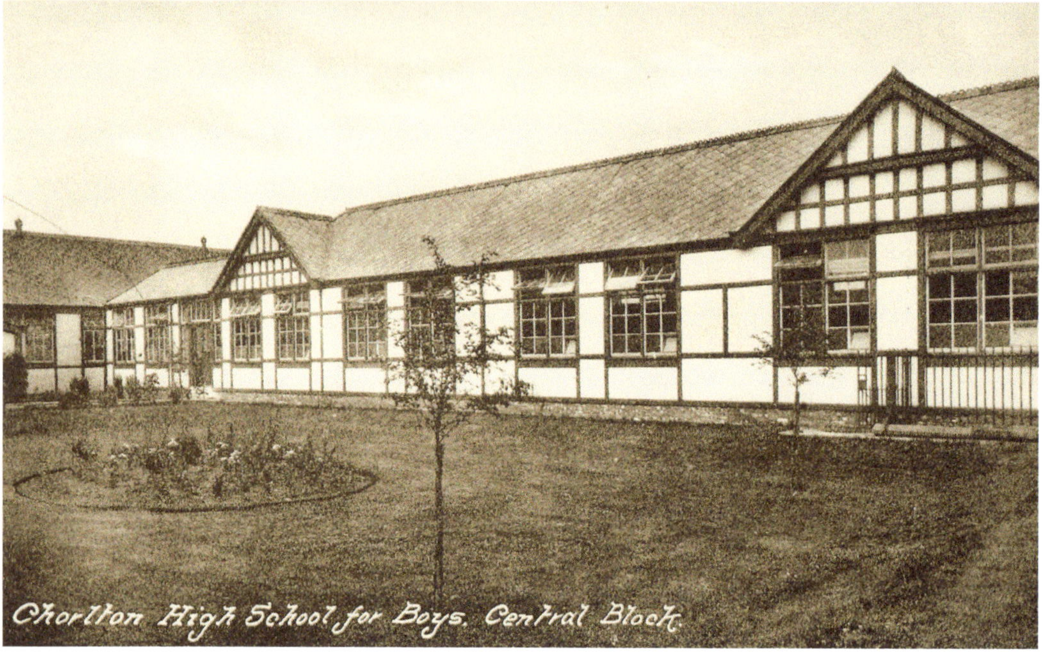

Chorlton High School for Boys, Central Block, *c.* 1930, and School Entrance from Nell Lane, 2017

This image of the central block shows the school in virtually pristine condition and so it can only be assumed that it was taken shortly after opening. The school consistently expanded and developed over the years, with a new biology laboratory and classrooms in September 1953; there were also further school improvements and expansion throughout the 1950s. In September 1954 there were 550 boys enrolled, with eighty-two in the sixth form; however, by the mid-1960s student numbers had fallen.

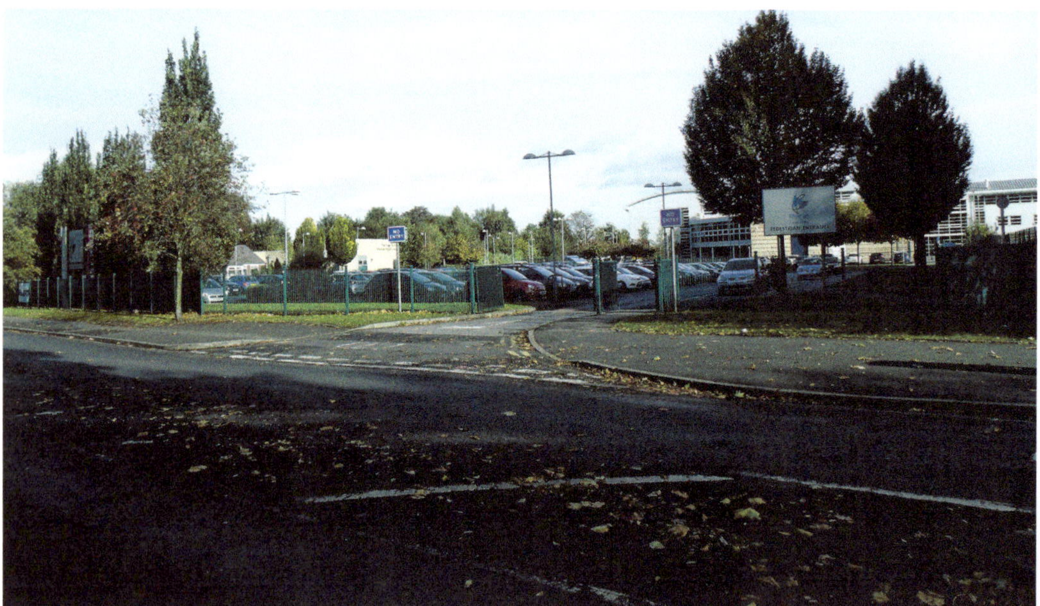

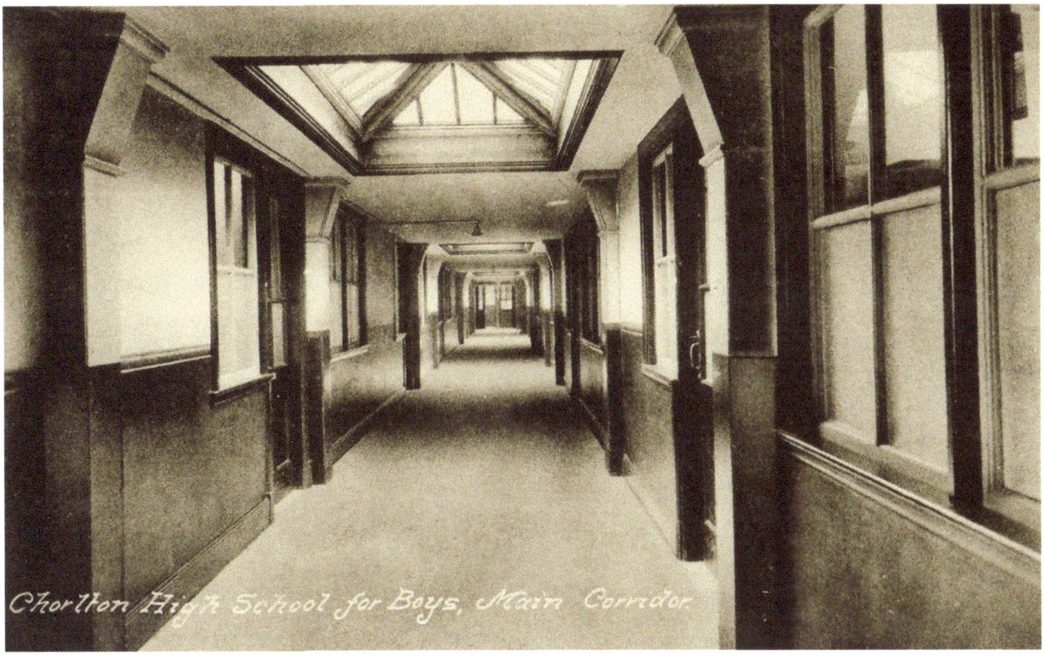

Main Corridor of Chorlton High School for Boys, *c.* 1930, and School Buildings and Mauldeth House, Nell Lane, 2017

This view of the main corridor of Chorlton High School for Boys also looks pristine. In the forty-three years of the school's existence more than 4,000 boys have passed through this corridor. By the mid-1960s plans for a new school had been shelved – a result of declining numbers. There were new plans for the school to be amalgamated with Chorlton High School at Nell Lane, which was achieved in 1967–68. The old school site on Corkland Road became redundant.

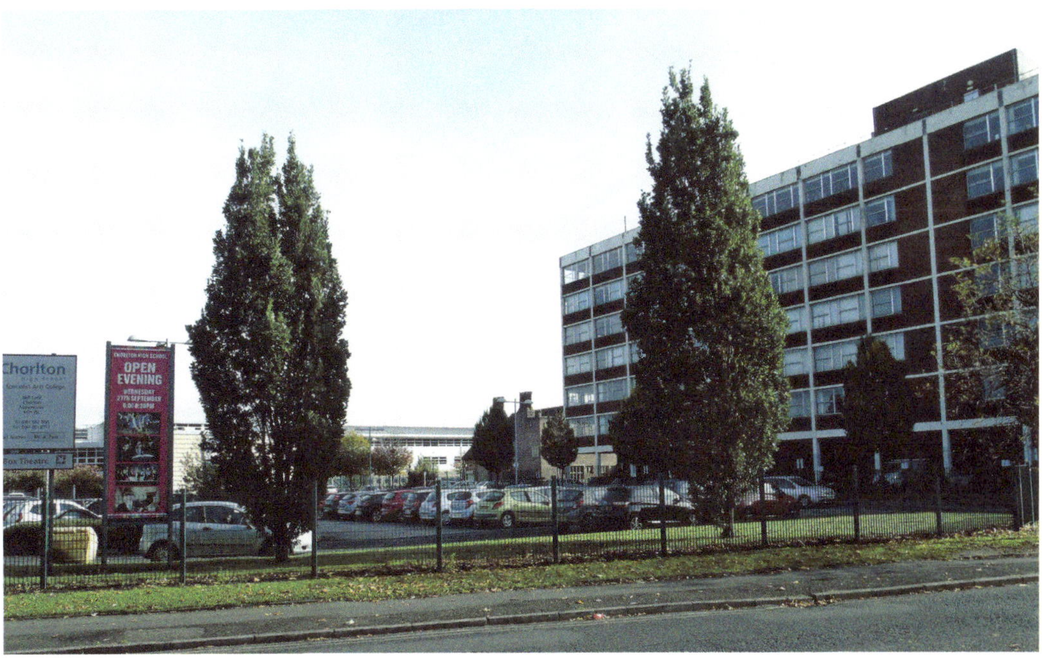

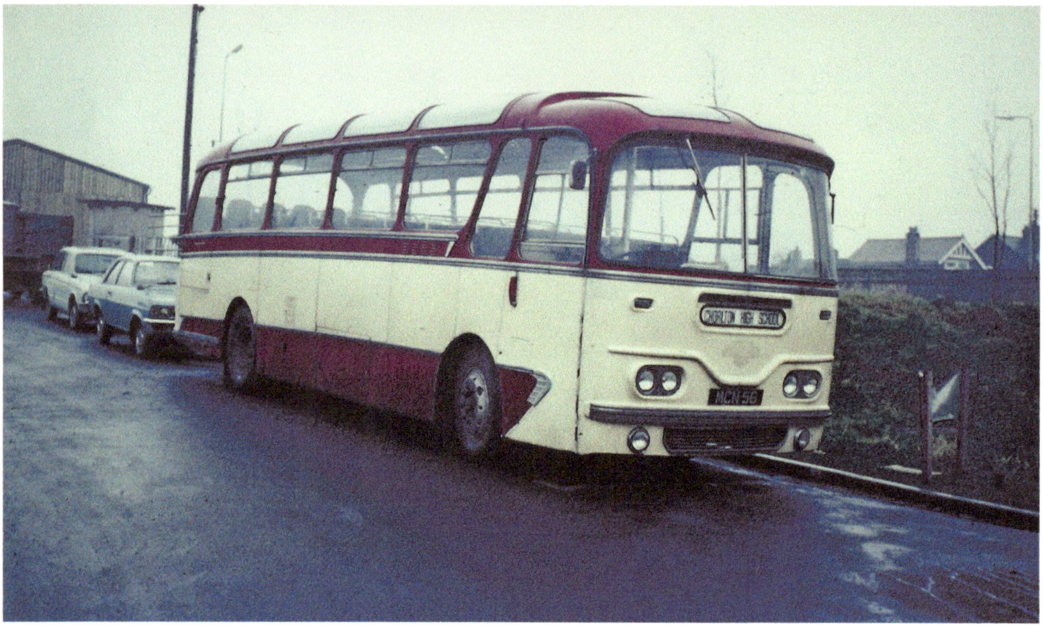

Leyland Leopard, Chorlton High School, 1975, and Metrolink Tram, Chorlton High School, Mauldeth Road West, 2017

This Leyland Leopard coach – registration No. MCN 56 – started its working life in the north-east of England in 1961–62, but some fourteen years later has found its way to Chorlton High School. It was hired out, in all probability for taking students to and from sporting and social events, as well as travel to school. Today the Metrolink tram system runs past the school, providing an efficient means of transport, although there are still regular bus services in the vicinity.

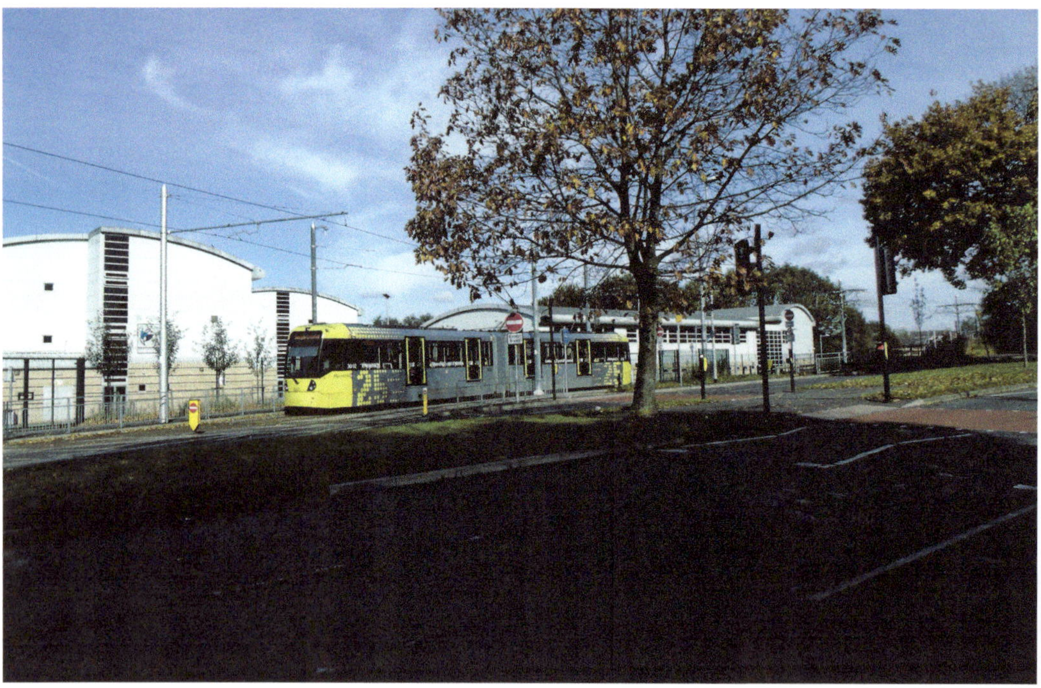

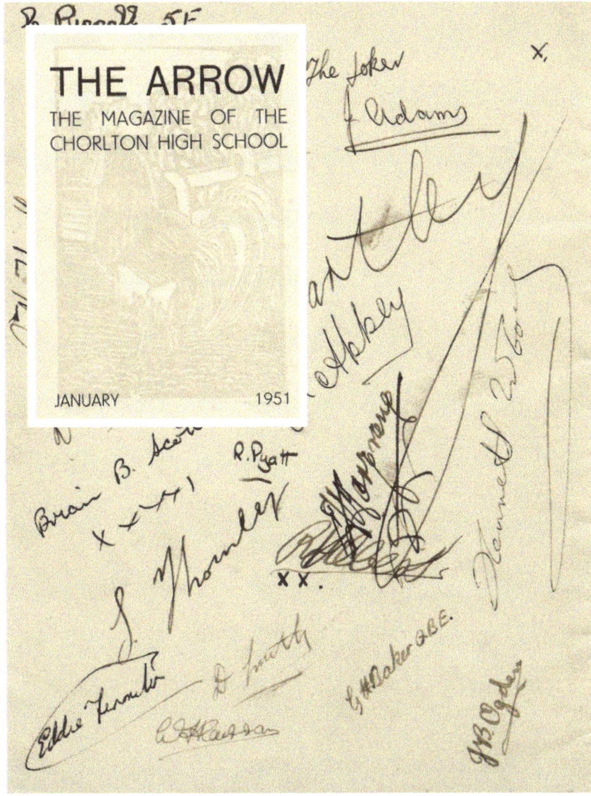

Autographs in *The Arrow*, January 1951, and New School Buildings from Mauldeth Road West, 2017. *Inset*: Title Page, 1951

There are several autographs on the back of the school magazine, *The Arrow*, although unfortunately some are illegible. However, here is a list of the ten signatures I managed to decipher: B. Ruggall 5F, G. Bentley, Brian B. Scott, G. H. Baker QBE, J. B. Ogden, D. Yale, S. Thornley, J. Adams, A. Hartley and R. Pyatt. A year later the school became a boys' grammar school and has undergone further changes since amalgamating with Chorlton High School in 1967. It is now a coeducational school with academy status.

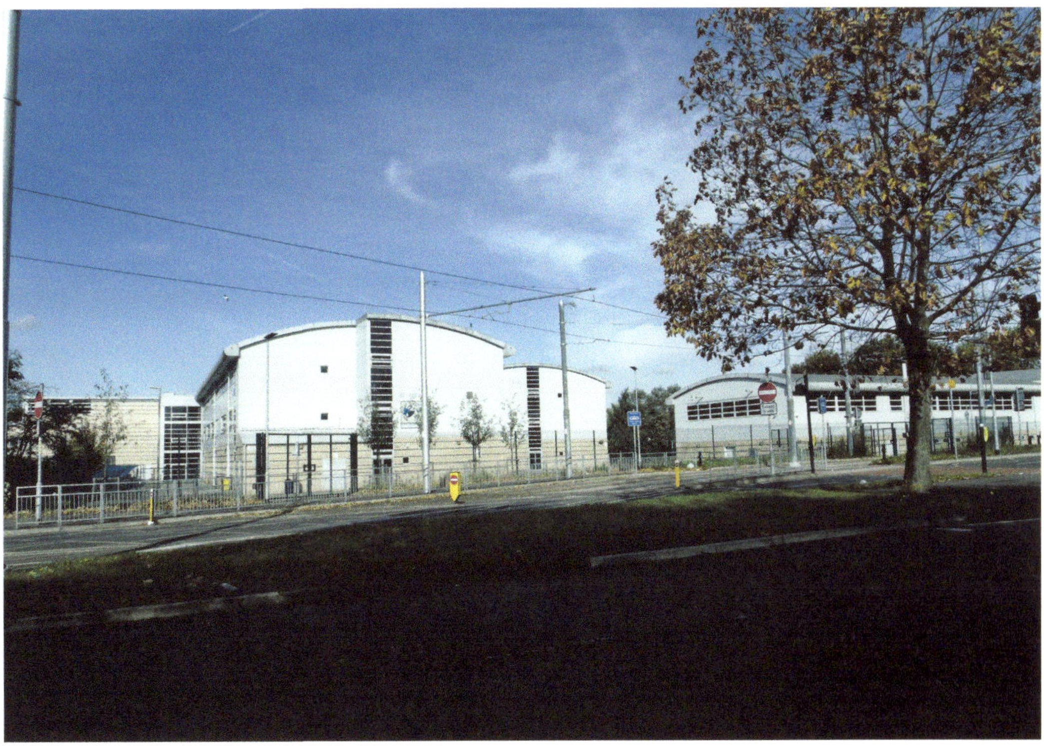

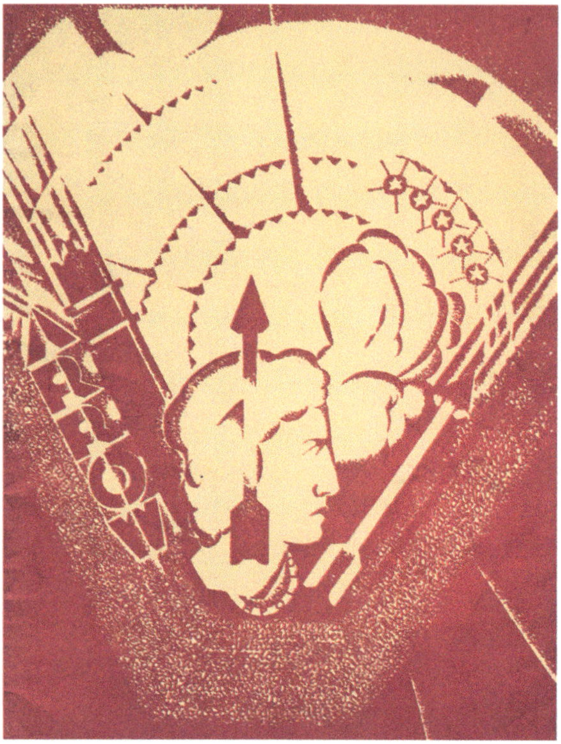

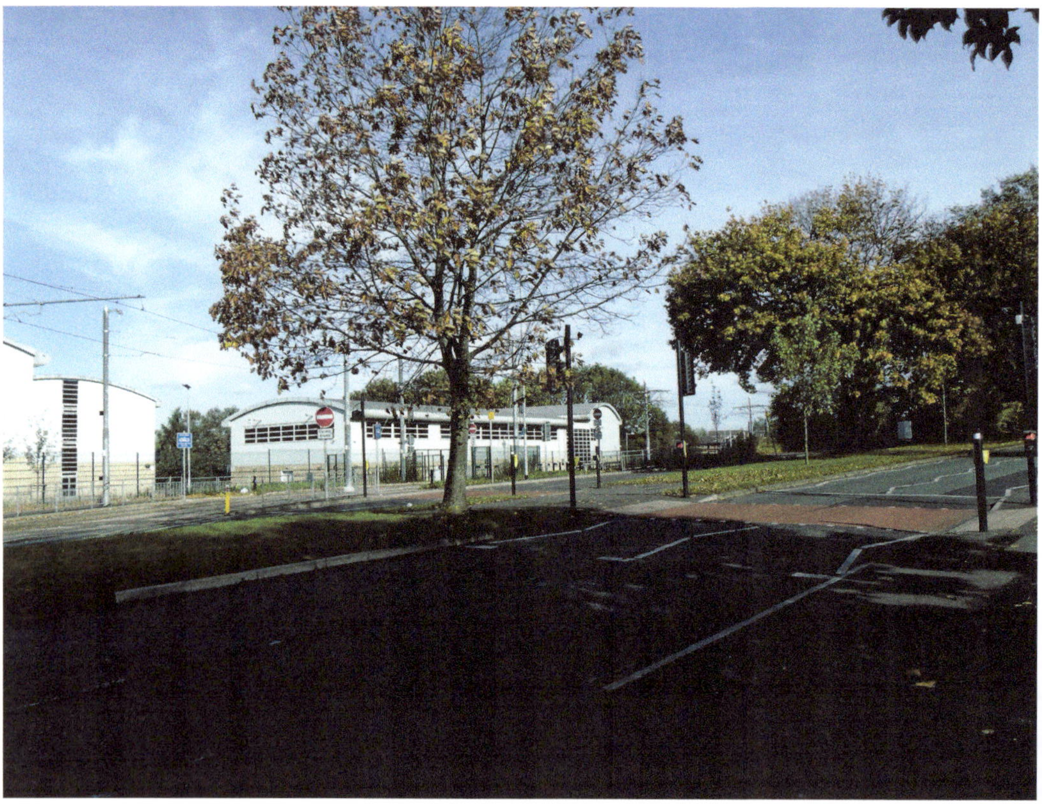

The Arrow, January 1951, and New School Buildings From Mauldeth Road West, 2017

In 2002 Chorlton High School became a specialist arts college, with the decision for the school to become an academy approved in May 2012. It officially became an academy on 1 January 2013. Today there are several new buildings across the site and there is no evidence of the original 1960s buildings. It shares a site at the junction of Mauldeth Road West and Nell Lane with Mauldeth House and Hough End Hall. Readers of *The Arrow* in 1951 were about to witness great academic changes.

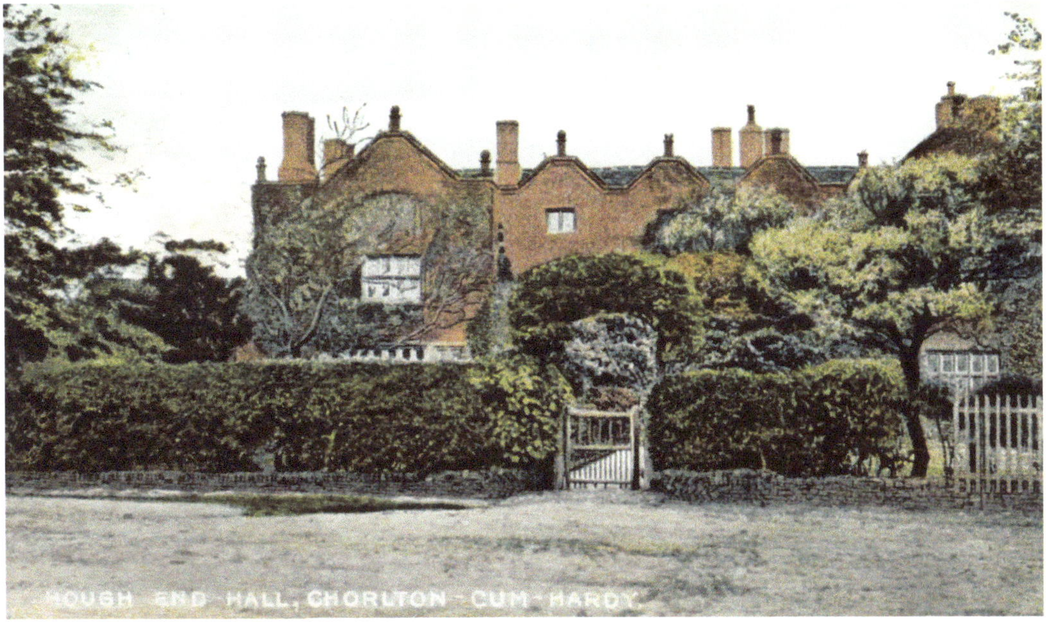

Hough End Hall, Nell Lane, *c.* 1910

Originally located in Withington, it was built in 1596, during the reign of Elizabeth I, by Sir Nicholas Mosley (1527–1612). It is a three-storey brick building with gabled wings, and is Grade II listed. It has been much altered over the years and is now surrounded by large concrete office blocks. Part of its grounds, along Mauldeth Road West, was the site of Alexandra Park Aerodrome until 1924 and is now the site of new buildings for Chorlton High School.

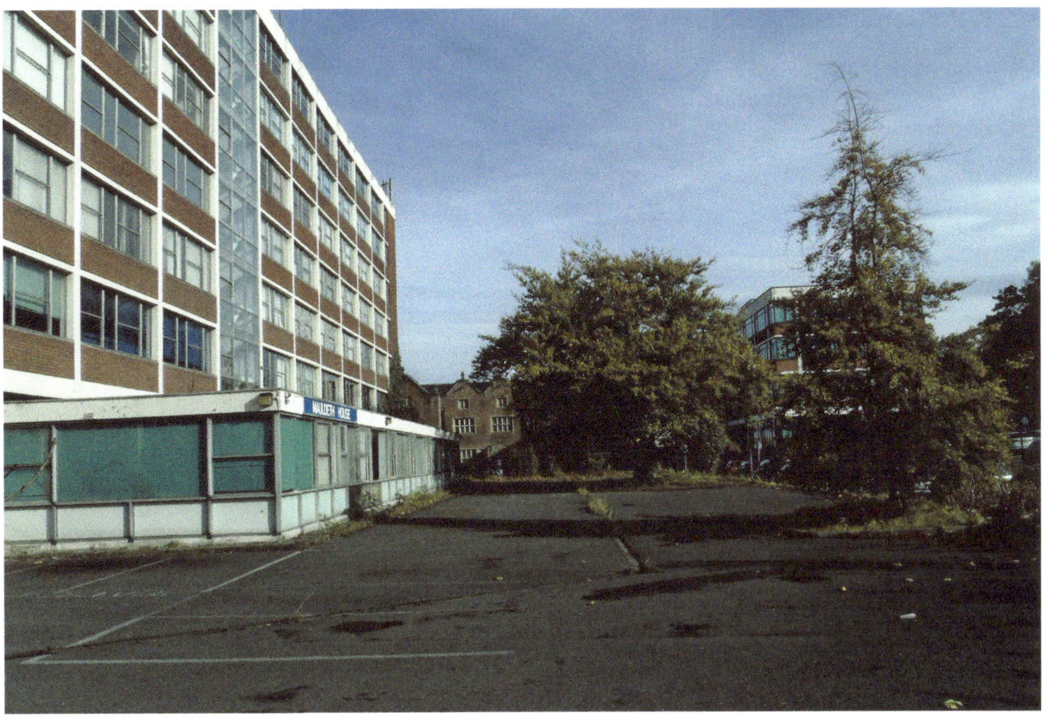

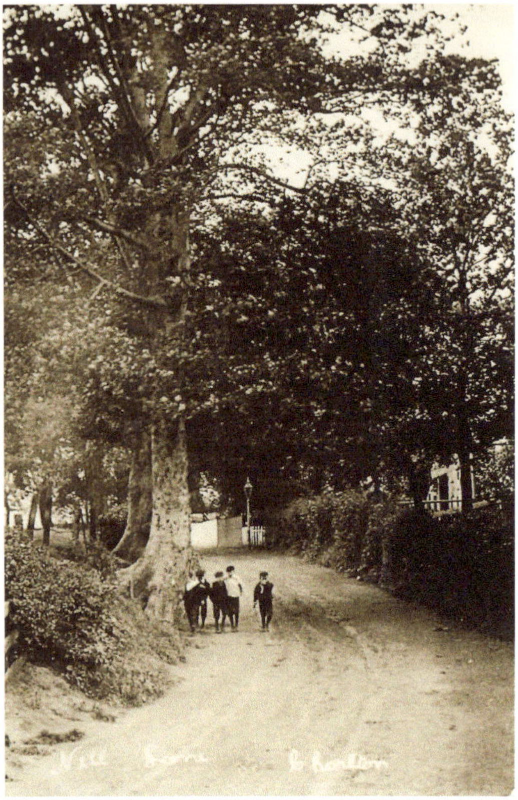

Nell Lane, Chorlton-cum-Hardy, *c.* 1900

Housing development took place along Sandy Lane and Nell Lane during the early part of the twentieth century, although more than 200 acres of land was still being farmed around Hough End Hall and between Withington and Chorlton-cum-Hardy. During the First World War an aerodrome was constructed on land to the rear of the hall, and in the 1920s housing and retail premises were built. Nell Lane still managed to retain its rural outlook, as shown above.

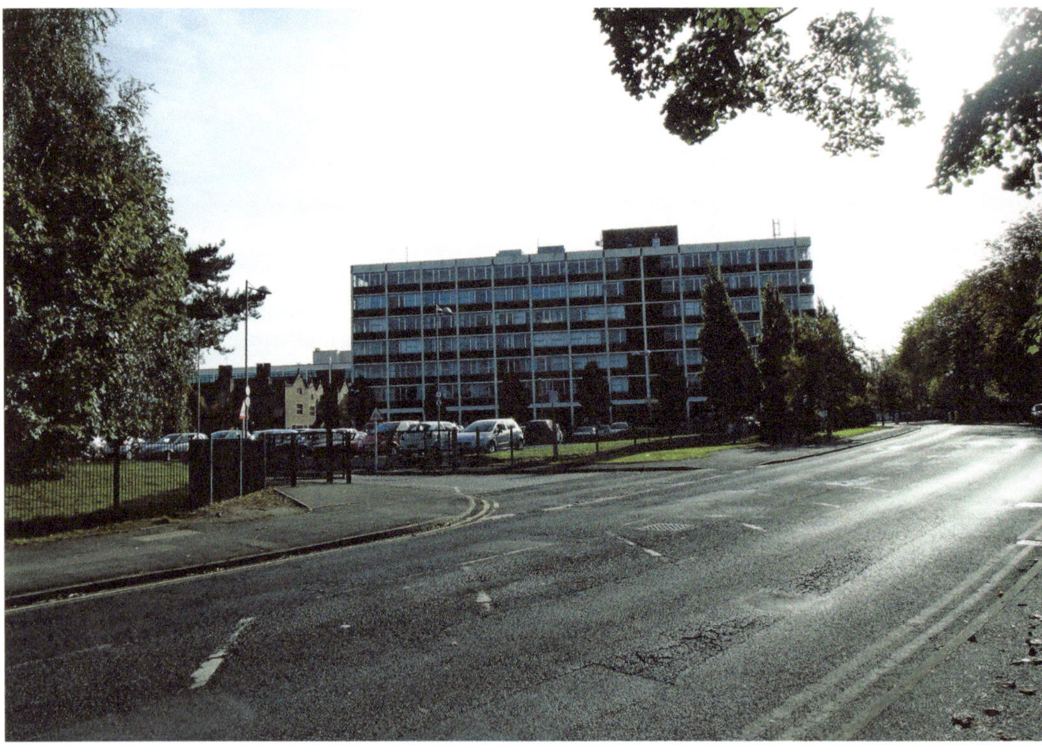

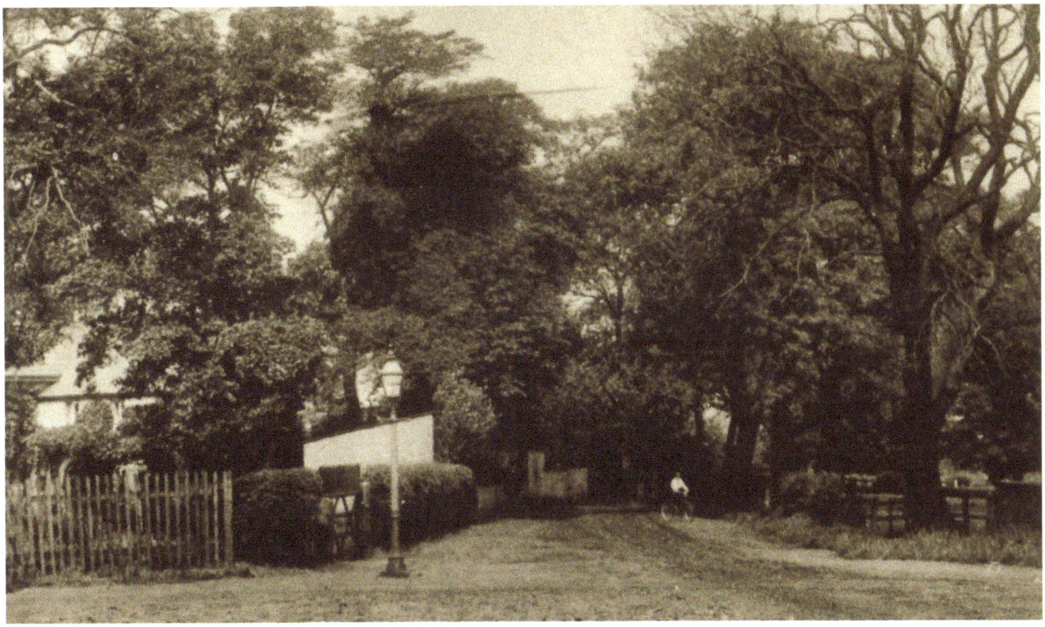

Nell Lane, Looking North, *c.* 1920

By the 1930s Chorlton Park was well established and Nell Lane had been widened. Local authority housing was constructed to the south of Hough End Hall, so the corner of Nell Lane and Mauldeth Road West was thus dominated by houses and the Southern Hotel, which became a 'landmark' here (see *inset*). By the 1940s and '50s the amount of farmland in the area was much reduced and had been taken over by housing and later schools and office facilities.

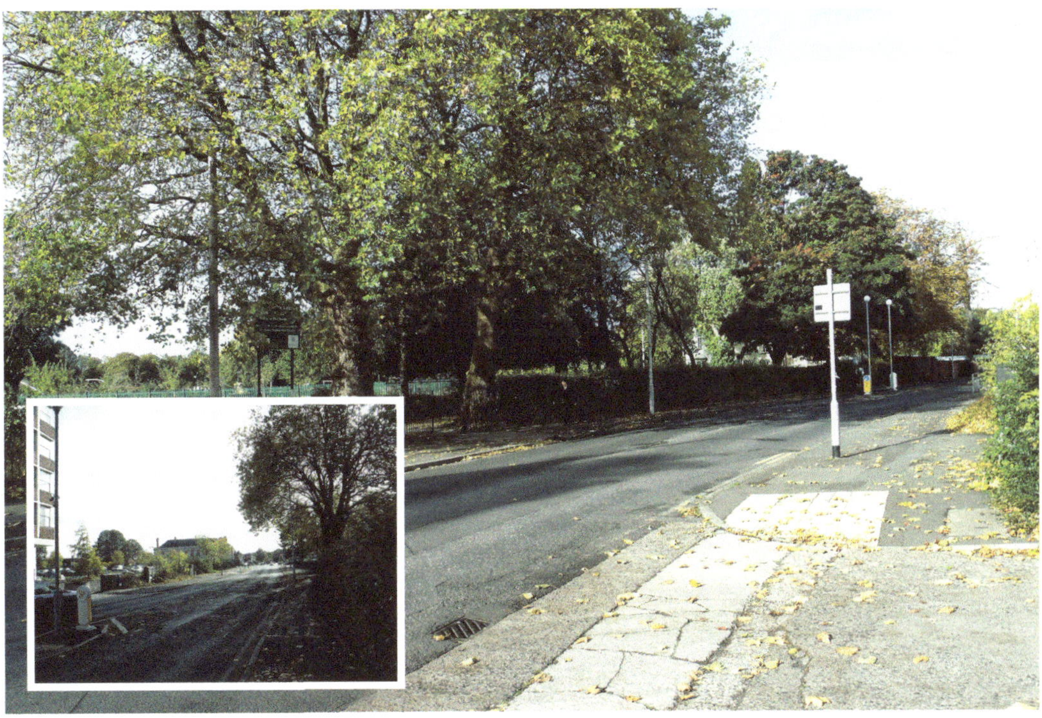

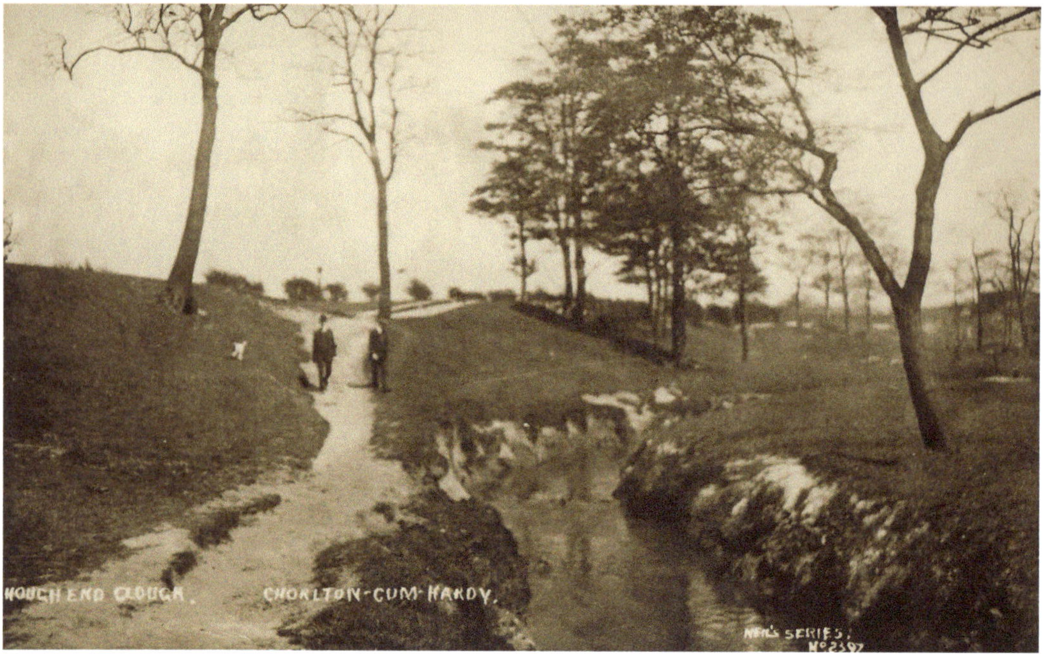

Hough End Clough, Chorlton-cum-Hardy, 1922

The Anglo-Saxon word *hof* means 'a dwelling' in modern English, with *ende* meaning 'a boundary' – the hall and its grounds stand close to the boundary between the townships of Chorlton-cum-Hardy and Withington. The hall was once the seat of the Mosley family, who moved to Rolleston Hall in Staffordshire in the mid-seventeenth century. The clough follows the course of Red Lion Brook and is adjacent to Hough End playing fields and an area of woodland.

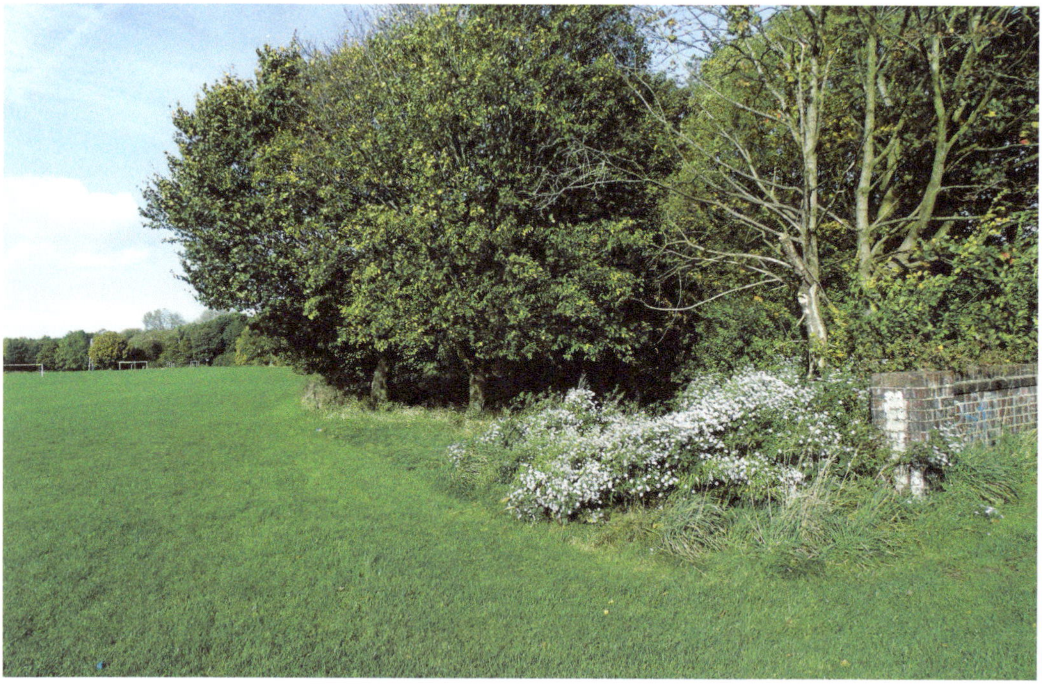

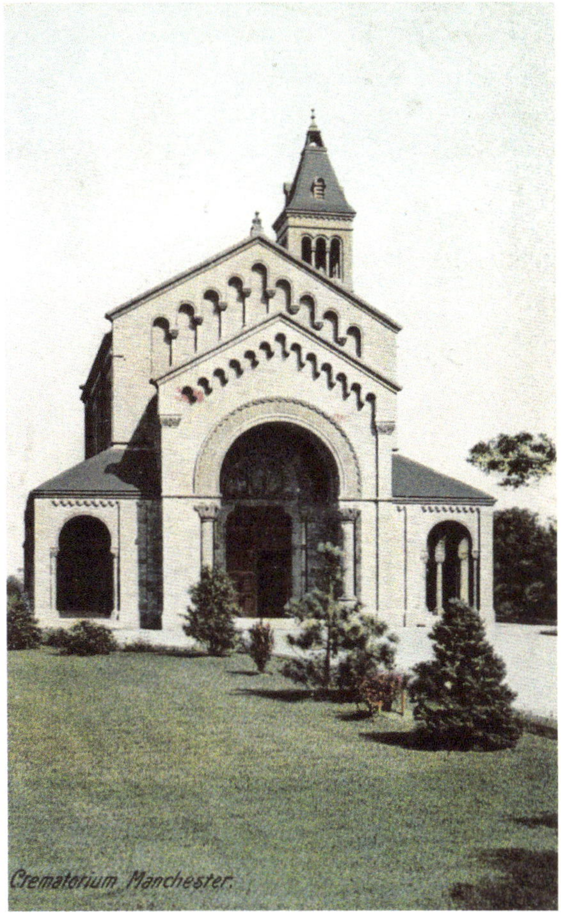

Manchester Crematorium, Barlow Moor Road, 1909

This was first opened in 1892 – only the second in this country at the time. The Manchester Cremation Society was founded in 1888 and believed in conserving the land. They were in favour of Manchester having its own crematorium. Manchester Crematorium has two chapels, with the old chapel (designed by Edward Salomons and A. Steinthall) opening in 1892 and seating around 120. It is Grade II listed and has an organ and stained-glass windows. The new chapel was opened in 1954, seating around sixty.

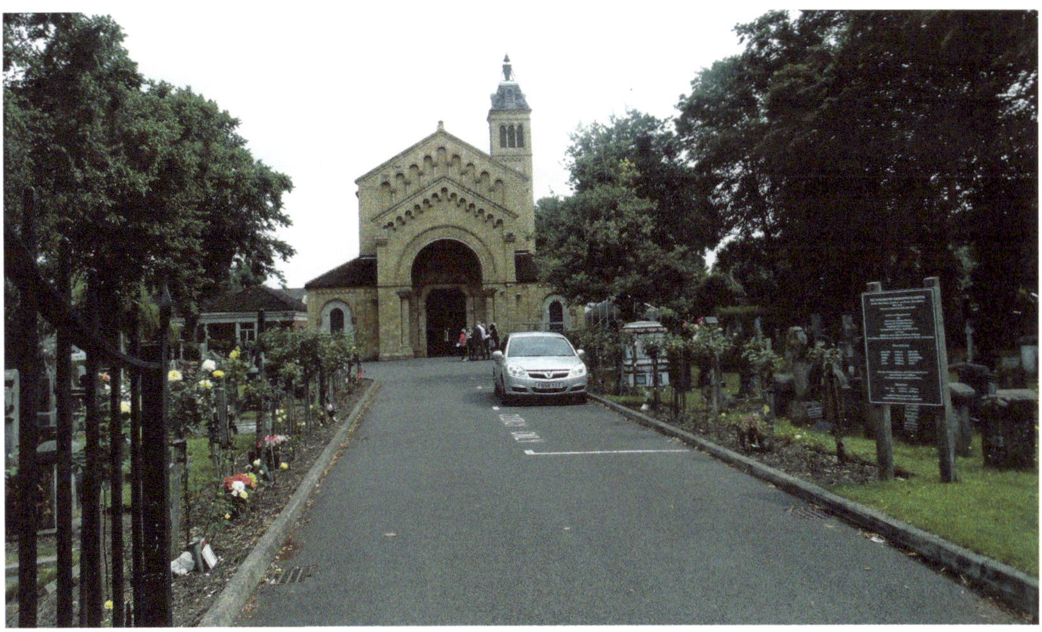

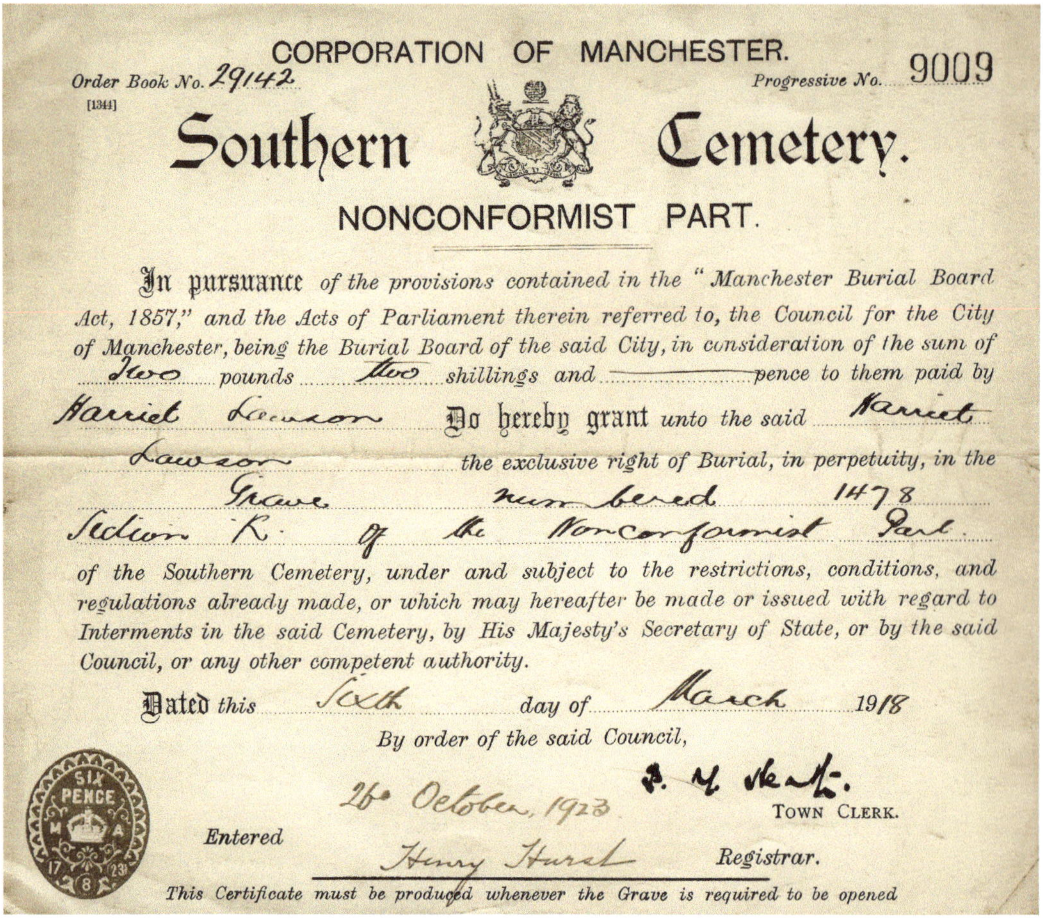

CORPORATION OF MANCHESTER.

Order Book No. 29142 Progressive No. 9009

[1344]

Southern Cemetery.

NONCONFORMIST PART.

In pursuance *of the provisions contained in the "Manchester Burial Board Act, 1857," and the Acts of Parliament therein referred to, the Council for the City of Manchester, being the Burial Board of the said City, in consideration of the sum of* Two *pounds* two *shillings and* —— *pence to them paid by* Harriet Lawson Do hereby grant *unto the said* Harriet Lawson *the exclusive right of Burial, in perpetuity, in the* Grave numbered 1478 Section K of the Nonconformist Part *of the Southern Cemetery, under and subject to the restrictions, conditions, and regulations already made, or which may hereafter be made or issued with regard to Interments in the said Cemetery, by His Majesty's Secretary of State, or by the said Council, or any other competent authority.*

Dated *this* Sixth *day of* March 1918

By order of the said Council,

SIX PENCE M A 17 8 23

26 October, 1923

TOWN CLERK.

Entered Henry Hurst *Registrar.*

This Certificate must be produced whenever the Grave is required to be opened

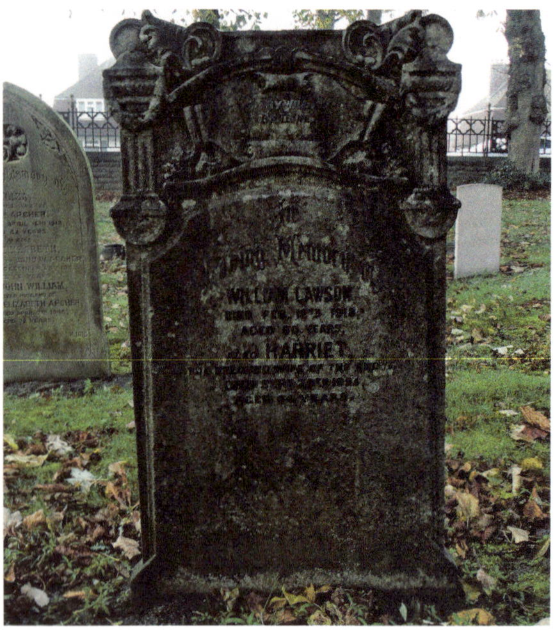

Southern Cemetery: 1918 Grant of Burial and the Headstone of William Lawson (d. 1918) and Harriet Lawson (d. 1923)

Southern Cemetery, which opened on 9 October 1879 to the cost of £38,340, is the largest municipal cemetery in the United Kingdom and the second largest in Europe. The cemetery is Grade II listed and contains six Grade II-listed buildings, including four chapels (one Jewish). Buried here is philanthropist John Rylands, aviator John Alcock, artist L. S. Lowry, entertainer Wilfred Pickles, and former Manchester United manager Sir Matt Busby. It was designed by the city surveyor from 1857–79, James Gascoigne Lynde, with buildings by H. J. Paull and was extended in the twentieth century.

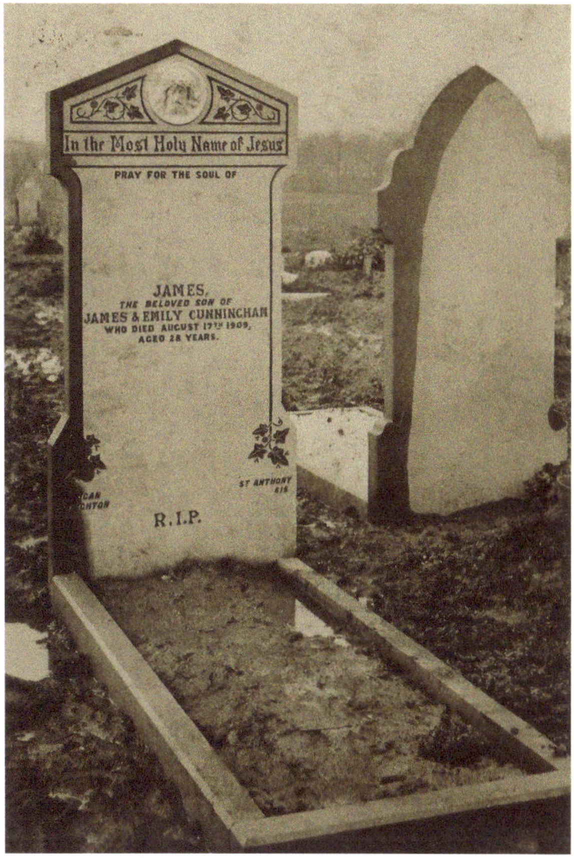

Final Resting Place of James Cunningham, 1909, and the Jewish Section of Southern Cemetery, 2017
Southern Cemetery has the record of James Cunningham, who died on 30 December 1909 and is buried in the Nonconformist section of the cemetery. He was aged fifty-nine. His son, also James, died on 17 August 1909 aged twenty-eight. His memorial is shown in the above photograph, which was a common form of Victorian and Edwardian remembrance practice. Both their deaths were registered initially at neighbouring Chorlton upon Medlock, part of the parish of South Manchester since 1896.

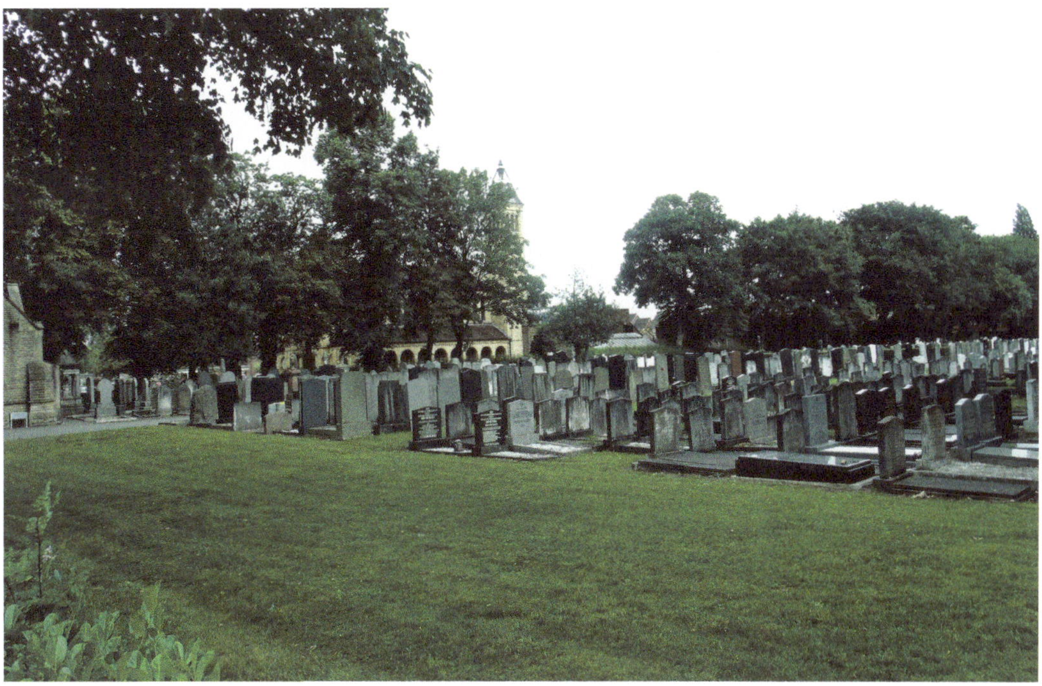

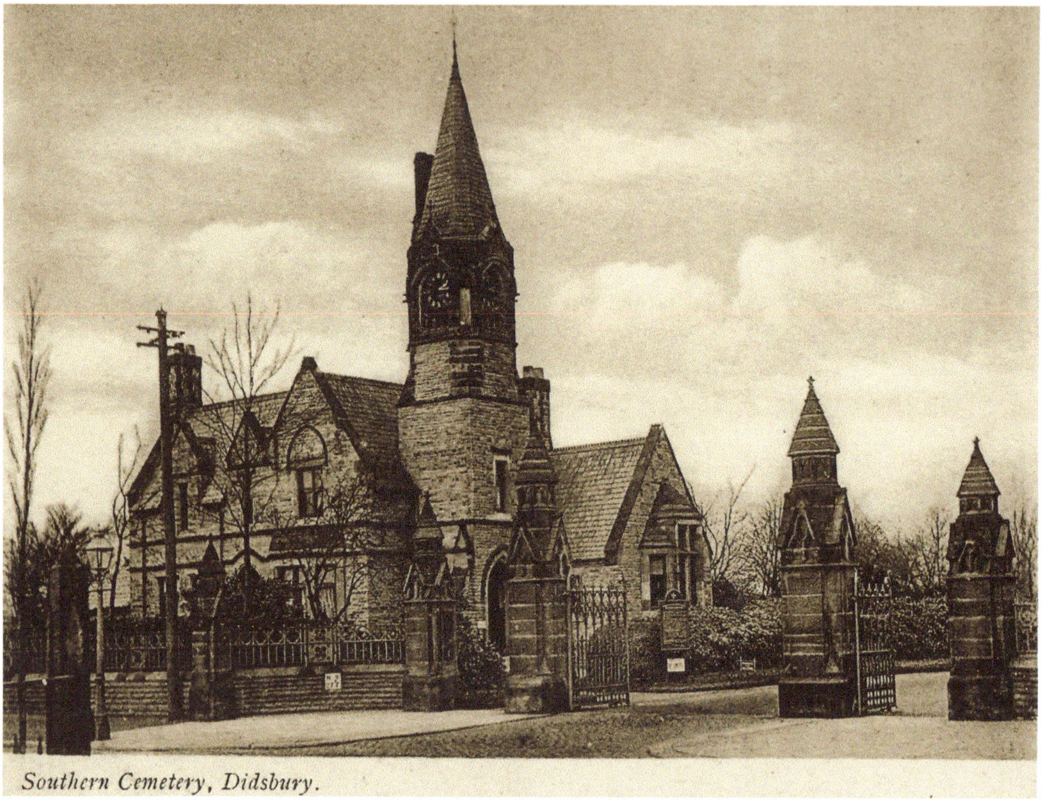

Barlow Moor Road Entrance of Southern Cemetery, Chorlton-cum-Hardy, *c.* 1900

The main entrance, at the centre of the south-west boundary of the main section of the cemetery, is Grade II listed. On both sides of the entrance lies a registrar's office and a lodge – both Grade II listed. With the entrance, they date from 1879. The two-storey stone buildings are in the Gothic style and each have a tower and short spire. There are three mortuary chapels – Grade II listed – which vary in design and are also Gothic in style; these date from 1879.

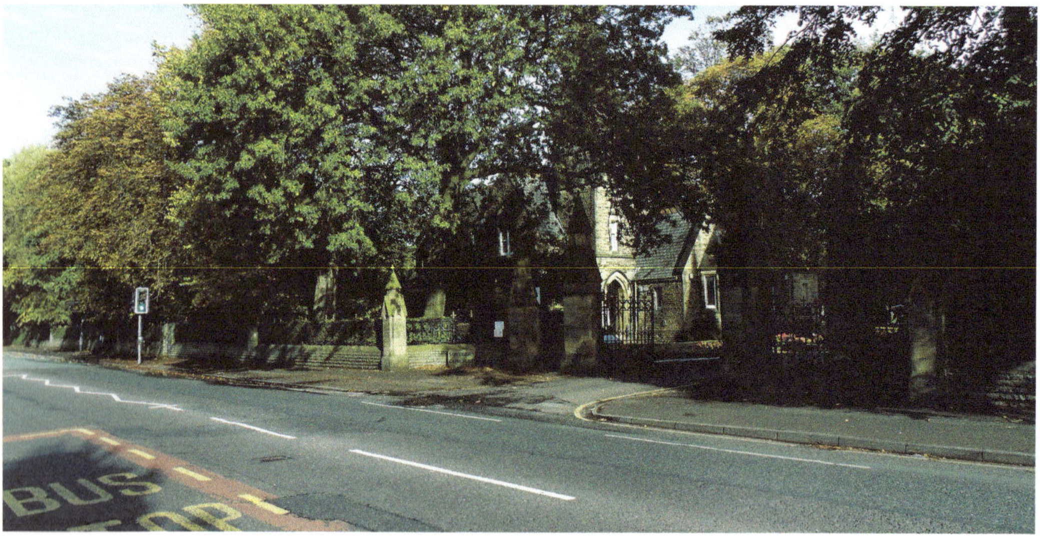

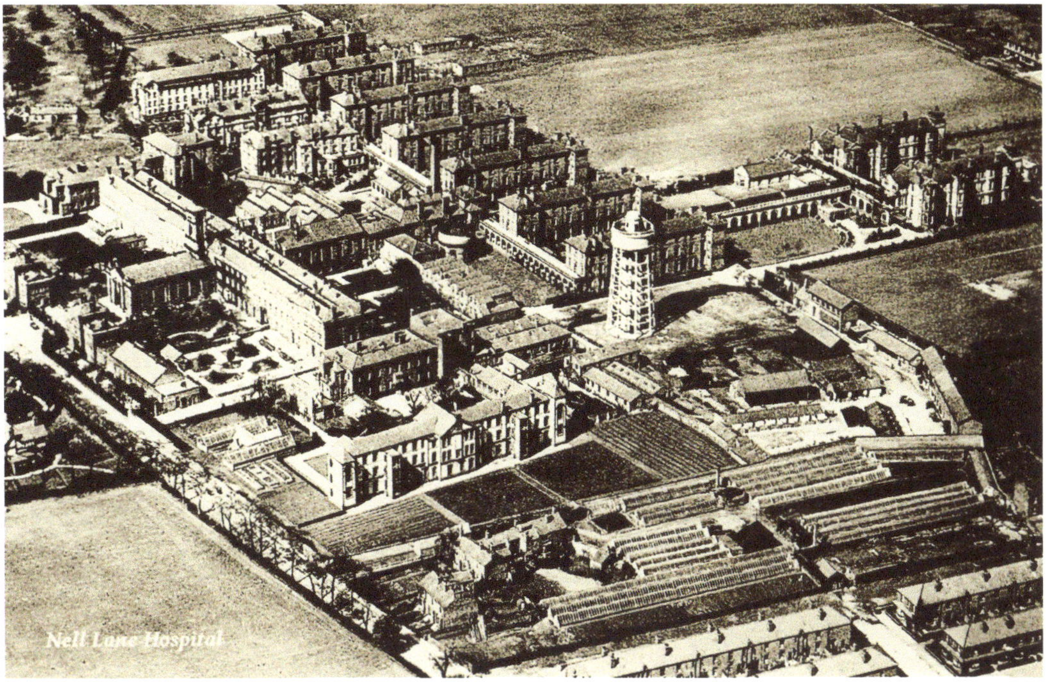

Nell Lane Hospital, *c.* 1930

The first Chorlton Union Workhouse was located on Stretford New Road, near Leaf Street, and housed 300 inmates. The building became too small to cope with the district's rapidly growing population and the guardians decided to construct a new workhouse at Nell Lane, Withington, which opened in 1855. The site also included the Chorlton Union Cemetery, which served the Chorlton Union area, as well as the workhouse and hospital, until 1920. In 1926 Southern Cemetery expanded to the north-east of Nell Lane.

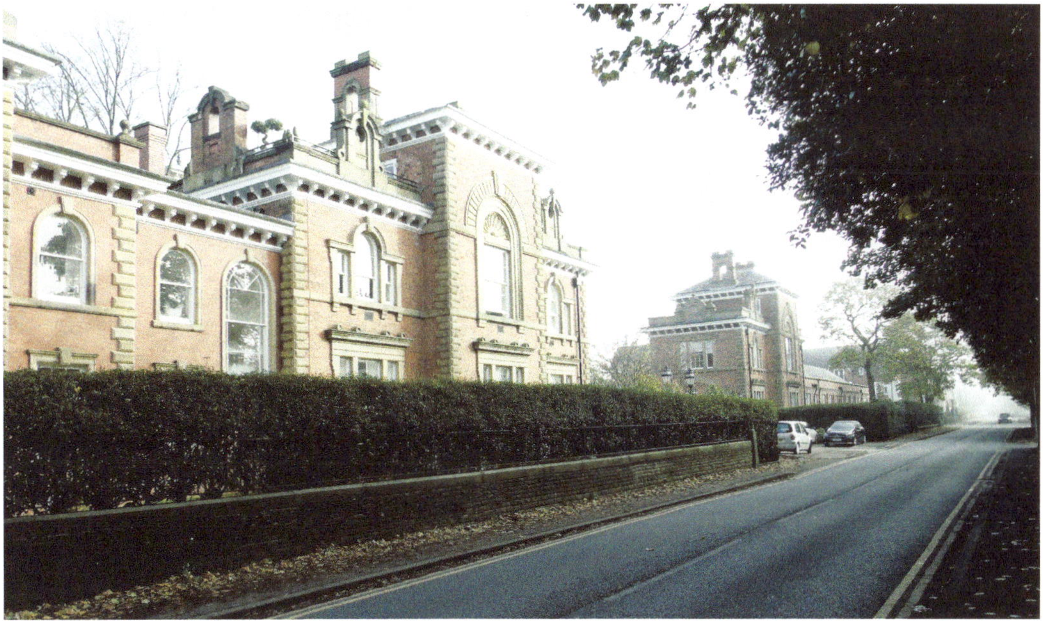

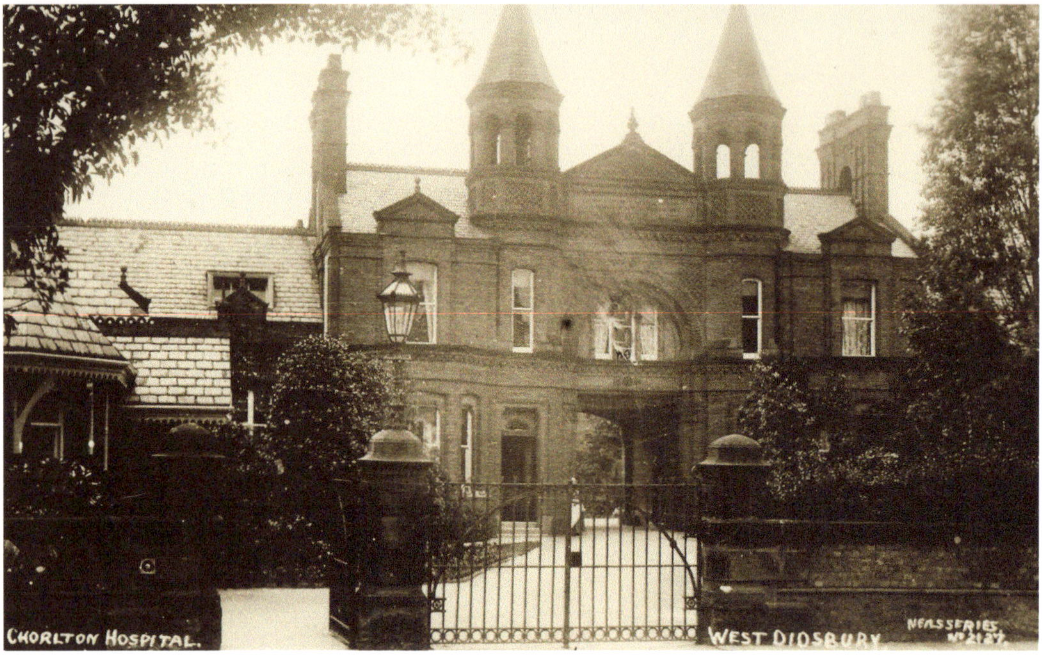

Chorlton Hospital, Nell Lane, *c.* 1900

The Chorlton Poor Law Union was founded in January 1837, with nineteen elected guardians representing the twelve parishes of Ardwick, Burnage, Chorlton-upon-Medlock, Chorlton with Hardy, Didsbury, Gorton, Hulme, Levenshulme, Moss Side, Rusholme, Stretford and Withington – all in south Manchester. The new workhouse at Withington cost £53,000 and could accommodate up to 1,500 inmates. In 1864–66 it became a hospital for the poor, designed by architect Thomas Worthington. The frontage and chapel were Italianate in style. In 1915 the workhouse was renamed Withington Hospital.

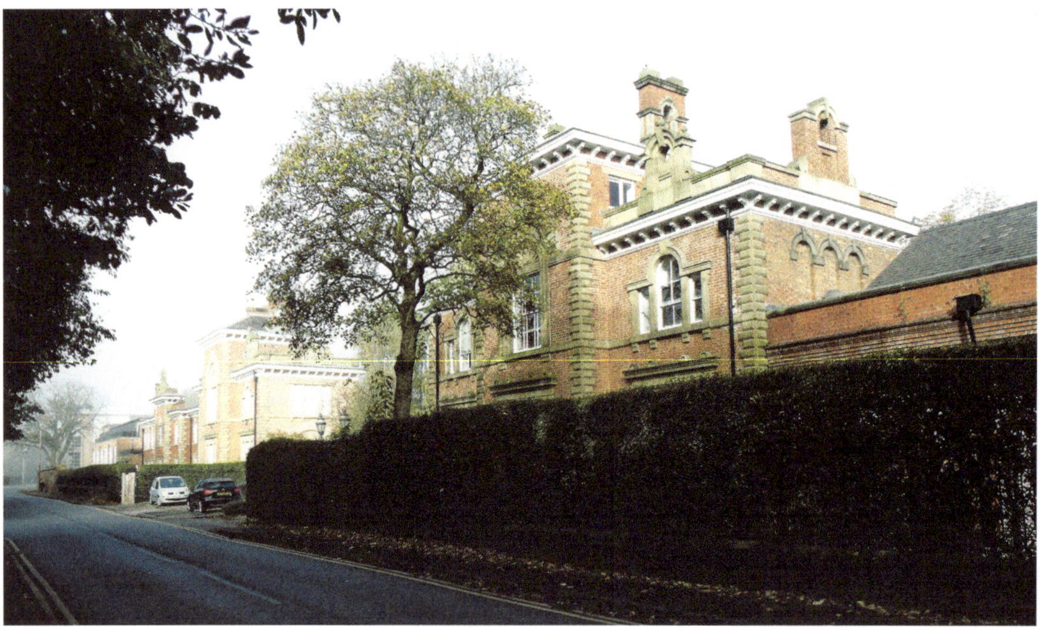

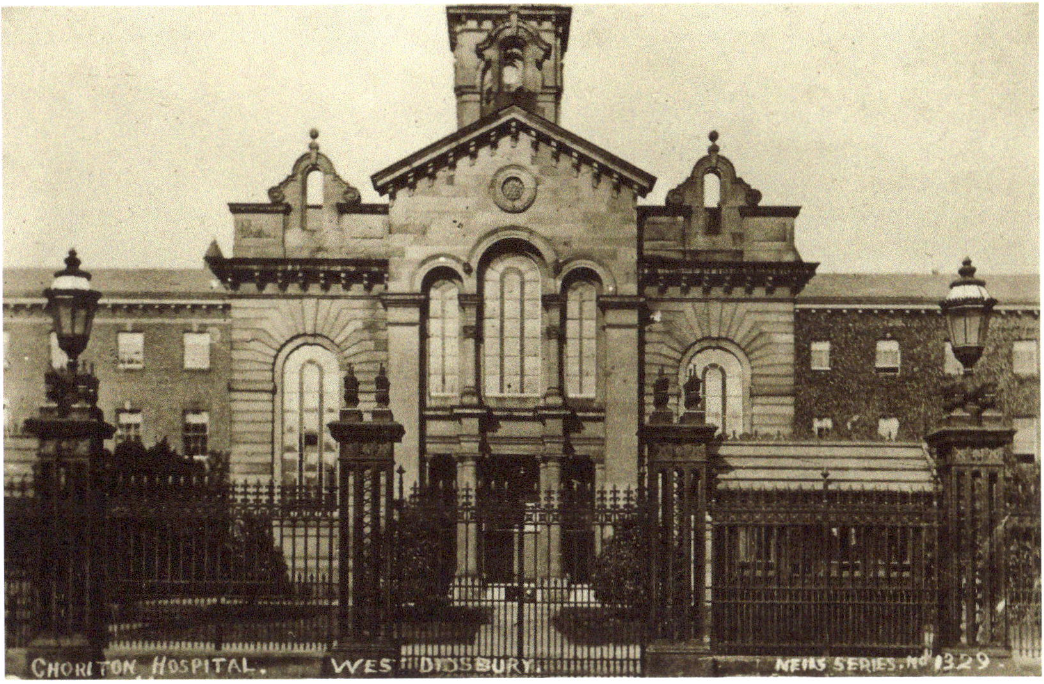

Chorlton Hospital, Nell Lane, *c.* 1900

After the Local Government Act 1929, the hospital was developed and extended by the City of Manchester. By 1948 it was one of the largest general hospitals in the country and was once part of the largest teaching hospital in Europe, under the supervision of the University of Manchester's medical school. Its cemetery formally closed in 1970, with remains reinterred at Southern Cemetery. Some had already been removed when Princess Road was built over the old cemetery site.

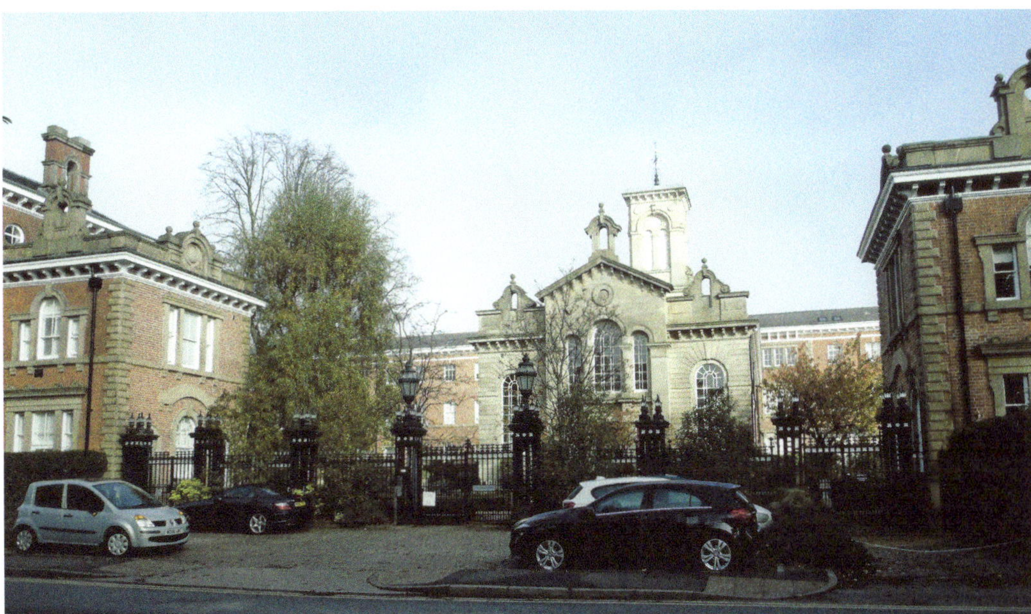

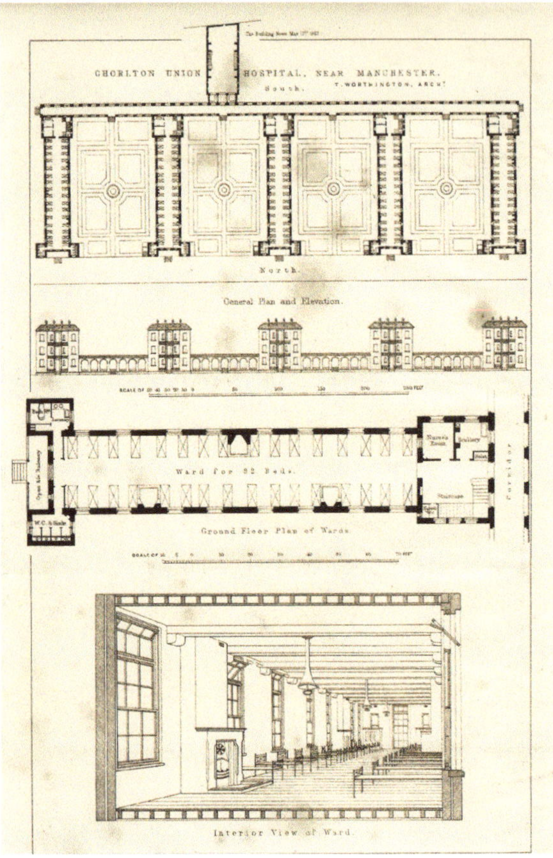

Chorlton Union Hospital Blueprint by Thomas Worthington, 1867

It is now known as Withington Community Hospital and is located in a new hospital building to the south-east of the old site. Once all the old workhouse buildings had been occupied by the original hospital (above) a smaller workhouse was built on the opposite side of Nell Lane, which closed in 1928. The remaining hospital eventually closed in 2002, with three of its former buildings being granted Grade II-listed status. They have since been converted for residential occupation.

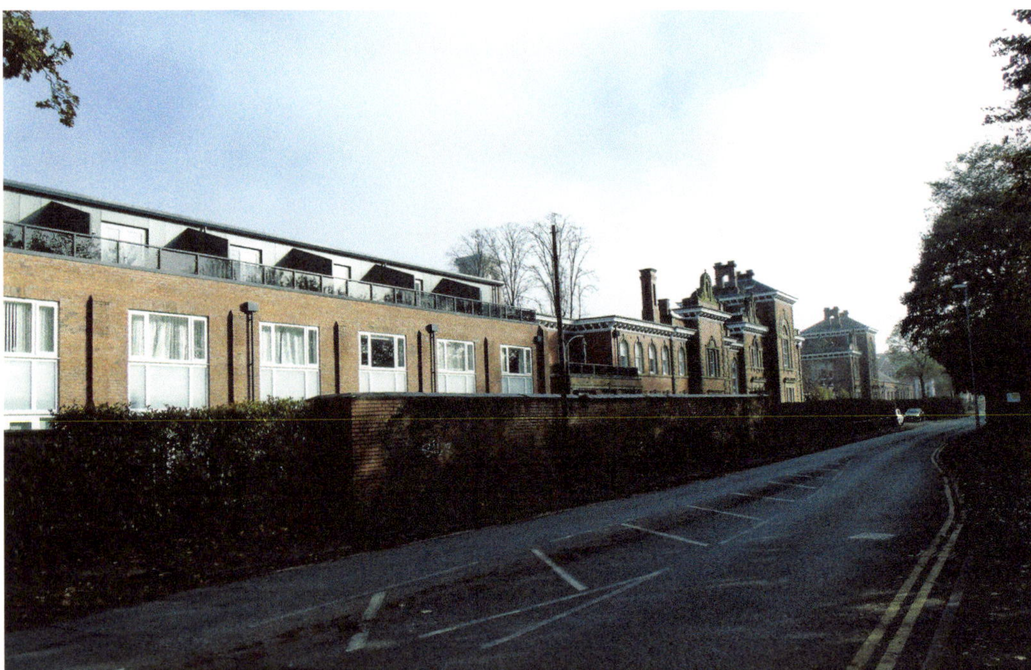

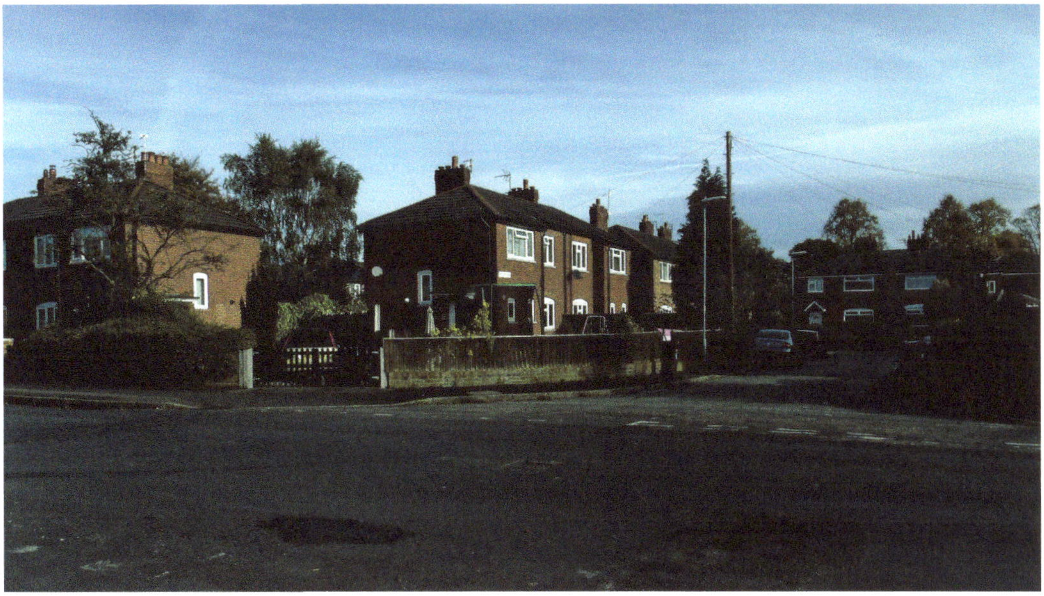

No. 9 Aycliffe Avenue, Chorlton-cum-Hardy and George Best on European Cup Final Teamsheet, 29 May 1968

The Manchester United footballer spent ten years periodically lodging at No. 9 Aycliffe Avenue. Famously, when he first arrived in Manchester in 1961, he became homesick and returned to Northern Ireland, but came back with some persuasion. He lodged with Mrs Mary Fullaway and had David Sadler as a roommate. Best eventually bought a house in Bramhall (named Que Sera), but sold it to return to the home of his former landlady in 1972. Soon after, his career with United came to an end.

BENFICA

(*Colours:* White Shirts, White Shorts)

1. JOSE HENRIQUE
2. ADOLFO
3. HUMBERTO
4. JACINTO
5. CRUZ
6. JAIME GRACA
7. COLUNA (Captain)
8. JOSE AUGUSTO
9. TORRES
10. EUSEBIO
11. SIMOES

Team Manager: Mr. Otto Gloria.

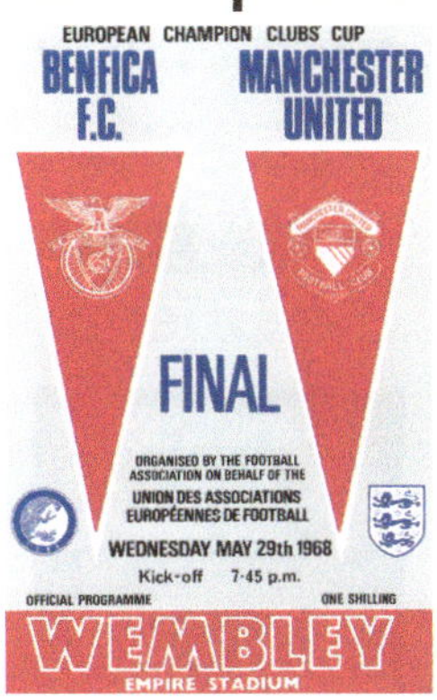

MANCHESTER UTD.

(*Colours:* Blue Shirts, Blue Shorts)

1. ALEX STEPNEY
2. SHAY BRENNAN
3. TONY DUNNE
4. PAT CRERAND
5. BILL FOULKES
6. NOBBY STILES
7. GEORGE BEST
8. BRIAN KIDD
9. BOBBY CHARLTON (Captain)
10. DAVID SADLER
11. JOHN ASTON

Team Manager: Mr. Matt Busby.

Team Trainer: Mr. J. Crompton.

EXTRA TIME: If scores are level after 90 minutes' play an extra half-hour will be played.
REPLAY (*if necessary*): It will take place at Arsenal F.C., Highbury, London, next Friday (31st May), k.o. 7.30 p.m.
Replay prices: £4, £3, £2, £1, standing 10s.
Tickets for replay will be on sale at the Arsenal to personal applicants only on Thursday, 30th May from 10 a.m. until 8 p.m. Also on Friday (providing tickets are still available) from 10 a.m. till 2 p.m.

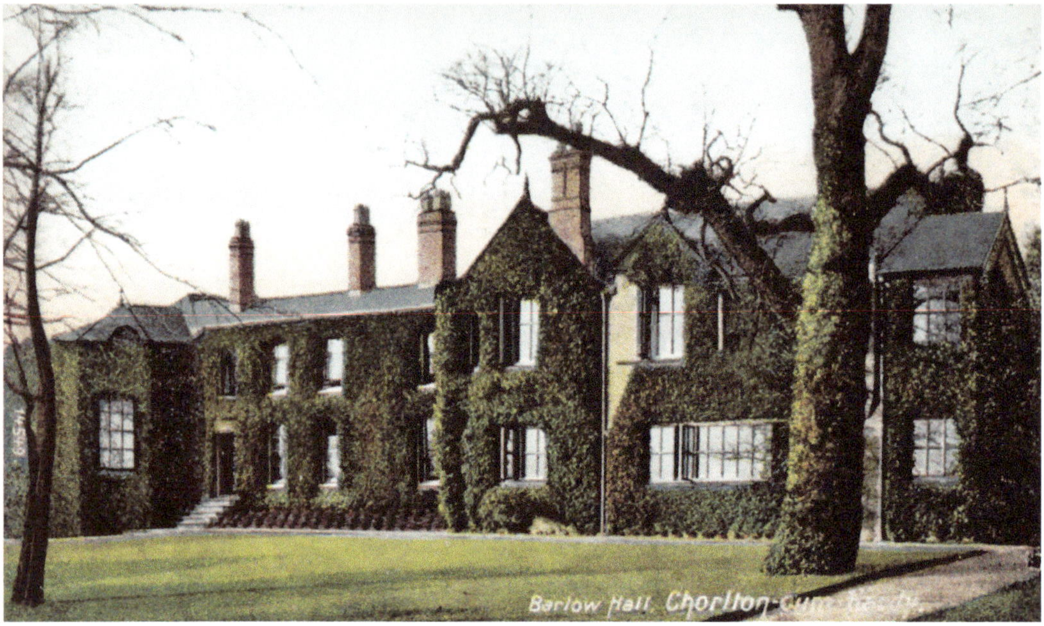

Barlow Hall, Chorlton-cum-Hardy, *c.* 1910

Barlow Hall was probably erected during the reign of Edward I (1272–1307) and rebuilt or renovated around the time of Henry VIII, when the hall was occupied by Alexander Barlow. Little of the original timberwork now remains exposed to view, having been coated with plaster and subjected to subsequent alterations. On the banks of the River Mersey, a watermill formed part of the manor that was occupied by descendants of the Barlow family until around 1800. Barlow Hall is now home to Chorlton-cum-Hardy Golf Club.

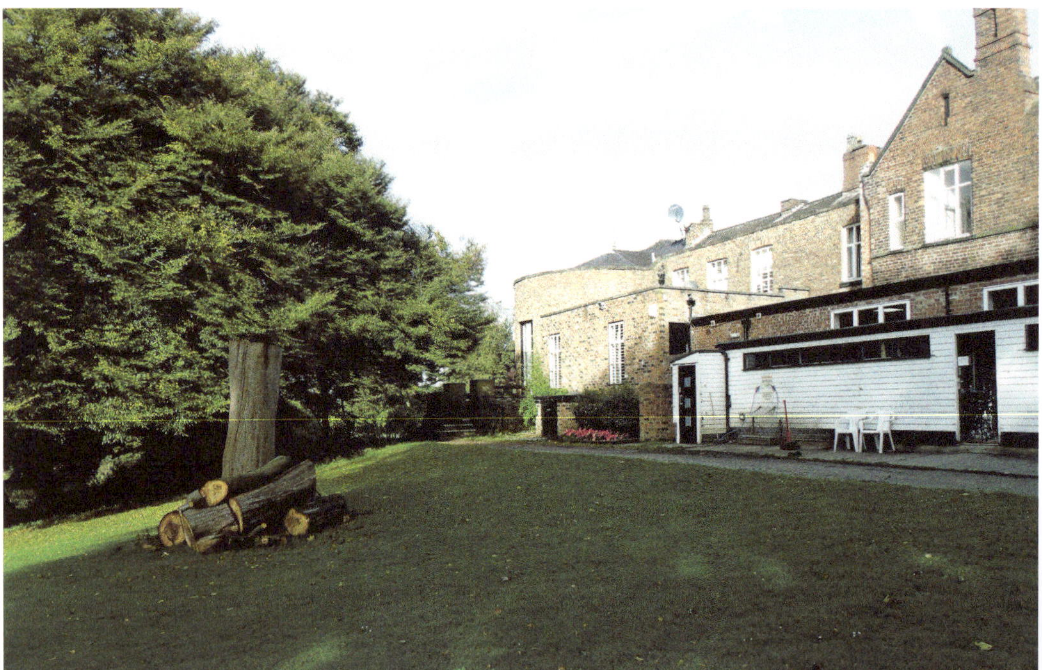

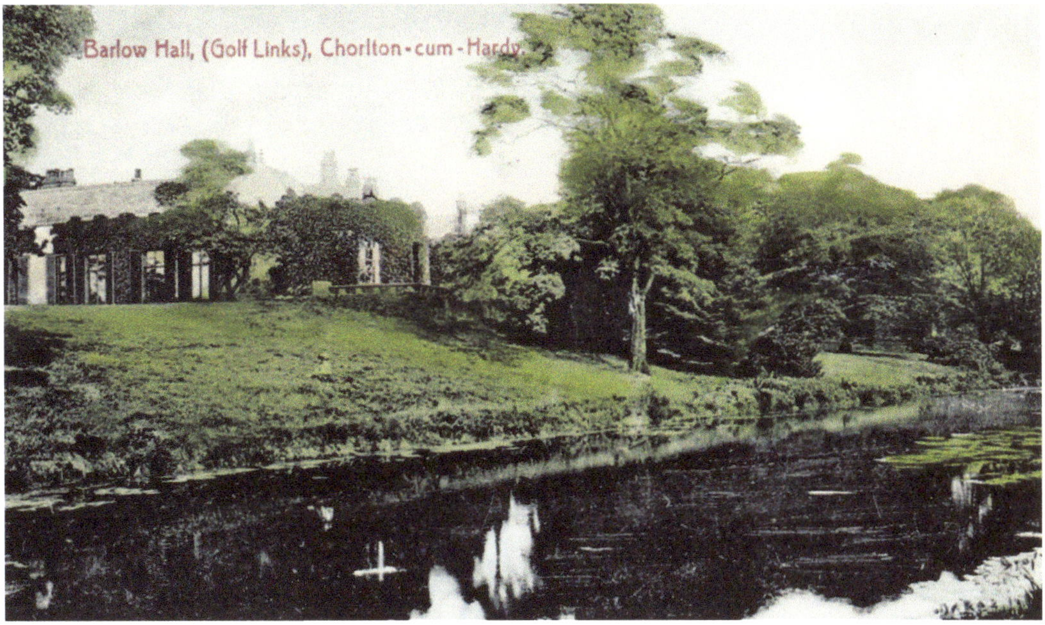

Barlow Hall Golf Links, Chorlton-cum-Hardy, *c.* 1910

Barlow Hall was the birthplace of St Ambrose Barlow. Sir Edward Barlow was born at Barlow Hall in 1565 and took the name Ambrose when he was ordained as a priest of the Order of St Benedict. On 25 April 1641 he was arrested and taken to Lancaster Castle. He was subsequently removed to Lancaster Gaol, where he confessed to being a Catholic priest and was hanged, drawn and quartered on Friday 10 September 1641. The nearby parish church and primary school are named after St Ambrose.

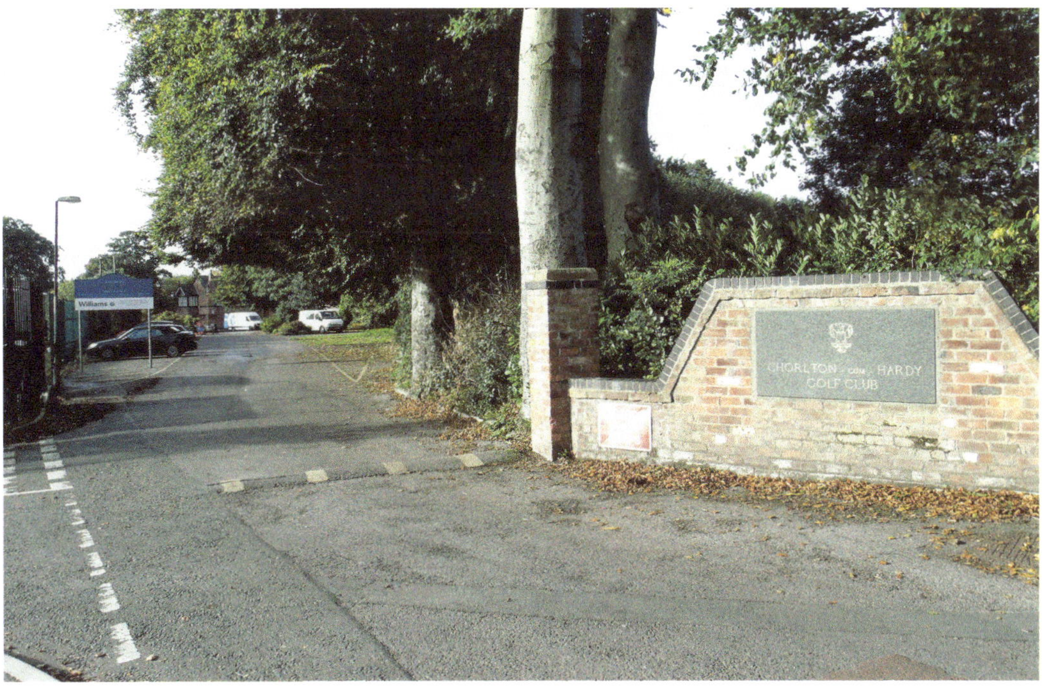

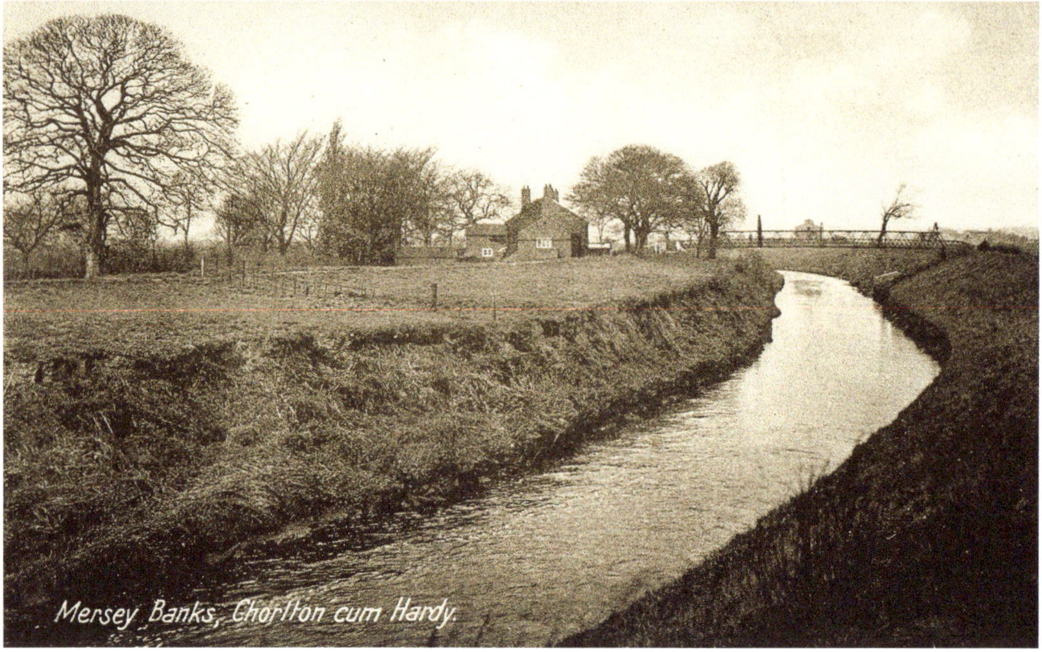

Mersey Banks, the Bridge Inn (Jackson's Boat) and Footbridge, *c.* 1910
The original building dates from 1663, with the present public house (built around the year 1800) incorporating some older structures. Originally known as the Bridge Inn, or Jackson's (ferry) Boat, the ferry that used to cross the River Mersey at this point was discontinued in 1816 when a wooden bridge was built. This was swept away in a storm and replaced by an iron toll bridge that opened on 14 October 1881. In the eighteenth century it was a regular meeting place of the Jacobites.

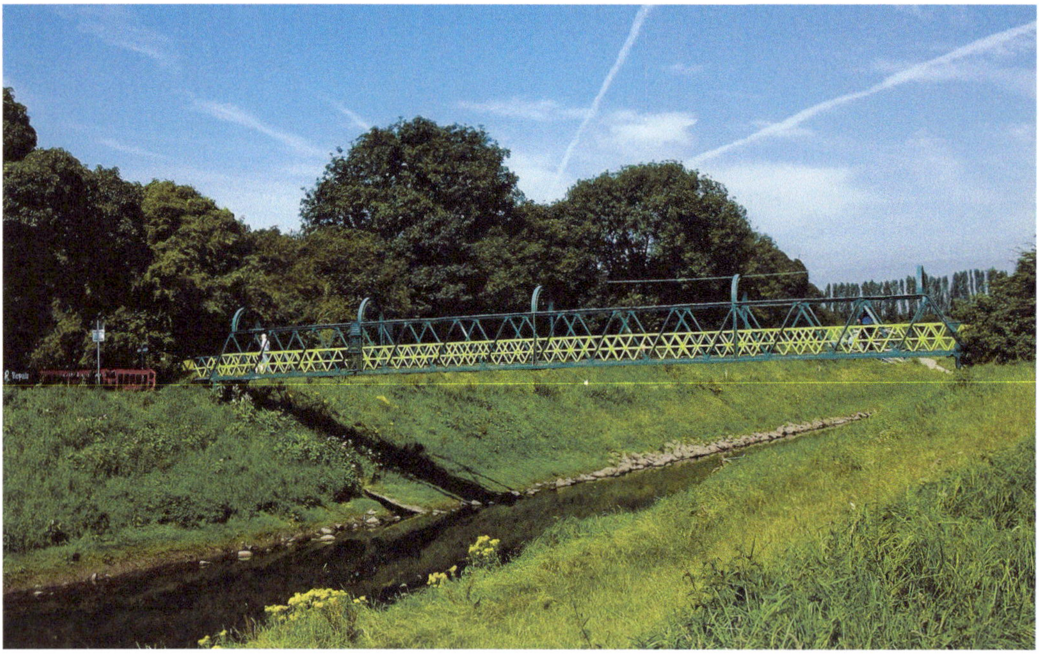

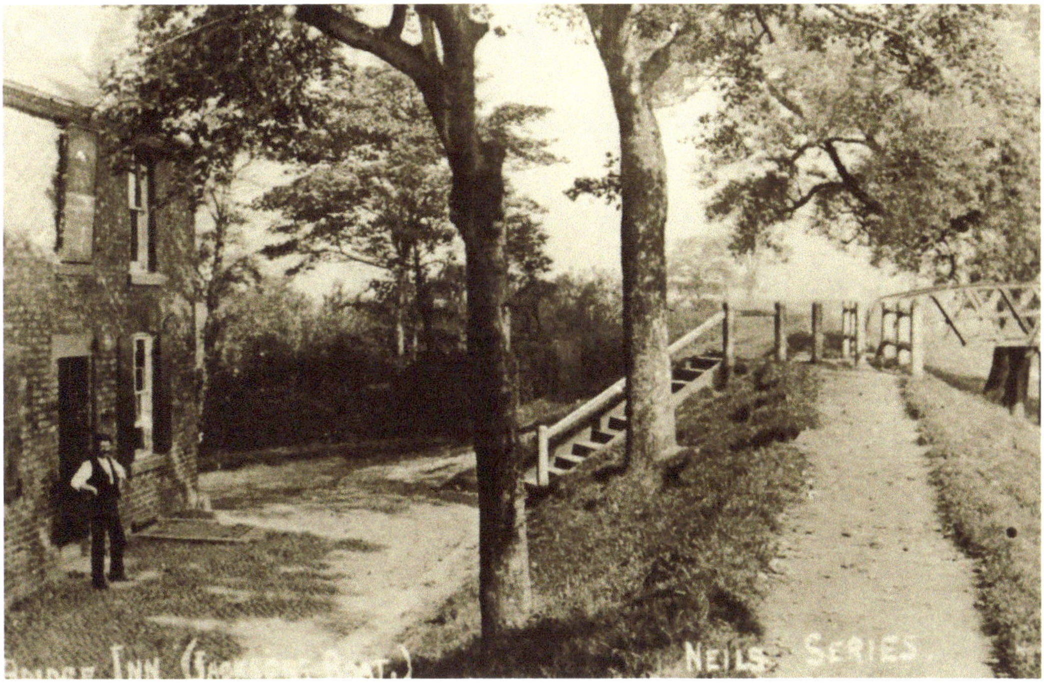

The Bridge Inn (Jackson's Boat), Looking Towards Sale, *c.* 1910

The oldest inn in the district is the Bridge Inn (previously called the Greyhound), which was constructed out of traditional wattle and daub building materials. It was demolished in the early seventeenth century; the newer building, dating from 1663, has undergone many alterations since. The local Jacobin club used it as a meeting place around the year 1730 and would drink to the king's health over a bowl of punch. Today, the public house, located off Rifle Road and now in Sale, remains popular.

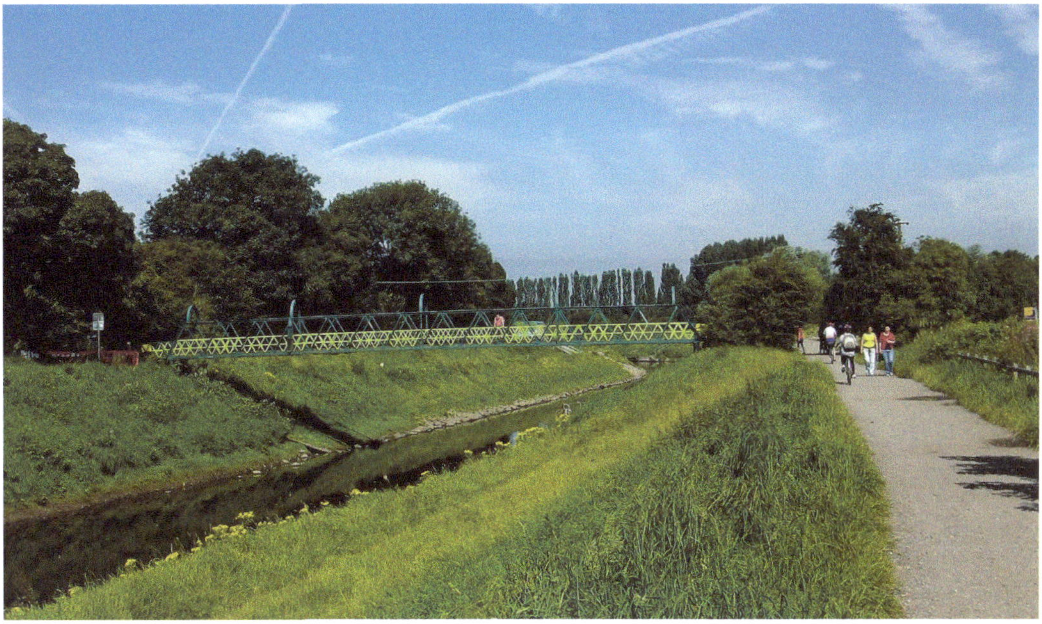

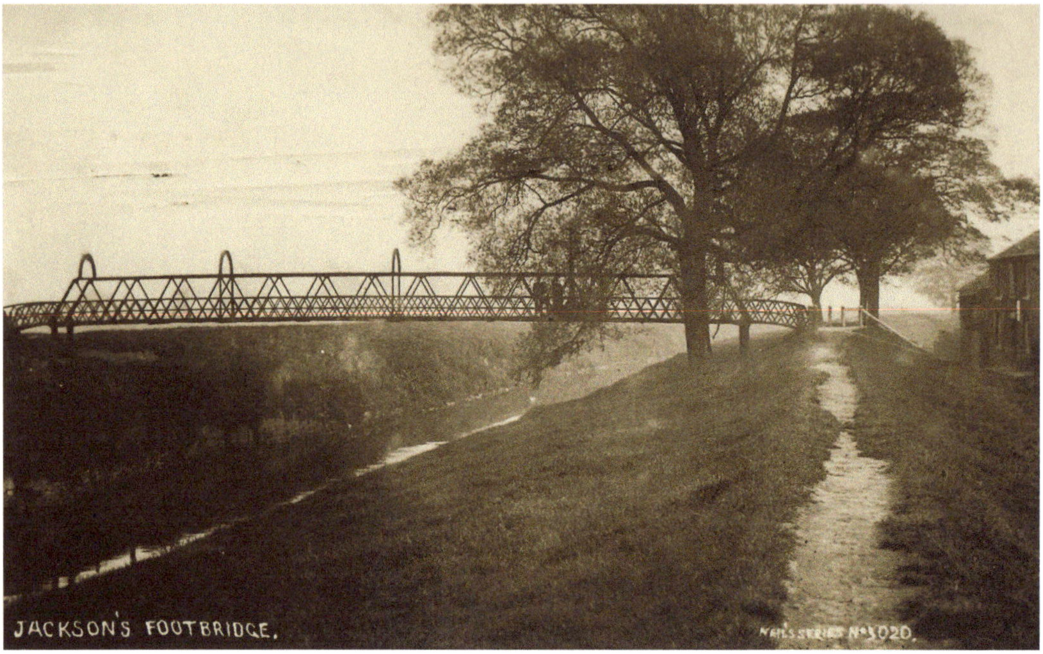

Jackson's Footbridge and the Bridge Inn (Jackson's Boat), Looking Towards Chorlton-cum-Hardy, 1911

This postcard image was sent from Chorlton on 7 June 1911 to Private E. K. Nuttall, drummer of the 35th Manchester Company, Boys' Brigade Camp, Penrhyn (near Llandudno). It makes interesting reading as the First World War was just over three years away, and father tells his son: 'Learn to obey orders then you will do well.' This (and the two previous) modern views are all taken from the Chorlton bank because of tree cover opposite, which also shades out the public house in this view.

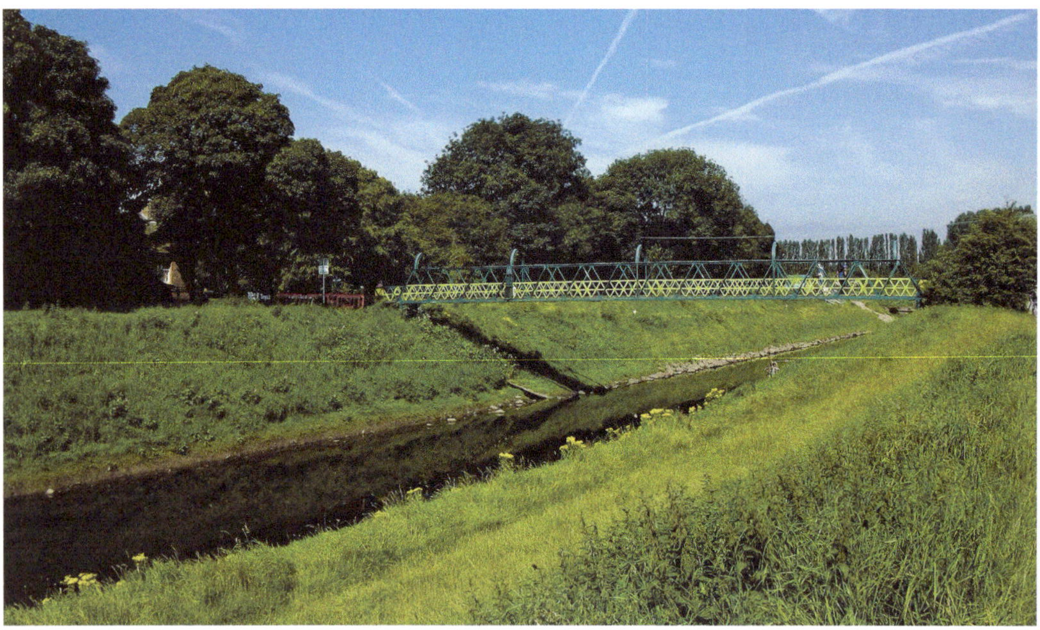

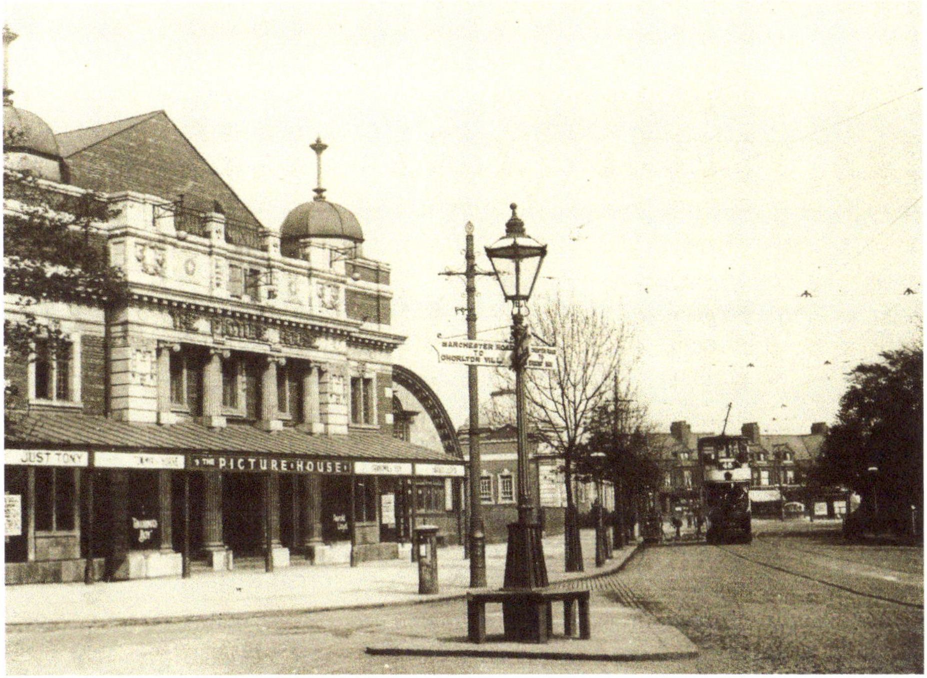

The Picture House, Manchester Road, Chorlton-cum-Hardy, *c.* 1920

Opening in 1920 as the Picture House, the Savoy cinema was the popular name for this building, despite a previous name being the Majestic. This appeared on the face of the building, later being covered by the 'Savoy' name (J. Lloyd). It then became the Gaumont and closed in 1962. Today the former cinema is owned by an undertaker's business and its stone frontage, columns and ornamentation – including twin domes – are all hidden behind a brick wall. The wrought-iron canopy has also gone.

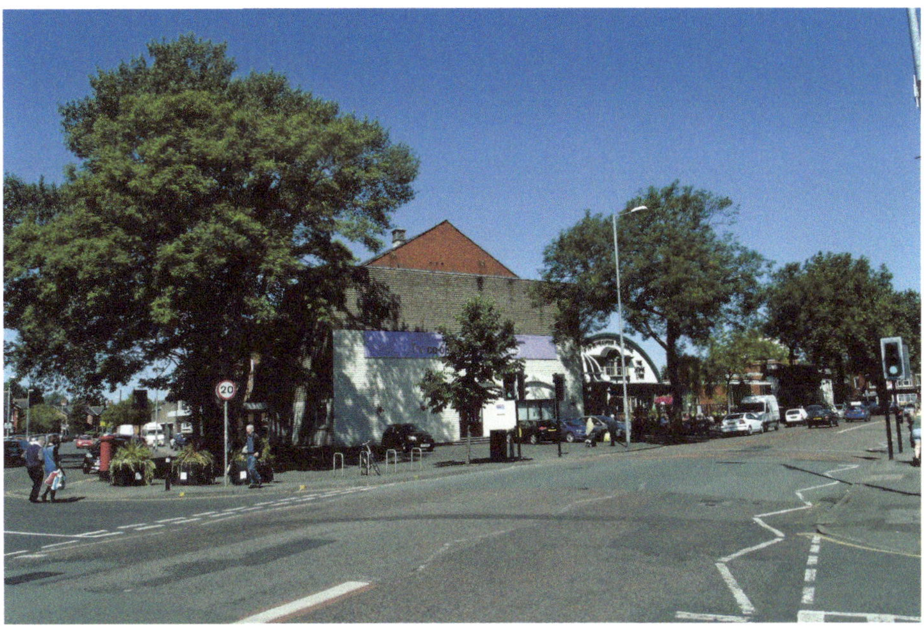

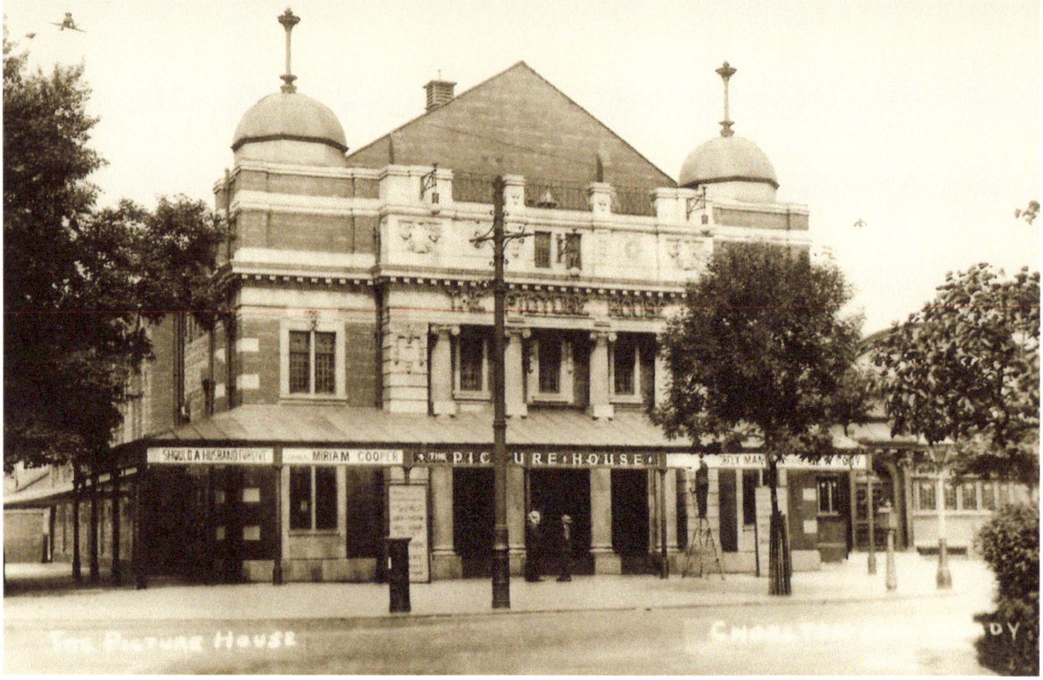

The Picture House, Manchester Road, 1922. ***Inset*****: Chorlton Library, 2017**

Possibly the biggest building in the township, the Picture House was located next to the temperance snooker hall that had opened in 1907 – now the Sedge Lynn public house. Sedge Lynn is the name of the house that once stood here, in its own grounds. Next to the Sedge Lynn is Chorlton Library (*inset*), which was opened on 4 November 1914 by the mayor. It was made possible by a donation of £5,000 from the steel magnate Andrew Carnegie and was built in classical style.

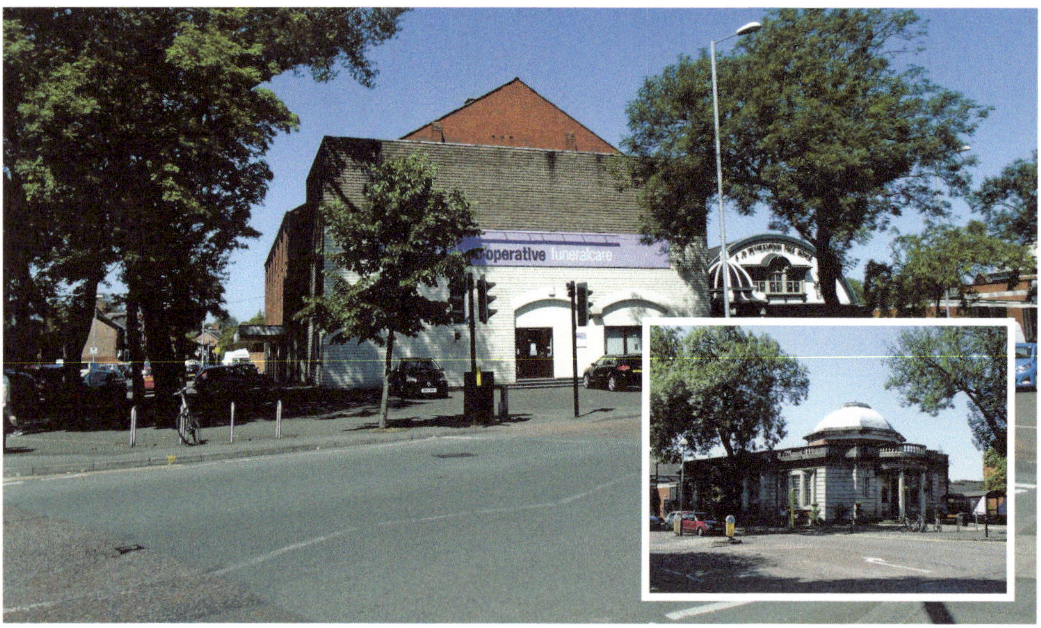

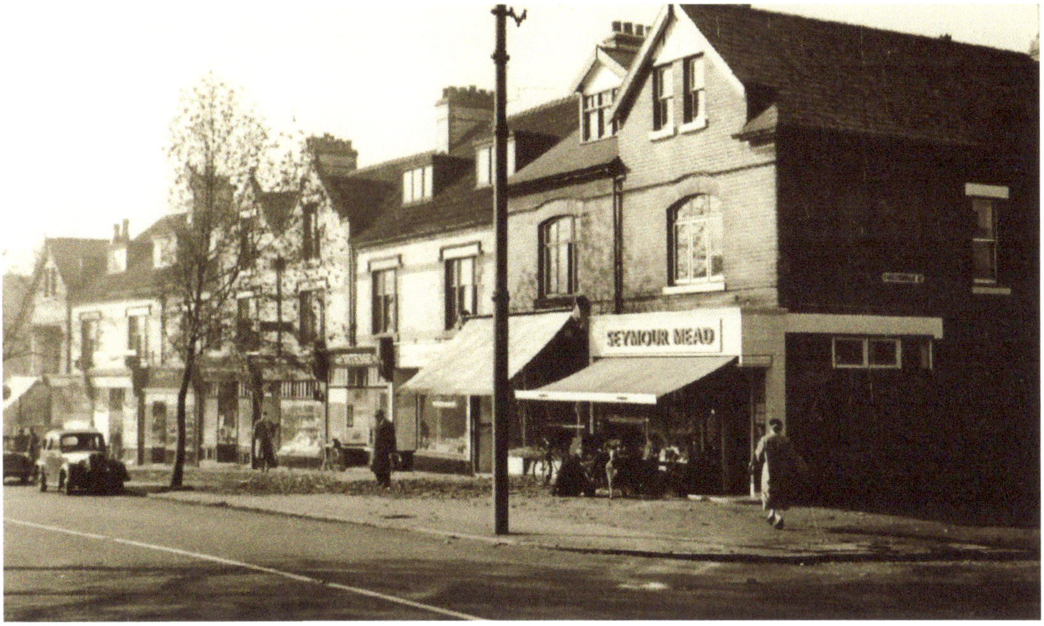

Manchester Road, Chorlton-cum-Hardy, *c.* 1950

This row of shops is located at Manchester Road's junction with Cheltenham Road. Seymour Mead is clearly visible at the corner of the terraced row and vintage cars park where modern ones park today. The photograph has been taken from the corner of the railway bridge as it begins to rise above the track, and the road can be seen sloping away – right to left. The corner shop is shuttered today, but there is still a range of shops along the terrace.

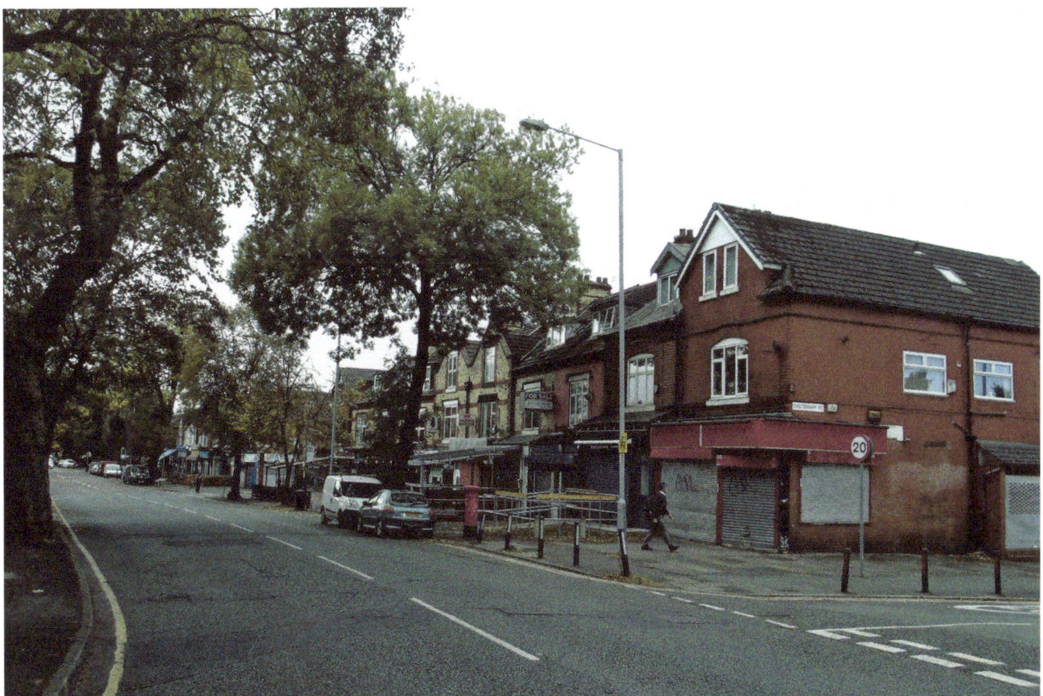

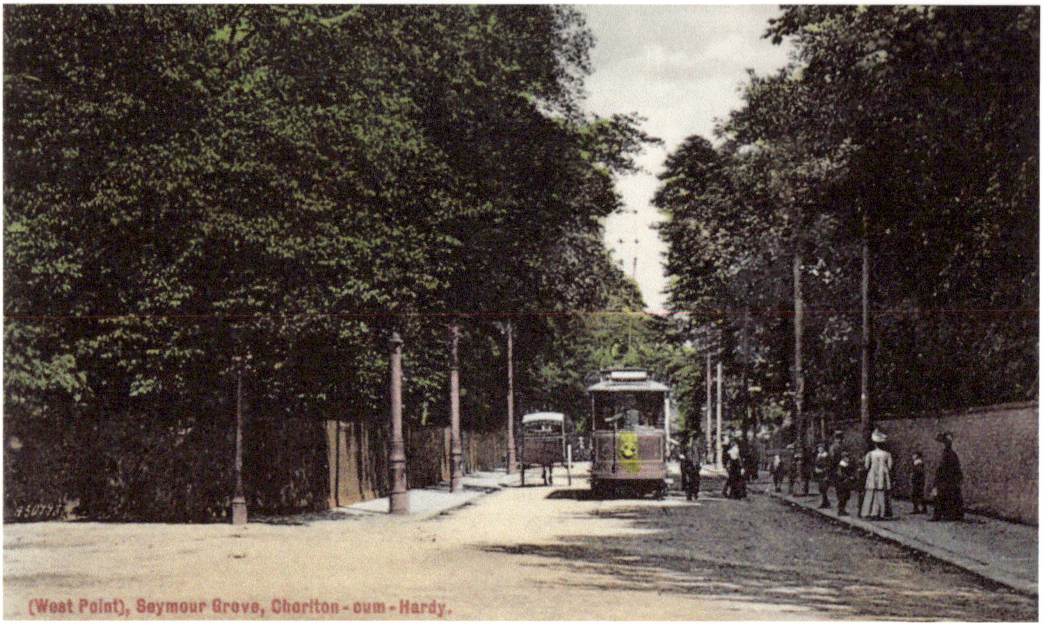

West Point, Seymour Grove, Chorlton-cum-Hardy, 1910

Before extensive suburban development in the district, there was once a footpath from West Point ('The Flash') to Brooks Bar in order to provide access between Hulme and the village of Chorlton-cum-Hardy. A brook ran alongside the footpath, which Samuel Brooks covered and used as a main sewer from his property – Whalley House – which was then drained into Black Brook. The brook frequently flooded the footpath during periods of heavy rain, resulting in the need to rescue travellers in the vicinity.

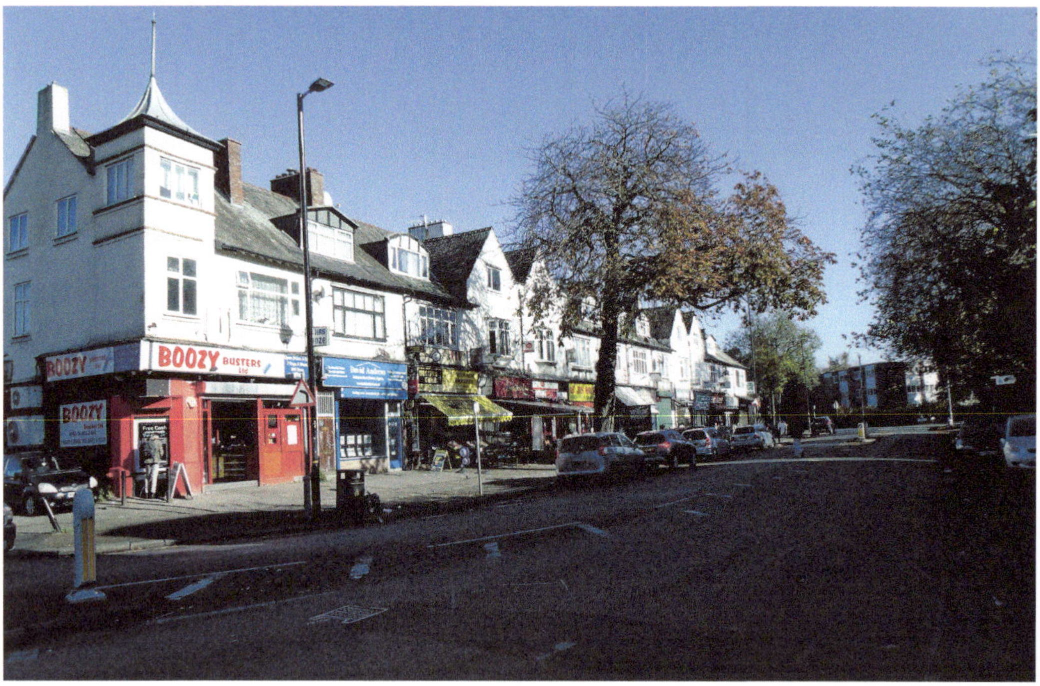

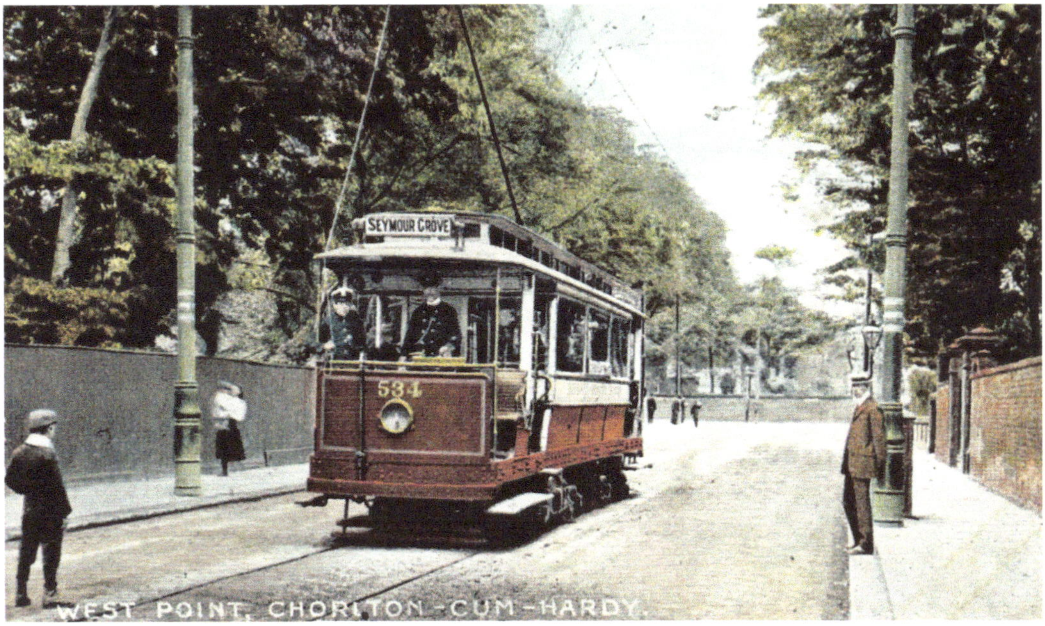

West Point, Chorlton-cum-Hardy, 1906

On 1 August 1876, PC Nicholas Cock was shot by the wall on the right by Charles Peace. Through the trees on the left (where the shops are now) was the mansion house of Darley Hall, which was believed to be the murderer's intended target when he was apprehended by PC Cock along Upper Chorlton Road. Charles Peace, a well-known petty thief and house burglar, operated by checking his intended target well in advance of a potential burglary.

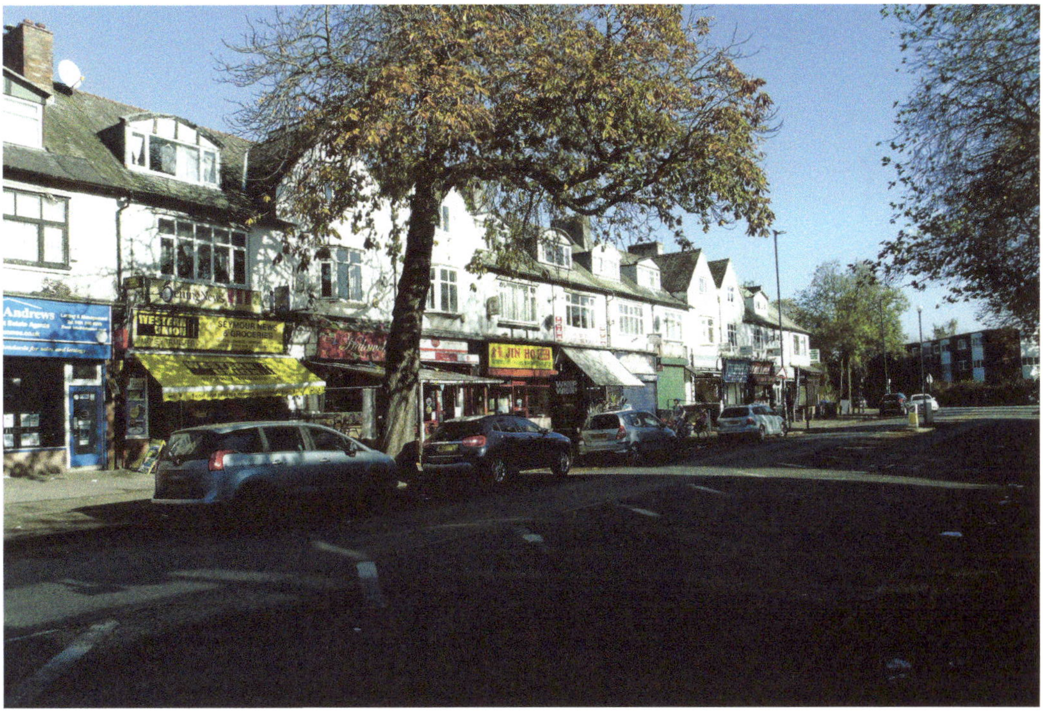

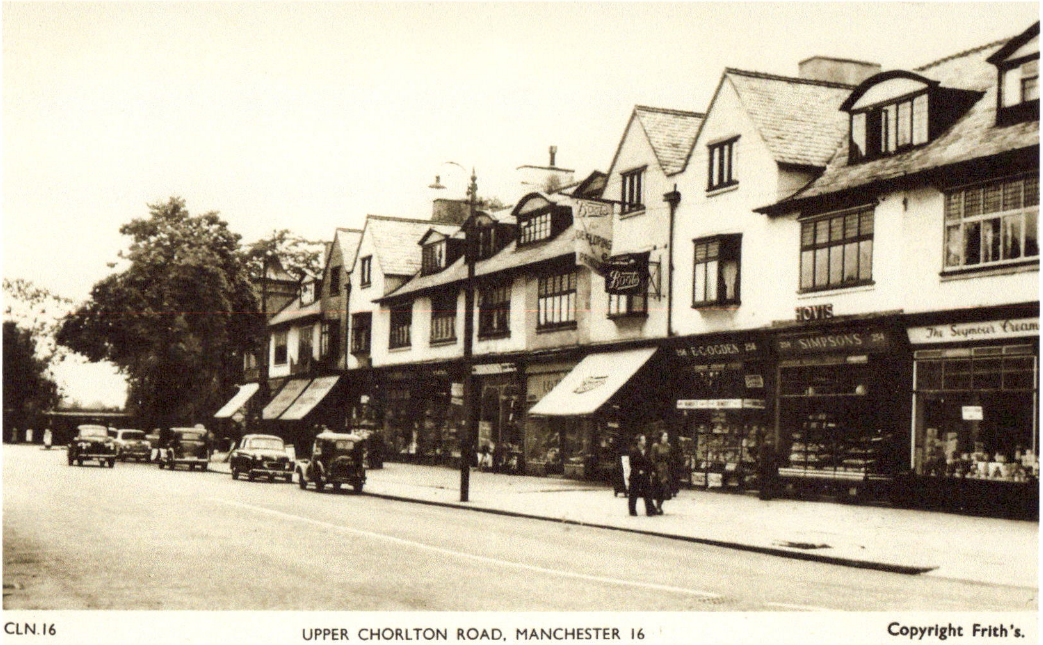

Shops in Upper Chorlton Road, West Point, 1962

PC Cock and his partner PC Beanland noticed Peace as he made his way towards Darley Hall, preparing for his house burglary. PC Cock left Beanland and backtracked along Upper Chorlton Road, apprehending Peace at the end of Seymour Grove. In response, Peace shot the policeman in the chest, with the latter dying from a pistol wound. Peace was eventually apprehended on another charge and confessed to the killing, thus pardoning an innocent suspect previously found guilty of the murder.

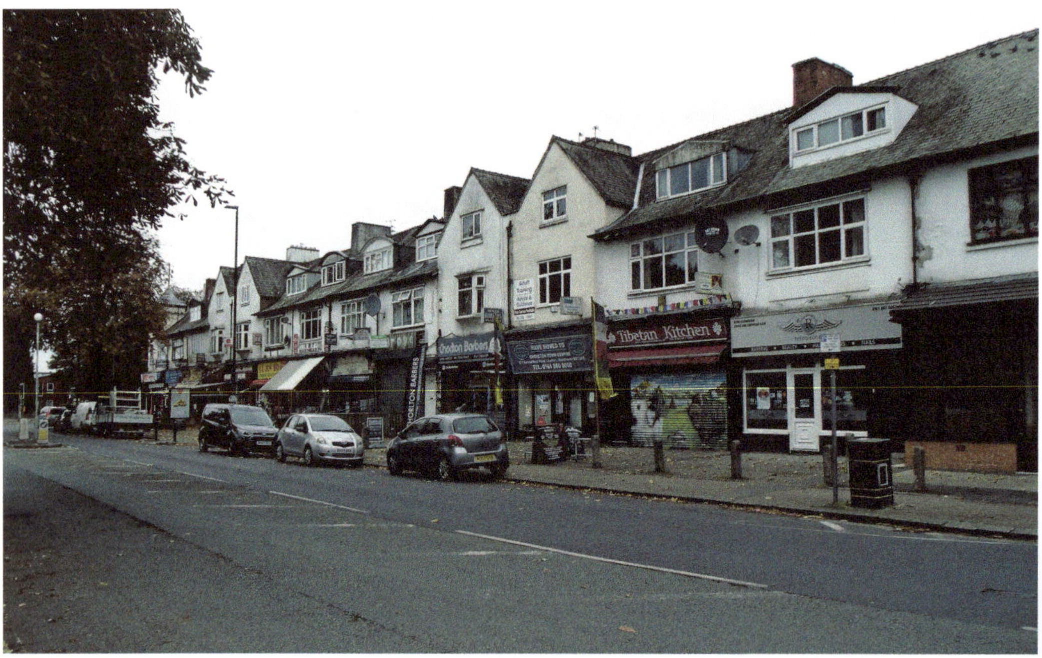

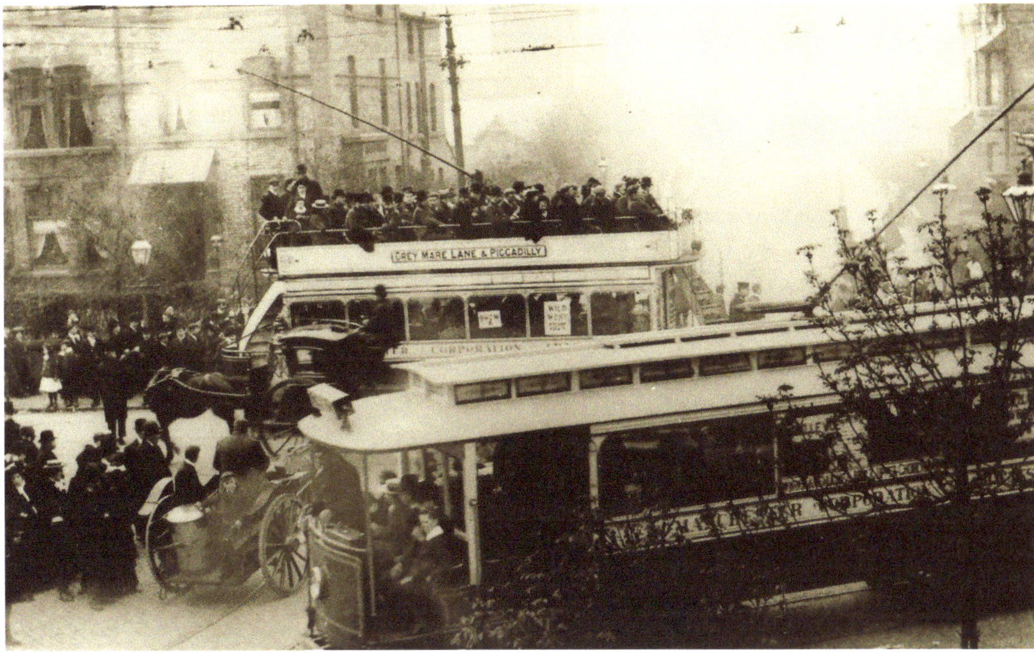

Brooks Bar, Old Trafford, 1903

In 1903 the tram route from Belle Vue, via Brooks Bar and Upper Chorlton Road was extended to West Point at Seymour Grove. Four years later it was extended again to Lane End, the junction of Sandy Lane and Barlow Moor Road. Before the establishment of the electric tram in the city, horse trams left Manchester from the Exchange, with passengers changing at Brooks Bar for the horse tram to Chorlton Green. The images look towards Shrewsbury Street and the former Unitarian church.

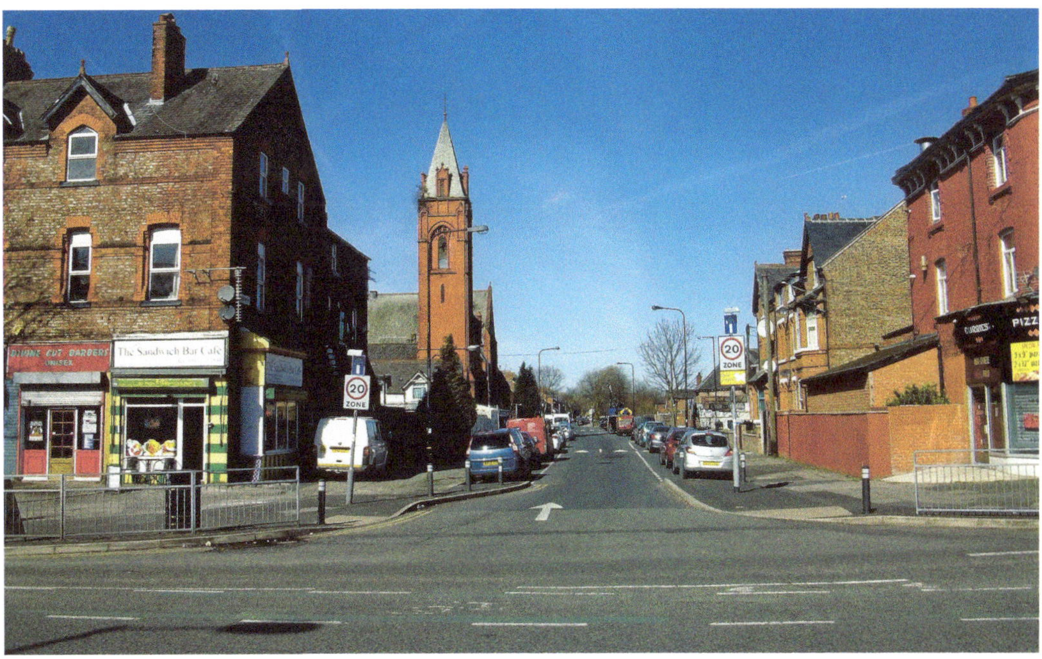

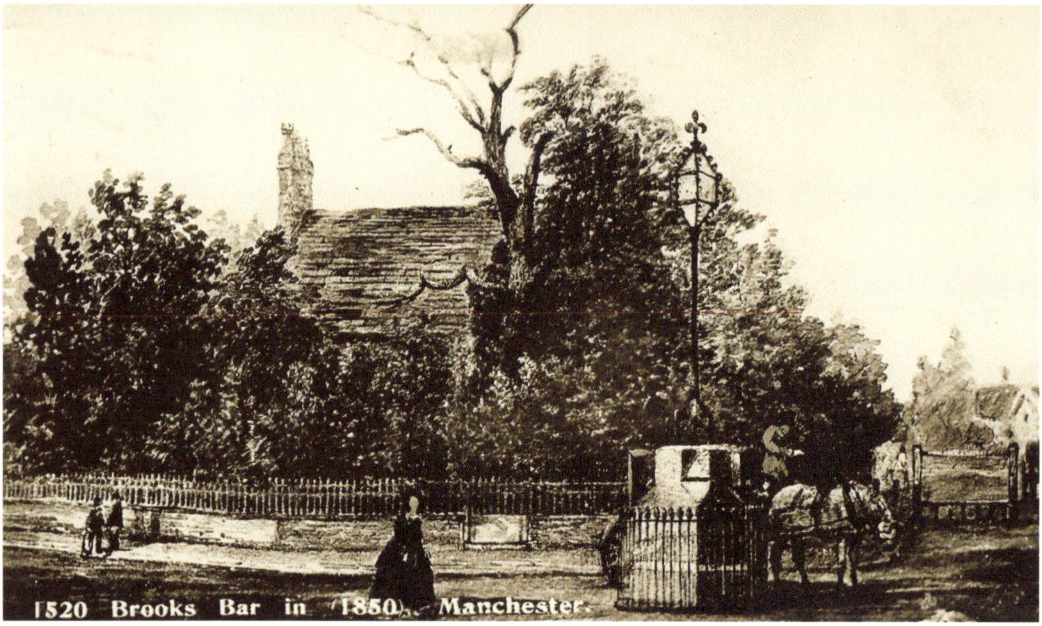

Brooks Bar, Old Trafford, 1850

Brooks Bar, at the junction of Withington Road and Upper Chorlton Road, is so named because it was where the Manchester entrepreneur Samuel Brooks placed his toll gate in 1850 (above). It remained here until it was removed on 10 June 1896. Brooks developed Whalley Range to the east of Old Trafford and bordering onto Chorlton-cum-Hardy. The name is suggestive of his family's origins. He is responsible for developing some of Manchester's earliest suburbs, giving his name to the Sale district of Brooklands.

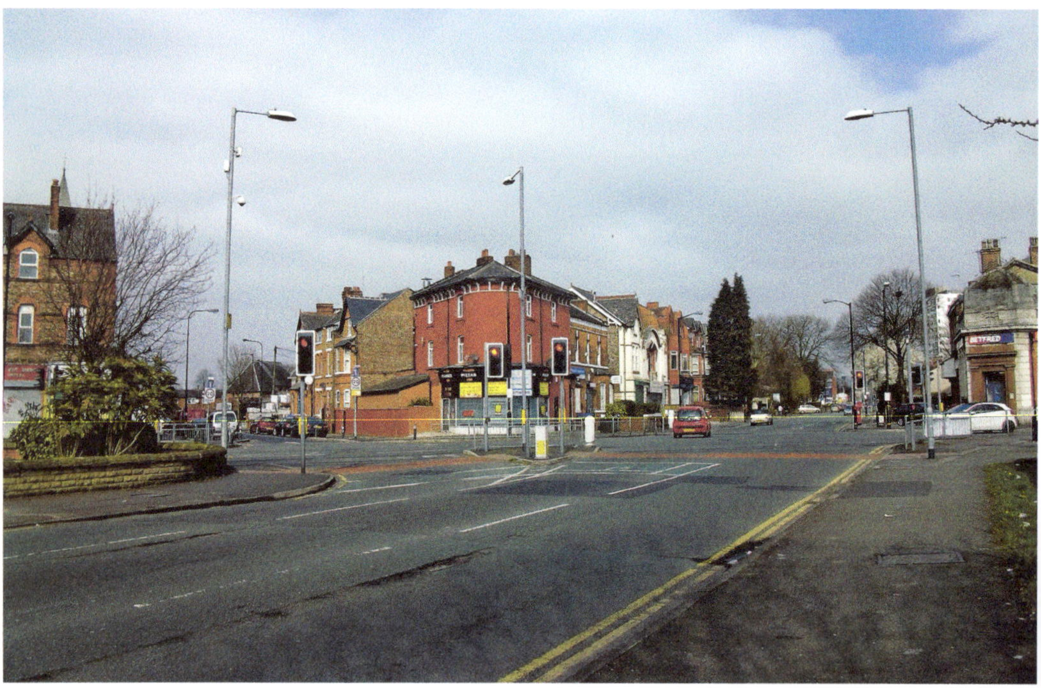

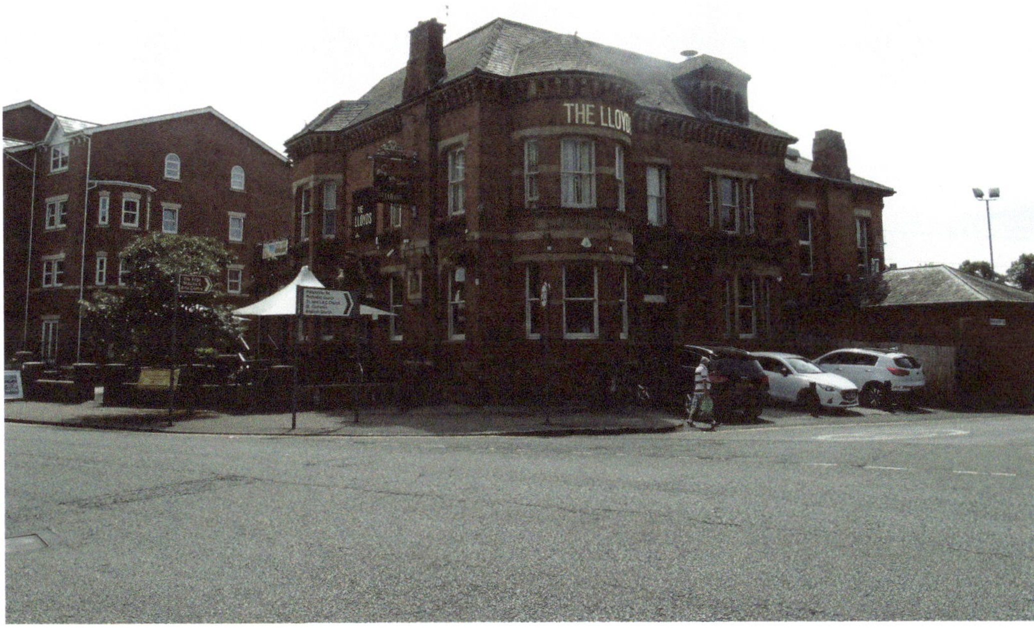

Lloyds Hotel, Junction of Wilbraham Road and Manchester Road, Chorlton-cum-Hardy, 2017
Within the Wilbraham Road and Edge Lane Conservation Area, the hotel is Grade II listed and was built around 1870, with the original stone signage stating that its name was once Lloyd and Platts Hotel. It was designed by E. J. Thompson of Manchester for George Lloyd and James Platt, catering for the 'grander' inhabitants of 'new' Chorlton. George Lloyd owned the land and James Platt built the hotel, but once the latter had died his name was removed and the hotel retitled. It had integrated tennis courts and a crown bowling green.

Sources

Chorlton History (http://www.oldchorlton.me.uk)

Lloyd, J., *Looking Back at Chorlton-cum-Hardy, Martledge, Barlow Moor and Hough End* (Altrincham: Willow Publishing, 1985).

Lloyd, J. M., *The Township of Chorlton-cum-Hardy. Chorlton, Hardy, Martledge, Barlow and Hough End* (Didsbury: Morten, 1972).

Manchester Archives & Local Studies, Central Library, St Peter's Square, Manchester.

Simpson, A., *The Story of Chorlton-cum-Hardy* (Stroud: The History Press Ltd, 2012).

Simpson, A. (https://chorltonhistory.blogspot.co.uk/)

Welcome to Chorltonville (http://www.chorltonville.org)

About the Author

Steven lives in the Flixton area of Manchester. He has an academic background in twentieth-century history and the history of the National Health Service. Steven has always had an interest in local history and genealogy, and has written several journal and magazine articles on these subjects as well as several *Through Time* volumes; he has also given many talks on these subjects. Steven is a former charge nurse and college lecturer. He is married to Sarah, and they have six children.